OXFORD STUDIES
IN MODERN EUROPEAN HISTORY

General Editors
SIMON DIXON, MARK MAZOWER,
and
JAMES RETALLACK

PRAISE FOR LIVING THE REVOLUTION

'Dr Willimott's book provides a lively insight into the attempts of some young people in early Soviet Russia to live out in practice the proclaimed ideals of the new Communist regime. He describes vividly the hopes inspiring their experiments in collective living, their successes, frustrations and failures, and how ultimately those experiments were integrated into the emerging totalitarian structure of the Stalinist regime.'

Geoffrey Hosking, University College, London

'*Living the Revolution* is about those youthful citizens of the new Soviet republic—men and women—who sought to remake their lives by throwing in their lot with the Bolsheviks. It is, to be sure, a critical analysis of their many projects. But, unlike previous historians who all too easily dismissed them as "utopian," it revivifies the spirit of those efforts, putting the reader in touch with the emotional energy of the revolution. Here, at last, is a rigorously researched yet unapologetically sympathetic account of the multiple initiatives undertaken in the first decade of Soviet power to bring the revolution into the workplace, the classroom, and the home.'

Lewis Siegelbaum, Michigan State University

'Beautifully written, meticulously researched, and bursting with narrative appeal, Willimott's study of early Soviet communes demonstrates that a hundred years after the Russian Revolution not all has been said about the revolution's layers, complexities, and legacies. From the very first sentence—a question to his readers—Willimott draws us into an energetic world of enthusiasm, idealism, and activism, but also of disappointment, fracture, and conflict. He convincingly shows that neither did spontaneous self-experimentation end with the advent of Soviet power, nor was every aspect of revolutionary utopianism irrevocably lost during the Stalin years. Rather he weaves a fine net of dense description, in which he brings the elusive communes to life, while subtly quoting, probing, and pushing existing scholarship on the period and indeed beyond.'

Juliane Furst, University of Bristol

Living the Revolution

*Urban Communes & Soviet
Socialism, 1917–1932*

ANDY WILLIMOTT

OXFORD
UNIVERSITY PRESS

OXFORD
UNIVERSITY PRESS

Great Clarendon Street, Oxford, OX2 6DP,
United Kingdom

Oxford University Press is a department of the University of Oxford.
It furthers the University's objective of excellence in research, scholarship,
and education by publishing worldwide. Oxford is a registered trade mark of
Oxford University Press in the UK and in certain other countries

© Andy Willimott 2017

The moral rights of the author have been asserted

First Edition published in 2017

Impression: 1

Published in the United States of America by Oxford University Press
198 Madison Avenue, New York, NY 10016, United States of America

British Library Cataloguing in Publication Data
Data available

Library of Congress Control Number: 2016935942

ISBN 978–0–19–872582–4

Printed in Great Britain by
Clays Ltd, St Ives plc

For my parents

Acknowledgements

Many individuals and institutions helped to inspire this book and get it to this point.

Thanks to the UK Arts & Humanities Research Council for funding my first explorations into the world of the urban communes and communards, and to the Leverhulme Trust for granting me a three-year early career research fellowship and the time to bring the book to fruition.

Thanks to the team at Oxford University Press, especially the commissioning editor, Robert Faber, and assistant commissioning editor, Cathryn Steele, for their support, enthusiasm, and professionalism. Thanks to my copy-editor, Elizabeth Stone, for her keen eye and skill. Thanks also to the anonymous readers for their constructive criticism and detailed engagement with the early manuscript. The readers subsequently identified themselves as Christopher Read and Mark Steinberg.

Thanks to those who agreed to read all or part of the manuscript, offering valuable comments along the way, including Edward Acton, David Brandenberger, Michael David-Fox, Juliane Fürst, Geoffrey Hosking, Dan Healey, Francis King, Diane Koenker, Lisa Kirschenbaum, Kristin Roth-Ey, Stephen A. Smith, Lewis Siegelbaum, and Matt Worely.

Thanks to the fellow researchers and scholars who put up with me in Moscow and St Petersburg, especially those who elected to share an apartment with me at one point or another, including Alan Crawford, J. J. Gura, Samantha Sherry, Simon Huxtable, and Alessandro Iandalo. Thanks to George Gilbert and Scott Siggins for sharing their enthusiasm for all things Russian. Jonathan Waterlow deserves particular thanks—not only for his friendship and good company over the years, but for reading and commenting on the manuscript for this book and countless other things, often at short notice.

Thanks to the School of History at UEA, where, surrounded by the inspiring architecture of Denys Lasdun and Norman Foster, I first decided to embark on my inquiries into modern dreamers and alternative forms of living. And thanks to the UCL School of Slavonic & East European Studies, where I held my Leverhulme fellowship, engaged in many interesting debates, and wrote much of this book.

I owe a debt of gratitude to several scholars at these two institutes, especially Peter Waldron, whom I was fortunate to have as a passionate and knowledgeable supervisor, and Matthias Neumann, who was an early and enthusiastic backer. Both are now dear friends. Cathie Carmichael was also a positive secondary supervisor to my postgraduate work. Also, particular thanks to Simon Dixon—a witty, supportive, fun, and yet thorough and challenging mentor. And Susan Morrissey was a source of wisdom throughout my Leverhulme fellowship. All read more than their fair share of book proposals and early drafts, too.

Thanks also to my new colleagues at the University of Reading for providing me with a warm welcome and helping to minimize disruption to the final stages of editing.

Thanks to those that have presented alongside me at conferences and to those that commented on various commune-based research papers over the years, be it at the Annual Conference of the Association of Slavonic, East European & Eurasian Studies (ASEEES) in Los Angeles, Washington, New Orleans, Boston, Austin, and Philadelphia; the Annual Conference of the British Association of Slavonic & Eastern European Studies (BASEES) in Cambridge; the International Council for Central and East European Studies (ICCEES) World Congress in Stockholm and Tokyo; gatherings of the Study Group of the Russian Revolution (SGRR) in Belfast and Norwich; or the Russian studies seminars of UCL SSEES and Oxford.

Thanks to those behind the wonderfully titled Russian Archive Training Scheme (RATS), especially Polly Jones and Alexander Titov, who introduced me to the repositories of Moscow and St Petersburg several years ago, and have remained good friends ever since.

Thanks to the staff of the libraries in which I went on to conduct research: the UCL SSEES Library and the British Library, in the UK, and the Russian State Library (a.k.a. 'the Lenin Library') and the State Public Historical Library, in Russia. Thanks also to the staff of the archives and museums in which I conducted research: RGASPI, RGASPI-m, GARF, TsGA, OKhDOPIM, SPbETU, and MRGPU im. Herzen. Galina Mikhailova Tokareva (RGASPI-m) and Ekaterina Matveevna Kolosova (MRGPU im. Herzen) deserve honourable mention.

Thanks to Veronika Bowker and Anastasia Khachemizova for offering answers to linguistic anomalies that had me stumped, and for providing me with warm Russian hospitality on numerous occasions.

Above all, a special thank you to Jennifer Helen Davey, my strongest critic, my fiercest friend, and my partner in all things.

And a special thank you to my parents. I dedicate this book to them, as I said I would: a poor reimbursement for their unfaltering love and support.

Andy Willimott

London

Contents

List of Illustrations

Acronyms in Archival Citations

GARF	*Gosudarstvennyi arkhiv Rossiiskoi Federatsii* (State Archive of the Russian Federation)
MRGPU im. Herzen	*Muzei istorii Rossiiskii gosudarstvennyi pedagogicheskii universitet im. A. I. Gertsena* (Museum of History, A. I. Herzen State Pedagogical University)
Muzei istorii SPbETU	*Muzei istorii Sankt-Peterburgskogo gosudarstvennogo elektrotekhnicheskogo universiteta, 'LETI'* (Museum of History, St Petersburg State Electro-technical University, 'LETI')
OKhDOPIM	*Otdel khraneniia dokumentov obshchestvenno-politicheskoi istorii Moskvy* (Divisional Repository of the Social-Political History of Moscow)
RGASPI	*Rossiiskii gosudarstvennyi arkhiv sotsial'no-politicheskoi istorii* (Russian State Archive of Socio-Political History)
TsAG Moskvy	*Tsentral'nyi arkhiv goroda Moskvy* (Central Archive of the City of Moscow)
TsDAHOU	*Tsentral'nyi derzhavnyi arkhiv hromads'kykh ob'iednan' Ukrainy* (Central State Archive of Public Organizations of Ukraine; former Party Archive)
TsGAMO	*Tsentral'nyi gosudarstvennyi arkhiv Moskovskoi oblasti* (Central State Archive of the Moscow oblast)

ABBREVIATIONS IN ARCHIVAL CITATIONS

f.	*fond*	(collection)
op.	*opis'*	(inventory)
d.	*delo*	(file)
l.	*list*	(folio)
ll.	*listy*	(folios)
ob.	*obrorot*	(verso)

A Note on Names and Transliteration

All Russian names have been rendered into the Latin text in accordance with the Library of Congress system of transliteration, except when another spelling has become standardized in English, for example, Krupskaya instead of Krupskaia, Trotsky instead of Trotskii, and Mayakovsky instead of Maiakovskii.

Let the old whine on!—
Our ranks are young.
We
    Shall surely enter
Into the high noon of the commune.

Vladimir Mayakovsky,
March of the Komsomols
(1923)

Introduction
Making their Revolution

Have you ever wondered what it would be like to be part of a revolution? What it would be like to experience the energy and the promise of a new beginning, to be swept up in the tides of change, to embrace the prospect of a new world? You might have imagined the hopes and dreams that pulsed through the veins of the activists and idealists at the heart of this book. These were young hopefuls who declared the formation of urban communes—revolutionary examples of socialist living—inside whatever domestic lodgings they could lay their hands on after the October Revolution. 'If not us, then who?' was the driving thought that motivated many of those who came to form these cohabiting alliances. It also perfectly encapsulated the sense of possibility felt during the opening years of the revolution.[1] Here, impatient for change, would-be radicals experimented with the ideas of collectivism, equality, and the rational reorganization of living. They tried to bring this thing called socialism to life. And, in turn, they helped to initiate a trend that continued to captivate aspiring Communist Youth League (Komsomol) and party members across the opening decade of the Soviet Union. This book tells the history of these collective activists and the history of the urban commune as a revolutionary initiative.

This is a tale of revolutionary aspiration, appropriation, and participation at ground level. In many ways, by asserting their choice to live collectively and in ways they defined as socialist, the subjects of this book tried to *be the change* they wanted to see in the world. Or, in the words of the father of Russian revolutionary literature, Nikolai Chernyshevsky, they were determined to 'strive toward it, work for it, bring it nearer', to make the promises of revolution a reality.[2]

By paying close attention to the urban communes and the people that created these groups, this book will chart the production and consumption of socialist ideology among aspiring revolutionaries. It will explore the connection between Soviet socialism and the articulation of popular identities, as well as the evolution of Soviet political culture—understood as the field of ideas, beliefs, and conceptions that helped shape the revolutionary agenda.[3] According to traditional visions

---

[1] 'Esli ne my, to kto zhe?', *Komsomol'skaia Pravda*, 16 April 1927, 4.

[2] Nikolai Chernyshevsky, *What Is to Be Done?*, trans. Michael R. Katz (Ithaca, NY: Cornell University Press, 1989), 379.

[3] Cf. Steven Best and Douglas Keller, *Postmodern Theory: Critical Interrogations* (London: Macmillan, 1991); Peter Schöttler, 'Historians and Discourse Analysis', *History Workshop Journal*, no. 27 (1989), 37–65.

of the Soviet Union, popular experience and public reception mattered little after 1917. By rights—at least according to these interpretations—the urban communes should not have existed. But such versions of the Soviet Union can themselves only exist when real life is distilled to the point of abstraction. As ever, by focusing on politics and political outcomes in isolation we miss something: we fail to appreciate the arenas in which politics are played out and the effect that these arenas can have on politics along the way. For, as we will see, in reality the urban communes operated in-between autonomy and authority, and their actions reveal the messy, quotidian manner by which the supposedly unambiguous, orderly, and structured visions of Soviet socialism actually came into being.[4]

The urban communes were the product of a revolution that vowed to change the world. Erupting out of the political and social chaos of the failed tsarist state, the October Revolution gave birth to the first socialist state in history and ushered in far-reaching reforms designed to tackle social inequality, injustice, and exploitation. Capitalism, liberalism, and the Church were declared enemies of state. They were to be replaced by a radically new political order founded on the principles of Marxist ideology—a system that pledged to pass all the means of production into common ownership, equalize pay, and elevate the working class into positions of authority. A new type of state and society was supposed to emerge through the imagined virtues of the proletariat and the untapped potential of collective human harmony. This was just the sort of uncompromising break with the past that many had come to demand during the uncertainty of 1917. As the earliest socialist decrees were passed, and as the first pamphlets, posters, and banners of the Bolshevik-led government began to adorn the streets, many ordinary people started to ask: What could this new world look like and what might revolution mean for us?

At work, in markets, gathered around newspaper kiosks and samovars, groups of people excitedly discussed new possibilities. Buoyed by a sense of enfranchisement, many overturned symbols of the old order. Some workers carted their bosses out the door in wheelbarrows—a well-established form of labour protest and self-empowerment dating back to the uprisings of 1905. Others formed committees to requisition control of their factories, directly implementing the rhetoric of 'workers' control'.[5] Teenagers rejected the authority of their parents; women were emboldened to challenge the patriarchy; and many others joined nascent discussion circles and grassroots organizations—all in the name of the October Revolution.[6]

---

[4] Andy Willimott, 'Everyday Revolution: The Making of the Soviet Urban Communes', in Adele Lindenmeyr, Christopher Read, and Peter Waldron (eds), *Russia's Home Front, 1914–1922: The Experience of War and Revolution* (Bloomington, IN: Slavica, 2016), 431–54.

[5] Stephen A. Smith, *Red Petrograd: Revolution in the Factories 1917–1918* (Cambridge: Cambridge University Press, 1983), esp. 55–7, 192, 193, 196, 199.

[6] See Anne E. Gorsuch, *Youth in Revolutionary Russia: Enthusiasts, Bohemians, Delinquents* (Bloomington: Indiana University Press, 2000); Wendy Z. Goldman, *Women, the State & Revolution: Soviet Family Policy & Social Life, 1917–1936* (Cambridge: Cambridge University Press, 1993); Isabel A. Tirado, *Young Guard! The Communist Youth League, Petrograd 1917–1929* (New York: Greenwood Press, 1988); Matthias Neumann, *The Communist Youth League and the Transformation of the Soviet Union, 1917–1932* (London: Routledge, 2011).

The parameters of this new world were still being formed in both a practical sense and in the minds of those people that now found themselves citizens of socialism.

This was the environment that gave birth to the urban commune, with revolutionary activists starting to rethink, among other things, their domestic habits and the way they conducted their everyday lives. They set about putting into practice their own conceptions of what it meant to be part of this 'new dawn'. In the tenements and basic housing of the early Soviet landscape, these enthusiasts were dramatically reimagining the home. Innocuous features of domestic life—from internal walls to personal ornaments—became associated with 'bourgeois individualism' and had to be rejected. This was their understanding of materialist philosophy—direct and to the point; the delay between thought and action was barely perceptible. They were questioning the fundamentals of life and looking to the potential of revolutionary change. While the Bolsheviks sought to consolidate governmental power, the making of socialist revolution remained an open project in the eyes of these activists. This book is formed around the hopes and experiences of these early Soviet citizens: those that came to embrace new possibilities, those that believed History was on their side.

*

If you were to visit Petrograd in the winter of 1919–20 and take a walk through the northern outskirts of the city, away from the neoclassical grandeur of Nevsky Prospekt, you would find three polytechnic students who had just declared the formation of a 'commune' within the confines of a simple dormitory room. In the corner of this room sits a small tin, or 'common pot' (*obshchii kotel*), alongside a noticeboard and a large basket of clothes. Look beyond the humble nature of this abode, with its exposed wooden floor and signs of structural neglect, and you soon notice that these young activists are in the process of establishing a system of pooled resources and shared duties. As a gesture of equality, linen, socks, and underwear are provided at the common expense, while household tasks, including meal preparation—usually limited to bread, potatoes, soup, and porridge—are undertaken by all cohabitants. A general roster, written on the noticeboard, ensures that they each take their turn performing these duties. In the centre of the room a small table serves as a place for collective meals, group meetings, study, and political discussion. Sometimes fellow students and neighbours are invited to debate the merits and practical implications of socialism around this table. On such occasions, the beds, which are pushed up against the walls, provide the necessary extra seating. The peaceable sharing of this multipurpose space seems to be equated with the socialist practice of mutual cooperation and 'rational management'.[7]

This dormitory was just one of numerous urban residences where you could witness a group of young people experimenting with the revolutionary ideas of their day. The first urban communes consisted of a few like-minded individuals looking to share resources, materials, income, and, most important of all, modern socialist visions. They embraced one of the key tenets of Marxism: 'From each

[7] N. A. Filimonov, *Po novomu ruslu, vospominaniia* (Leningrad: Leninizdat', 1967), 3–15.

according to his ability, to each according to his needs!' Contemporary reports reveal that many groups also wrote 'founding charters' (*ustavy*) dictating the outline of a socialist lifestyle, which often included a commitment to collective decision-making, the 'rational organization' of daily schedules, and participation in wider revolutionary activities. They also tended to set strict guidelines on admittance and expulsion procedures, with all members expected to display a firm commitment to the basic principle of collectivism.[8] The activists that united in these cohabitative alliances, often active in Komsomol and party campaigns, would have been aware that the Bolsheviks were encouraging agricultural communities to experiment with such organizational methods and collective ideals in the Soviet countryside at this time. They were evidently inspired to try their hand at something similar in the city. Plus, as we shall see, they were also influenced by a Russian radical tradition that placed a lot of weight on group activity and collective action. And their actions did not go unnoticed. Within a year of the October Revolution, some newspapers were reporting that the urban communes had started to release domestic life from 'the bourgeois yoke'.[9]

Despite their practical engagement with socialist ideology and the interest they garnered from the press and other contemporaries, the urban communes have largely remained on the margins of Soviet history. While they have not entirely escaped the attention of historians—occasionally appearing in brief asides concerning the 'anomalies' of revolution—we still know very little about these groups.[10] No study has presented a comprehensive account of their origins, activities, or development. As a result, there has been a tendency to think of the communes as conductor-less orchestras or pupil-led classes—one of those arresting but ultimately superfluous and fleeting examples of revolutionary utopia. Indeed, anyone who has read *Revolutionary Dreams* might be forgiven for thinking that the urban communes were part of what Richard Stites saw as an intriguing moment in Soviet history when random and isolated utopian experimentation sprang to life, quite separate from the statist ambitions of the Bolshevik-led revolutionary project. Stites presented the array of utopian practices seen across the opening decade of the Soviet Union as some sort of alternative to the harsh realities of the socialist state, especially when compared to that which was to come under Stalin. In his view, these utopian practices were among the most important things to emerge out of the October Revolution. This approach distinguishes between the ambitions of the 'dreamers' and the general political development of the October Revolution. It celebrates the child-like beauty and innocence of utopian action. But it also

---

[8] 'Rabochaia zhizn', *Pravda*, 12 August 1919, 4; 'Pervaia rabochaia domovaia kommuna', *Pravda*, 12 August 1919, 2.

[9] 'Po kvartiram rabochikh', *Kommunar*, 9 October 1918, 3. *Kommunar* was a daily newspaper published in Moscow under the auspices of the Central Committee of the All-Union Communist Party (Bolsheviks). This publication keenly followed the emergence of the urban commune phenomenon before its staff and stories were subsumed within larger circulations in mid-1919.

[10] The best of these accounts can be found in Richard Stites, *Revolutionary Dreams: Utopian Vision and Experimental Life in the Russian Revolution* (New York: Oxford University Press, 1989), esp. 213–19.

encourages us to excise such creations from their natural habitat, and instead place them among the clouds.[11]

When I first started to research the lives of the communes, I expected to find a short-lived story of utopian folly. I thought I would discover a few radical individuals involved in some sort of counterculture, much like the hippie communities of 1960s America. Maybe, I thought, the urban communes represented an attempt to establish some sort of idyll not dissimilar to the Hutterites or other religious colonies, cutting themselves off from mainstream society while they awaited the advent of the Second Coming or a Golden Dawn.[12] But what I discovered was far more interesting and dynamic. Following the voices of these activists—who frequently referred to themselves as 'communards' (*kommunary*) and 'civic agitators' (*obshchestvenniki*)—I soon realized that they were deeply involved in the revolutionary processes and social changes taking place around them.[13] Far from isolating themselves, the communes and communards were often in communication with local Bolshevik organizations and the Soviet press. Many sought and went on to hold party and/or Komsomol membership. It became apparent that these activists were searching for both themselves and the wider meaning of revolution.

As the first full and documented account of the urban communes, this book cannot avoid telling a tale of popular experience and revolutionary practice. The communards lived their beliefs, testing them in a daily struggle. The story of their lives should be read as an example of grand revolutionary visions understood and digested at the human level. It comments on the connection between ideas and reality, people and state, institutional power and social agency. By telling their story, this book adds texture to Soviet ideology and brings revolution to life. But the experience of such groups can also help us to better account for the manner of the Soviet state's early development, connecting revolutionary process and outcome. Indeed, as I began to uncover the lost world of the urban communes and communards, I was reminded time and again that the past can be just as messy and complicated as the present. As the communes came into focus, a picture of tangible, even prosaic, revolution began to emerge.

*

Communards sought to interpret, navigate, and carve out their own political identities in a world that was still in flux. They also brought ideas and ideology to bear on their immediate problems. In one instance, a group of workers vowed to form a commune alliance over their lunch break, aware that together they might

---

[11] Stites, *Revolutionary Dreams*, esp. chs 10–11.

[12] For example, see Timothy Miller, *The 60s Communes: Hippies and Beyond* (New York: Syracuse University Press, 1999); Rosabeth M. Kanter, *Commitment and Community: Communes and Utopias in Sociological Perspective* (Cambridge, MA: Harvard University Press, 1972); Kanter (ed.), *Communes: Creating and Managing the Collective Life* (New York: Harper & Row, 1973); Robert S. Fogarty, *All Things New: American Communes and Utopian Movements 1860–1914* (Chicago, IL: University of Chicago Press, 1990).

[13] O. Snar, 'Zadachi momenta', *Iunyi kommunist,* no. 16 (1919), 1–3; Iu. Verber, 'Krasnovorotskaia', *Krasnoe studenchestvo,* no. 6 (1929), 20–1.

improve the state of their factory-based living quarters.[14] The material hardship of their surroundings provided the inescapable context for their interpretation of socialist goals.[15] Similarly, in 1918, a group of ten activists spontaneously formed a commune in apartment block 22, Preobrazhenskaia Gate (now Preobrazhenskaia Square), to the northeast of Moscow. Here, amid the ruins of a dilapidated apartment, with peeling wallpaper, draughty windows, and no running water, the prospect of renovation—the work that had to be undertaken to make this abode habitable—was understood in revolutionary terms. It was seen as a means of overcoming both the social standing of the previous 'bourgeois' occupants and the material backwardness of Russia.[16] Through acts such as these—more than the official campaigns of the period—Marxist visions came to life. This was historical progress.

Equally, returning to the three-person dormitory commune in the northern quarter of Petrograd, we should note that this venture had actually emerged from what was essentially a particularly lively study group. These students—part of that demographic perhaps most susceptible to new ideas—were stirred into action by the prospect of being part of something of grand historical significance. At the same time, while they looked to use their shared resources to promote the socialist ideal of collective enlightenment and collective betterment, these same individuals also enjoyed holding impromptu parties: drinking, dancing, and, at least on one occasion, attracting the attention of the police.[17] The world of the urban commune, then, was not without contradictions and capricious behaviour. As the journalist and activist Ella Winter noted on her travels through Soviet Russia, the urban communes were not always steadfast or uniform in their convictions. She had herself noticed that while some communes condemned 'ephemeral sexual connections and an unbridled sex life', others proved quite promiscuous and dissolute. And, as with the polytechnic students, mischief and deviance was far from uncommon.[18] This was, in other words, socialism in real life. It was immediate, indeterminate, and imperfect.

While, at first glance, the urban communes and communards of this period might seem to fit into Stites's somewhat linear and tragic depiction of Soviet utopia and experimental living, the reality was unquestionably more complex. Stites certainly captured the hope and optimism that many young activists and communards must have felt, but, in his rendering, their revolution always appeared one step removed from the construction of the first socialist state.[19] By looking at the everyday functioning and nitty-gritty realities of the urban communes and communards, this book presents a grounded view of utopianism, activism, and revolutionary dreaming in the early Soviet state. Indeed, for one thing, the actions of the urban communes and communards were a product of revolutionary hope, but they were also fundamentally linked to their belief in the statist-revolutionary project—the idea that a new and

---

[14] Iu. Ber, *Kommuna segodnia, Opyt proizvodstvennykh i bytovykh kommun molodezhi* (Moscow, 1930), 59–60.

[15] Cf. Diane P. Koenker, *Republic of Labor: Russian Printers and Soviet Socialism, 1918–1930* (Ithaca, NY: Cornell University Press, 2005), 17.

[16] 'Po kvartiram rabochikh', 3.   [17] Filimonov, *Po novomu ruslu, vospominaniia*, 13–15.

[18] Ella Winter, *Red Virtue: Human Relationships in the New Russia* (London, 1933), 144–6.

[19] Stites, *Revolutionary Dreams*, esp. ch. 11.

interventionist socialist state could create the conditions for a harmonious, rational, and modern world. These were true believers in the cause. Very few could be said to offer a rosy alterative to the Bolshevik project. In that respect, this book might also carry a warning: Be careful what you wish for. For, as well as presenting a tale of hope and optimism, this book reveals how an activist trend and an approach to life came into existence and evolved alongside Bolshevik ideology and in-between the apparatuses of the state.

SPACES, LOCATIONS, NUMBERS

The urban communes existed in many different shapes and sizes. Some of the first commune groups emerged, like our polytechnic example, inside the dormitories of Russia's institutes of higher education. Petrograd, in particular, served as a seedbed for young student communes between 1918 and 1920.[20] It was home to a number of educational institutes and a vibrant student community, even during the shortages and general hardship of civil war. With the Bolsheviks introducing a system of class-based positive discrimination (*vydvizhenie*), and with the establishment of workers' faculties (*rabfaki*) in September 1919, the everyday politics of revolution was ripe within these institutes.[21] The dormitories of the pedagogical institutes that became the Herzen University in 1920, alongside various other Petrograd academies, and subsequently the educational establishments of Moscow, also witnessed the formation of student communes.

Other commune groups established themselves in the apartments, hostels, and workers' barracks of urban Russia. These groups looked to extend collectivism to city life. They tended to be made up of radical workers and youths taking action into their own hands; new urban migrants searching for a cause; and returning Red Army soldiers looking to extend their experience of comradely cooperation.[22] The first of these arrangements arose as the Bolsheviks issued decrees sanctioning 'revolutionary housing repartition' (*revoliutsionnyi zhilishchnyi peredel*), which legalized the seizure of residential property in the name of the proletariat.[23] In principle, local soviets were supposed to lead the reclamation of housing space: overseeing the movement of the hitherto deprived Russian masses from their dishevelled hovels into the spacious homes of the former elite.[24] In practice, however, reports

[20] Cf. N. B. Lebina, *Povsednevnaia zhizn' sovetskogo goroda: normy i anomalii, 1920/1930 gody* (St Petersburg: Letnii Sad, 1999), 164–5.

[21] Peter Konecny, *Builders and Deserters: Students, State, and Community in Leningrad, 1917–1941* (Montreal: McGill-Queen's University Press, 1999), esp. ch. 2; Susan K. Morrissey, *Heralds of Revolution: Russian Students and the Mythologies of Radicalism* (New York: Oxford University Press, 1998), epilogue.

[22] For an example of Red Army activists, see M. Zagarnyi, 'Pis'mo kommunara', *Molodaia gvardiia*, no. 3 (1930), 79–81.

[23] 'Pereselenie v burzhuaznye doma', *Kommunar*, 17 October 1918, 2.

[24] See John N. Hazard, *Soviet Housing Law* (New Haven, CT: Yale University Press, 1939); Gregory D. Andrusz, *Housing and Urban Development in the USSR* (Basingstoke: Macmillan, 1984); Victor Buchli, *An Archaeology of Socialism* (New York: Berg, 1999).

show that the process of eviction and resettlement was frequently left to workers' organizations, housing commissions, factory committees, and even urban commune activists.[25] Some Bolsheviks expressed concern about the potential ramifications of such practices. They worried that local initiative might lead to uncontrollable revolutionary excess. But these symbolically rich and cathartic acts often remained in the hands of local groups. Emerging from this environment, it is not surprising that the 'housing problem' became an integral part of commune life.[26] Indeed, this remained the case even after the policy of 'revolutionary housing repartition' was officially curtailed with the introduction of the New Economic Policy (NEP) in 1921.

The actual number of cohabitants within a single commune could vary. As the Soviet novelist, playwright, and journalist Vera Panova recalled from her brief experience of commune life in the early 1920s, these groups could start with as few as three or four friends joining forces to reject the family home.[27] They settled in single dormitory rooms, small apartments, or subdivided residential arrangements. Space was often at a premium. In one instance, a commune of six young men and one woman was recorded residing in a factory barrack room of just twenty-five square metres.[28] After 1919, as the political emergency and economic restrictions of civil war began to ease, some commune groups became more ambitious. Occasionally they would spill across multiple rooms or take over neighbouring rooms, if they managed to attract new members. In some instances, communes grew their membership into double figures. And in still rarer instances, the most successful and ambitious groups expanded into the low hundreds, filling large sections of residential blocks and occasionally whole buildings.[29] From even the smallest of seeds, the most ambitious visions could emerge.

These larger communes might be said to share many of the characteristics of a residential cooperative—a vision that can be linked back to the model communities established by Robert Owen in New Lanark and New Harmony at the beginning of the nineteenth century. The resultant cooperative movement, which took root in Britain and France against the backdrop of a brutalizing industrial revolution, offered collective security to participants who agreed to join together in common association, selling goods under the umbrella of a community store or a community-owned outlet. Indeed, aware of these origins, some urban commune groups did try to establish a relationship with their local cooperative establishments. The spirit of socialism was not always shared, however. One particularly engaged commune tried to solicit the help of their local cooperative as they embarked upon creating a public canteen within their residential block. But just before they were due to open, the members of this cooperative, in a particularly un-comradely act, broke in and stole the group's utensils. Expecting to cater for up to 400 people, the commune was left with the woefully inadequate sum of six bowls and a handful of

---

[25] I. Gromov, 'Zhilishchnaia nerazberikha', *Kommunar*, 1 November 1918, 3.

[26] Gromov, 'Zhilishchnaia nerazberikha', 3.

[27] V. F. Panova, *O moei zhizni, knigakh i chitateliakh* (Leningrad, 1980), ch. 25.

[28] Ber, *Kommuna segodnia*, 35.   [29] See 'Kommuna', *Pedvuzovets,* 28 November 1929, 4.

cutlery.[30] Needless to say, the canteen was not a success and relations between the commune and cooperative remained poor thereafter.

This unfortunate incident aside, the Bolsheviks' ambiguous attitude toward the cooperative movement both before and after 1917 helped to make space for the most ambitious commune creations. And, in this sense, the urban communes and communards should be understood as part of a largely unmandated social phenomenon or revolutionary trend. Contemporary reports suggest that a few hundred urban communes were formed across Petrograd and Moscow during the opening years of revolution.[31] Built on personal alliances and friendships, they remained prone to splits, arguments, and periodic disintegration. One urban commune even managed to fall out and disband in just seven hours.[32] But, all the same, within the dormitories of higher education and the housing facilities of Soviet industry, communes continued to form and spread their message. They looked to expand on the social and cultural causes of the October Revolution.

During the years of NEP (1921–27), they established a small but firm foothold within these establishments and, in the process, secured themselves a place in Soviet public discourse. When asked, some activists reported that they had first encountered the idea of forming a commune in the local newspaper or on the bulletin boards of their place of study or work.[33] At the same time, the Soviet national print media, particularly the youth press, started to publish more articles on and by the communards. As a result, hundreds more young idealists started to establish their own communes in other parts of the Soviet Union. Groups appeared in Kiev and Dnepropetrovsk, in Ukraine, and then in Vladivostok and other urban industrial sites to the east.[34] They were forming wherever significant urbanization was taking place, sometimes setting up base in makeshift tents because housing construction tended to lag behind demand in such places.

Toward the end of the 1920s, as Soviet industrialization geared up, and as the revolutionary discourse on collectivism, egalitarianism, and solidarity reached a new peak, the number of urban communes started to grow dramatically. Recalling Lenin's support for the *subbotniki*—a movement of volunteers that partook in additional social work in their free time—the party also encouraged its organs to foster a greater level of local initiative and social activism.[35] As a result, in some places, urban communes successfully acquired the support of factory foremen, Komsomol cells, and even local authorities.[36]

---

[30] Timofeev, 'Staryi byt, novym bit', *Krasnoe studenchestvo*, no. 4 (1930), 26.

[31] For example, see 'Rabochie i kommuny', *Kommunar*, 24 December 1918, 3; 'Gorodskie kommuny', *Kommunar*, 27 December 1918, 3.

[32] E. Mikulina, 'Kommuna sliudianits', *Molodaia gvardiia*, no. 8 (1931), 68.

[33] Kuper, 'V kommunakh dal'nego vostoka', *Krasnoe studenchestvo*, no. 4 (1930), 27.

[34] Kuper, 'V kommunakh dal'nego vostoka', 27. In the same issue of *Krasnoe studenchestvo* (no. 4, 1930), see Kokorii, 'Krupitsy opyta'; E. Ershov, 'Nuzhen kollektiv'; and Pavlov, 'Dnepropetrovsk', 26–7.

[35] See David Priestland, *Stalinism and the Politics of Mobilization: Ideas, Power, and Terror in Interwar Russia* (Oxford: Oxford University Press, 2007), esp. ch. 3.

[36] *Rossiiskii gosudarstvennyi arkhiv sotsial'no-politicheskii istorii* (hereafter, RGASPI), f. M.1, op. 4, d. 42, ll. 23–32 (Komsomol Central Committee discussion on support for groups partaking in political and cultural campaigns, 23 January 1930).

From humble origins, the urban communes developed into what the Komsomol termed a 'network of activists' by the end of the 1920s.[37] Newspapers started to report numbers in the thousands, and then tens of thousands.[38] With signs of greater external input, this growth reached a peak during the First Five-Year Plan. One snapshot survey of central European Russia conducted in May 1931 reported that 134,000 workers and activists were affiliated to a commune group of some kind, many based in the barracks attached to Soviet industry. This represented 7 per cent of the 1.8 million workers surveyed.[39] Despite this, the Soviet authorities failed to order a comprehensive, central report into the urban communes and their numbers. Drawing on a range of smaller contemporary studies, the research that goes into this book suggests that during the height of the urban commune phenomenon, somewhere between 7 and 14 per cent of all 'shock workers'—those engaged in the practice of collective competition over worker productivity rates—were involved in commune activities at some stage.[40] Numbers fluctuated from factory to factory, and across different industries. But with over 2 million Soviet workers engaged in these new labour practices by 1929, the communards were a significant minority of the urban population.[41]

As the urban commune became an ever more popular means of revolutionary participation, those involved gained increasing recognition as social activists. Come May 1930, the Central Committee of the Communist Party passed a resolution that requested greater attention be paid to groups voluntarily engaged in the 'reconstruction of life' (*perestroika byta*)—echoing Lenin's call to nurture workers' initiatives.[42] Among the studies produced in response to this resolution, the communes and communards were directly associated not only with domestic issues, but with a broad commitment to the social and cultural struggles necessary to drive forward the revolution.[43] This is how many contemporaries came to view the urban communes. One Soviet journal optimistically reported that the urban communes were the 'new shoots' of socialism 'for which Lenin had hoped'.[44]

[37] RGASPI, f. M.1, op. 4, d. 45, ll. 33–34 (Komsomol Central Committee discussion on '*perestroika byta*' and activism, 15 July 1930).

[38] 'Kommuny', *Komsomol'skaia pravda*, 18 January 1930, 4. For a contemporary report on numbers, also see A. Andropov, *Na novykh putiakh studencheskogo byta* (Moscow, 1930).

[39] Z. L. Mindlin and S. A. Kheinman (eds), *Trud v SSSR: statisticheskii spravochnik* (Moscow, 1932), 123; also cited in Lewis H. Siegelbaum, *Stakhanovism and the Politics of Productivity in the USSR, 1935–1941* (Cambridge: Cambridge University Press, 1988), 46.

[40] S. Samuelii, 'Rabotu proizvodstvennykh kommun i kollektivov—na novye rel'sy', *Partiinoe stroitel'stvo*, no. 15–16 (1931), 12; P. Dubner and M. Kozyrev, *Kollektivy i kommuny v bor'be za kommunisticheskuyu formu truda* (Moscow, 1930); S. Zarkhii, *Kommuna v tsekhe* (Moscow, 1930); V. Ol'khov, *Za zhivoe rukovodstvo sotssorevnovaniem, opyt vsesoiuznoi proverki sotssorevnovaniia brigadami VTsSPS* (Moscow, 1930); I. Zaromskii, 'Proizvodstvennye kollektivy—novaia forma organizatsii truda', *Voprosy truda*, no. 4 (1930), 19–20.

[41] On shock-work numbers, see Kenneth M. Straus, *Factory and Community in Stalin's Russia. The Making of an Industrial Working Class* (Pittsburgh, PA: University of Pittsburgh Press, 1997), 140.

[42] A. Kaishtat, I. Ryvkin, and I. Soschovik, *Kommuny molodezhi. Po materialam obsledovania i pod redaktsiei instituta sanitarnoi kul'tury* (Moscow, 1931), 3, 15–16.

[43] For example, see Kaishtat et al., *Kommuny molodezhi* and Ol'khov, *Za zhivoe rukovodstvo sotssorevnovaniem*.

[44] 'V nastuplenie!', *Smena*, no. 19 (1929), 1. This article references Lenin's description of the *subbotniki* in 1919. See V. I. Lenin, 'A Great Beginning: Heroism of Workers in the Rear. "Worker Subbotniks" ', in *Collected Works* vol. 29 (Moscow: Progress Publishers, 1965), 409–34.

DIALOGUE WITH REVOLUTION

In their various activities and numerous locations, the urban communes and communards tell us much about the October Revolution. Each commune holds up a mirror to the larger story of how revolution, state, and society developed after 1917. The image they reflect is often complicated and irregular, revealing the day-to-day realities of revolutionary practice. Like all Soviet citizens at this time, the communards were ultimately subject to party decisions and the powers of a small Bolshevik elite. But they also showed the readiness and capacity to condition revolutionary imperatives and ideological messages at ground level, especially during the 1920s. In other words, they were not the leaders of revolution, but they did have the ability to affect the manner by which revolutionary ideas came into being. What is most apparent from the communard experience, then, is that the development of the October Revolution was far from predetermined. Nor was it rolled out at will. Marx had not left the Bolsheviks with the blueprints to socialism, merely the will to stumble forth in search of new political methods and a new way of life. The modern, centralizing ambitions of the Soviet leadership should not blind us to the particular circumstances through which revolutionary messages had to emerge.

As this book will show, the urban communes and communards were involved in a dialogue with revolution, sometimes overtly communicating with local revolutionary representatives, official bodies, and the press. Starting with the latter, it should be noted that the communards were keen readers of the Soviet press. Many proudly advertised the fact that they subscribed to leading newspapers and journals.[45] These sources provided both digestible information and a means of presenting one's revolutionary identity to the wider world. The communards implemented and debated the ideas presented within these pages, sometimes subtly reworking them to suit their surroundings. Some showed remarkable self-assurance, inviting neighbours, peers, and complete strangers into the commune to discuss their interpretations of important revolutionary issues. Others helped form propaganda teams and agitation campaigns to spread the revolutionary ideas with which they were most engaged.[46] In this way, they helped to condition the local setting for revolution, while also lending weight to certain ideological messages—usually those relating to domestic reformation, collectivism, and teamwork. It might be said that these actions were helping to develop some form of social or ideological covenant with revolution: a connection between activist subject and official discourse that defined how the new socialist world would be publicly understood, how certain ideas would be read, and the way that certain individuals would find their place in this world.[47]

---

[45] See G. Levgur, 'Komsomol'skaia kommuna "Kauchuk"', *Iunyi kommunist*, no. 9 (1923), 26–7.

[46] P. Riazanov, 'Govorit kommuna LETI', *Krasnoe studenchestvo*, no. 2–3 (1930), 24.

[47] Cf. Joshua A. Sanborn, *Drafting the Russian Nation: Military Conscription, Total War, and Mass Politics, 1905–1925* (Dekalb: Northern Illinois University Press, 2003), 14–20, esp. 15–16. As Sanborn notes on the formation of national identity, while the (subject's) response is often weaker than the (official) call, it is still necessary to the formation of an ideological covenant.

Certainly, a cyclical relationship developed whereby the communards embraced the ideas and language of the press, and then some sections of the print media, noticing their potential, opened their pages to the urban communes. In a letter published by the Soviet journal *Iunyi kommunist* (*Young Communist*) in 1919, one activist and early communard publicly stated that those involved in the urban communes were leading the way in terms of revolutionary construction. Such spaces were needed, it was insisted, 'especially in big cities' where many people 'live in very bad conditions, renting room corners at exorbitant prices ... with little opportunity to read a book' or partake in revolutionary discussion. In contrast, the communes were shown to offer a space where occupants could read, learn, and better one another. Among other things, the activist draws upon Soviet calls for 'cultural revolution' (*kul'turnaia revoliutsiia*) and a Marxist understanding of material determinism within this letter. By sharing resources and pooling their money, he continued, the communards were laying 'the foundations of the communist system'.[48]

As they engaged with some of the key concerns of Soviet revolutionary discourse, we should note, many urban communes and communards began to press their local Komsomol cells and various other representatives. They urged them to take stock of their thoughts, experiences, and actions. Addressing the Komsomol directly, for example, the communard writing to *Iunyi kommunist* also insisted that the urban commune should be seen as a device to advance the revolutionary cause. The urban communes, he claimed, could bring great benefit to youth, institutions such as the Komsomol, and the wider Soviet state.[49]

This young activist was not alone in his bold assertions. Through the press and in person, many urban communards confronted the Komsomol and other bodies on issues that were important to them. Others still—quite sure of themselves—called upon various institutions and representatives to help replicate their example. As we will see in the coming pages, many groups tried to promote the creation and proper regulation of collective cafeterias and canteens within the universities; many became embroiled in the pursuit of new working methods and management systems within the factories; and some subjected themselves to outside scrutiny in the simple hope that they could make a bigger impact upon the revolution.

This points to a central tension at the heart of this book: the urban communes and communards were never fully endorsed by the Komsomol or the party, but they were not without their supporters (and therefore had a degree of influence) within the broader structure of these organizations. At the Third Congress of the Komsomol, in October 1920, delegates were already declaring that the cohabitant arrangements practised in the urban communes might help to reform the home and 'advance life in general'.[50] In 1921, delegates confirmed that the urban communes could 'protect youths from the corrupting influence of the street, the petty-mindedness of the

---

[48] Aktivnyi rabotnik, 'Kommuny molodezhi', *Iunyi kommunist*, no. 3–4 (1919), 10–11.

[49] Aktivnyi rabotnik, 'Kommuny molodezhi', 10–11.

[50] *Tovarishch komsomol. Dokumenty s"ezdov, konferentsii i TsK VLKSM, 1918–1968* (Moscow, 1969), vol. 1, 34.

family, and the heavy weight of ... [bourgeois] domesticity'.[51] By the end of the 1920s, the Komsomol and the youth press would become even more vocal about the merits of the urban communes.

While these comments did not lead to official endorsement or centralized funding, the urban commune did become a preserve of many rank-and-file Komsomol and party activists. One student commune, home to nearly 100 young activists, boasted that 92 per cent of its occupants held either Komsomol or party membership (51.7 per cent Komsomol and 40.3 per cent party).[52] Indeed, Aleksandr Kosarev, the future leader of the Komsomol, had himself been part of a small, three-person urban commune arrangement after October 1917. For Kosarev, who refused to live with his mother, the urban commune offered an escape from the political and ideological constraints of the family home.[53] Here he could start to develop his revolutionary identity and interact with people more like himself.

On the ground, party people and local representatives sometimes turned to the communes for help. Between January and February 1921, for instance, the party cell at the Automobile Society of Moscow (AMO) plant held a series of discussions in which the urban communes were presented as one potential means of promoting egalitarian relations within the workforce.[54] Komsomol representatives were also known to go round the factory praising the collective camaraderie of urban commune groups.[55] At the same time, in the Moscow machine-tool plant Red Proletariat (*Krasnyi proletarii*), one young Komsomol member named Anikeev reported that he and some friends had formed a commune that managed to secure the support of the local factory committee and party cell.[56] They convinced these representatives that the urban commune was a means of promoting proletarian labour values within the factory. Both sides hoped that the commune would help to spread socialist working practices on the shop floor. The urban commune was not an unwelcome entity at this level, especially at a time when the revolutionary leaders were encouraging mass participation in revolutionary projects.[57]

This is not to say that the urban communes were popular with everyone. Some commune activists were accused of acting too enthusiastically and extending their activities too far. As unofficial bodies, the communes and their supporters were open to criticism and reprimand, especially if they developed too much influence over local representatives or factory foremen. It was sometimes thought that they could push the causes of collegial factory practices at the expense of command management. In some cases they also managed to antagonize their neighbours and

[51] *Tovarishch komsomol. Dokumenty s''ezdov, konferentsii i TsK VLKSM*, 64.

[52] P. Riazanov, 'Govorit kommuna LETI', *Krasnoe studenchestvo*, no. 2–3 (1930), 24.

[53] N. B. Lebina, *Povsednevnaia zhizn' sovetskogo goroda: normy i anomalii, 1920/1930 gody* (St Petersburg: Letnii Sad, 1999), 166.

[54] Simon Pirani, *The Russian Revolution in Retreat, 1920–24: Soviet Workers and the New Communist Elite* (London: Routledge, 2008), 53.

[55] E. Milich, 'Raspad', *Sotsialisticheskii Vestnik*, no. 5–6 (1923), 9.

[56] *Gosudarstvennyi arkhiv Rossiiskoi Federatsii* (hereafter, GARF), f. 7952, op. 3, d. 98, l. 7-ob. (Recollections of former Komsomol cell members at the Red Proletariat factory, 1920s). I am grateful to Simon Pirani for bringing this source to my attention.

[57] GARF, f. 7952, op. 3, d. 98, l. 7-ob.

fellow workers. Older workers, in particular, tended to look upon the communards as young whippersnappers, full of unwarranted confidence. Feeling threatened, some displayed outright contempt toward the communards—do-good 'sons of bitches' that tried to force their way of life on others, surmised one worker.[58]

In their interactions with party organs and wider society, the urban communes and communards reveal much beyond themselves. They can be seen to illuminate the connecting points between ideology and popular experience. At its core, this book shows how the urban communes and communards tried to enact ideological messages. On occasion, we will see, they helped to press the revolutionary agenda of their local representatives. In some cases, they grounded revolutionary ideas, drew attention to important revolutionary shortfalls, and made demands of the political leadership. In this way, they could stall, accelerate, abort, or implement certain aspects of the revolution.[59] Whether or not it was their overt intention, the actions of these groups sometimes helped to decide which revolutionary messages gained the most traction in institution, workplace, and society. On the other hand, sometimes their activism merely initiated friction and tension. Still, the inconsistencies, limitations, failures, and confrontations that emerged as a result of communard action help to expose the realities of ideological reception.

THEMES OF REVOLUTION

This study works on three levels. Firstly, it looks upon the urban communes as an example of everyday revolutionary experience. The principle aim here is to shed more light on common and popular engagements with revolution, adding texture to our understanding of the early Soviet state. Secondly, it explores how the urban communards and their contemporaries could read, interpret, and appropriate socialist ideology. Here we will witness subtle ideological misreading, cases of local preference, and the complicated interaction between material reality and revolutionary dreams. Thirdly, it asks what impact these daily experiences and interpretations had upon the development of the Soviet state. It considers the effect that the urban communes and communards had on their local environment, Soviet discourse, and the wider revolutionary agenda. Taken together, these intersecting concerns offer a new social history based on popular interaction with state imperatives.

In its simplest form, this book makes an argument about the past by telling a story.[60] It does not suggest that the urban communes and communards were *the*

---

[58] Ber, *Kommuna segodnia*, 46.

[59] Cf. J. Arch Getty, *Practicing Stalinism: Bolsheviks, Boyars, and the Persistence of Tradition* (New Haven, CT: Yale University Press, 2013), 186.

[60] This description of the micro-history or micro-narrative approach is articulated in Jill Lepore, *Story of America. Essays on Origins* (Princeton, NJ: Princeton University Press, 2012), 15. Further work undertaken in this manner includes Joan W. Scott, *Gender and the Politics of History* (New York: Columbia University Press, 1999); Jacques Rancière, *Nights of Labour* (Philadelphia, PA: Temple University Press, 1989); Carlo Ginzburg, *The Cheese and the Worms: The Cosmos of a Sixteenth-Century Miller*, trans. John Tedeschi and Anna C. Tedeschi (Baltimore, MD: Johns Hopkins University Press, 1982); Natalie Z. Davis, *Women on the Margins: Three Seventeenth-Century Lives* (Cambridge, MA:

driving force of revolution. Nor does it subscribe to a pseudo-Hobbesian notion that blind individual agency is the cause of all change.[61] But it does suggest that the tale of the urban communards can help us better understand how Soviet socialism began to take shape after 1917. Through the communards we can begin to unpack and more accurately interpret both the way that Soviet citizens expressed revolutionary visions and how the Soviet state implemented socialist policy. In doing so, this book illuminates a number of connecting revolutionary themes present and identifiable in the daily lives of many Soviet citizens across the opening decade of the revolution. The full spectrum of revolution can be seen through the prism of communard activity.

Among these themes, the Russian concept of *byt* was particularly important to the urban communards. Frequently translated as 'the everyday' or 'way of life', the English language can scarcely portray the daily grind or the sense of manifest banality with which this Russian word was associated at the time of the October Revolution. In essence, it came to refer to 'the established order of things'—those inherited and inescapable assumptions about what is natural in life. One of Russia's greatest modern poets, Vladimir Mayakovsky, expressed it best when he said: 'Everything stands as it has been for ages. *Byt* is like a horse that can't be spurred and stands still.' For a revolutionary, *byt* was the feeling that 'One foot has not yet reached the next street', and maybe it never will. Encompassing morality, habit, custom, and convention, all efforts to escape the pervasive spectre of *byt*, claimed Mayakovsky, were like 'attempts to heat up ice cream': you might attempt to alter its structure, but you would always be left with a sticky mess.[62]

Yet the urban communards eagerly and determinedly associated their actions with what became known as the 'new way of life' (*novyi byt*). Visions of the 'new way of life' had been an important part of socialist revolutionary discourse before 1917. Inherent within the revolutionary imagination was the notion that one could modernize daily life by establishing new socialist ethics, habit, and behaviour. It was

---

Harvard University Press, 1995). Also see Levi Giovanni, 'On Microhistory', in Peter Burke (ed.), *New Perspectives on Historical Writing* (Cambridge: Cambridge University Press, 1991), 93–113. NB. In his magnum opus, *France 1848–1945* (Oxford: Clarendon Press, 1977)—a book that held up a series of mirrors on French history to reveal the kaleidoscopic reality of the past—Theodore Zeldin declared: 'I do not feel that I have ceased to be concerned with the universal by studying … in such detail'; vol. 2, p. 1156. *Living the Revolution* follows this work, using the daily experiences of the urban communes and communards to illuminate not just the fact of their existence, but the broader and often complex processes by which the revolution developed.

[61] Cf. Igal Halfin, *From Darkness to Light. Class, Consciousness and Salvation in Revolutionary Russia* (Pittsburgh, PA: University of Pittsburgh Press, 2000), 9–12. Citing the work of Lynn Hunt, Halfin suggests—somewhat unfairly but not without some insight on general historiographical trends—that too many historians of Soviet Russia have assumed that social and economic relations come before or determine cultural and linguistic practices.

[62] Cf. Roman Jakobson, *Language in Literature*, ed. Krystyna Pomorska and Stephen Rudy (Cambridge, MA: Harvard University Press, 1987), 273–300. Infamously, it was the shore of *byt* into which Mayakovsky finally crashed in 1930: his suicide note declared that the pain of his daily existence had become too much for him to bear. Also see Svetlana Boym, *Common Places. Mythologies of Everyday Life in Russia* (Cambridge, MA: Harvard University Press, 1994), esp. ch. 1, and Victor Buchli, *An Archaeology of Socialism* (New York: Berg, 1999), ch. 1 and, for a discussion of *byt* post-destalinization, ch. 7.

not enough to overturn the political order of Russia; the social order needed to go too. The issue of *byt* continued to occupy the minds of Soviet theorists and leading Bolsheviks during the opening years of revolution. Lev Trotsky's widely read *Questions of Everyday Life* (1923) proclaimed that standards of behaviour and new social norms were among the most significant challenges facing the new revolutionary state.[63] Nikolai Bukharin insisted that revolution had to encompass the characteristics, habits, feelings, and desires of each individual. This was, he continued, a revolution on course to tackle the 'manner of life'.[64]

However, while it remained a crucial aspect of revolutionary discourse, there was little consensus as to what this 'new way of life' should look like. Trotsky, for instance, disdained swearing, while fellow Bolsheviks, including Iosif Stalin, celebrated it as a sign of proletarian character. Some insisted that the 'new way of life' would emerge organically, as economic and social relations were transformed; others argued for a prolonged and sustained struggle launched from above.[65] Beyond the ideological tussles of Bolshevik grandees, however, the apparent importance and evident ambiguity of this discursive theme only encouraged activist debate.

For the urban communards, the 'new way of life' came to include domesticity, the family, sex, gender discrimination, and social attitudes. Picking up on the Soviet discourse surrounding the 'women question', many communards became particularly invested in the battle against 'the private kitchen'. After all, this was a gendered space, enforcing the role of 'hostess' on women. Figures such as Aleksandra Kollontai argued that the family kitchen enslaved women, kept them from the labour force, and provided limited nutritional value.[66] In short, Kollontai thought that the individual kitchen was both immoral and irrational. It was, therefore, branded as ideologically reactionary and fundamentally un-modern. The very process of cooking within the private kitchen was also portrayed as highly ritualized, with family recipes and habits being passed down through the generations. In this sense the kitchen was seen as a 'memory space' keeping traditional family structures and the old *byt* alive.[67] It follows that the communes and communards waged their war on the kitchen, as we will see, by promoting collective dining, using shared facilities, and lobbying for more public canteens and cafeterias.

The urban communards occasionally referred to their revolutionary visions under the term 'new life' (*novaia zhizn'*), which seems to have been less closely

    [63] L. Trotsky, 'Voprosy byta', in *Sochineniia*, vol. 21 (Moscow, 1927), 3–58.
    [64] N. Bukharin, 'Za uporiadochenie byta molodezhi', in *Komsomol'skii byt* (Moscow and Leningrad, 1927), 99, cited in Michael David-Fox, *Revolution of the Mind. Higher Learning among the Bolsheviks, 1918–1929* (Ithaca, NY: Cornell University Press, 1997), 106.
    [65] David-Fox, *Revolution of the Mind,* 106–7. Also see Stephen A. Smith, 'The Social Meanings of Swearing: Workers and Bad Language in Late Imperial and Early Soviet Russia', *Past and Present*, no. 160 (1998), 167–202.
    [66] A. Kollontai, 'The Family and the Communist State', speech delivered to the First All-Russian Congress of Women, 1918; reproduced in William G. Rosenberg (ed.), *Bolshevik Visions: First Phase of the Cultural Revolution in Soviet Russia,* 2nd ed. (Ann Arbor: University of Michigan Press, 2002), 67–76.
    [67] Catriona Kelly, *St. Peterberg: Shadows of the Past* (New Haven, CT: Yale University Press, 2014), 86–7. Also see Anya von Bremzen, *Mastering the Art of Soviet Cooking: A Memoir of Food and Longing* (London: Doubleday, 2013).

linked to daily customs and practicalities, and more overtly associated with the philosophy of life in general. The difference was subtle. The 'new way of life' included the creation of a 'red corner' (dedicated reading space) in an otherwise dishevelled apartment, while the 'new life' was symbolized by that most accessible wonder of the modern world, the radio. But as self-identified communards went to listen to this new marvel in the clubs and halls—some even purchasing crystal receivers in the hope of producing their own 'ham' sets—listening to the radio was still considered a group activity and, in its own way, a marker of socialist life.[68] And the same was true for that other modern wonder, the cinema—a visit to which became a vital component of commune life and an activity that was undertaken as a group. Falling either side of the *byt–zhizn'* divide, revolutionary discussions on 'cleanliness', 'hygiene', and 'health' also formed key parts of urban commune life.

Many of these activities also fell under the umbrella of 'cultural revolution'. Lenin noted the promise of 'cultural revolution'—the cultivation of socialist values, goals, and mores—through 'communal canteens, central laundries, crèches and the like'.[69] From this perspective, the idea was to create the human and material infrastructure that would allow a new culture and civilization to grow and flourish. It could be seen to include both the 'new way of life' and the 'new life', but 'cultural revolution' also encompassed themes such as 'enlightenment' (*prosveshchenie*), 'education' (*obrazovanie*), and 'upbringing' (*vospitanie*).[70] The urban communes and communards often embraced these broader themes through the lens of the political and 'cultural campaigns' (*kul'tpokhody*) of the post-revolutionary period. This entailed activists taking to the streets to promote, among other things, literacy and a basic understanding of Marxism. These events were viewed as part of a wider civilizing mission.

Looking beyond the walls of their apartments and engaging in wider activities, the urban communards soon found themselves at the forefront of a new and rapidly developing revolutionary concept: Soviet *obshchestvennost'*. This term had connotations of the public sphere, civil society, citizenry, and social duty. In the revolutionary context, it represented a vision of 'civic-mindedness' or 'civic work' quite specific to Soviet socialism.[71] This was civic agency permitted up to the point before it employed 'oppositionist' ideas or challenged the right of the Bolshevik

---

[68] See Stephen Lovell, *Russia in the Microphone Age: A History of Soviet Radio, 1919–1970* (Oxford: Oxford University Press, 2015), esp. ch. 2.

[69] V. I. Lenin, 'A Great Beginning', 409–34.

[70] David-Fox, *Revolution of the Mind*, 3–7. Also see Christopher Read, *Culture and Power in Revolutionary Russia: The Intelligentsia and the Transition from Tsarism to Communism* (London: Macmillan, 1990).

[71] The literature on this concept has only just begun to emerge. See Catriona Kelly and Vadim Volkov, 'Obshchestvennost', Sobornost': Collective Idenitites', in Catriona Kelly and David Shepherd (eds), *Constructing Russian Culture in the Age of Revolution, 1881–1940* (Oxford: Oxford University Press, 1998), 26–7; I. N. Il'ina, *Obshchestvennye organizatsii Rossii v 1920-e gody* (Moscow: Institut rossiiskoi istorii RAN, 2000); I. V. Gerasimov, *Modernism and Public Reform in Late Imperial Russia. Rural Professionals and Self-Organization, 1905–30* (London: Palgrave Macmillan, 2009); Sandra Dahlke, 'Kampagnen für Gottlosigkeit: Zum Zusammenhang zwischen Legitimation, Mobilisierung und Partizipation in der Sowjetunion der zwanziger Jahre', *Jahrbücher für Geschichte Osteuropas*, no. 50 (2002), 172–85; Neumann, *The Communist Youth League*, esp. 17–19, 126–30.

party to rule. Nonetheless, it offered a vision of social participation and provided a space for some activist initiative. Many urban communards rallied in support of socialist 'civic work' (*obshchestvennaia rabota*), which came to include aiding those fellow proletarian students and workers in need, helping the Komsomol organize local meetings, and producing 'wall-newspapers' (*sten-gazety*) or information for bulletin boards.[72] In other cases *obshchestvennost'* included haranguing non-socialist personnel in universities and factories, attempting to change the political culture of Soviet institutes, and supporting local revolutionary projects wherever possible.[73]

In fact, the most obvious feature of commune life, 'collectivism' (*kollektivizm*), was not necessarily a purely domestic concern. In its simplest form, 'collectivism' meant putting the common interest before personal preference. Popularized, in no small part, by the ascetic protagonists of Nikolai Chernyshevsky's revolutionary saga, *What Is to Be Done?* (1863), collectivism often took the form of self-denial. Lenin himself tried to fit this mould. 'A short, stocky figure ... [with a] snubbish nose', often dressed in 'shabby clothes', John Reed remembered Lenin as an 'Unimpressive idol'.[74] His appearance was often seen to reflect his regard for the honest and simple life. This might be seen as the collectivism of 'populist socialism', a label levelled at the likes of Saint-Simon, Wilhelm Weitling, and Robert Owen, who, it has been said, formed their revolutionary outlooks around a hankering for the supposedly virtuous communities and community attributes of the pre-capitalist and pre-modern world.[75] But the pre-revolutionary intelligentsia of Russia also bequeathed to October a collectivism obsessed with social, national, and utopian brotherhood.[76] This was, therefore, also a collectivism that extended beyond old community ties, embracing modern visions of unity and political consciousness. As a result, the collective endeavours of the urban communards extended beyond inward-looking, shared-living arrangements, and came to include a commitment to their broader social and revolutionary responsibilities. Inside the commune, individuals subjected themselves to the collective vote and the scrutiny of the group; outside the commune they applied themselves to what they saw as the 'common good'. These people tended to see themselves as the advocates of a rational, modern collectivism—the bearers of a proletarian social cohesion designed to advance the modern socialist state.

Studying the urban communes and communards in their various discursive and contemporary engagements can also shed light on a number of important themes that have been at the heart of recent studies on the Soviet Union and the modern world. First and foremost, we can see that their undertakings frequently spoke to notions of 'self', 'personhood', and 'subjectivity'. Research in this area has sought to advance our understanding of how state-sponsored rhetoric and modern visions

---

[72] Chlen kommuny, 'Kommuna studentov-vodnikov', *Krasnyi student*, no. 4–5 (1924), 44–5.

[73] E. Petrov, 'Akademizm i obshchestvennost'', *Krasnyi student*, no. 6 (1925), 12.

[74] John Reed, *Ten Days that Shook the World* (London: Penguin Books, 1977), 128.

[75] For a brief discussion of these ideas in relation to the Soviet Union, see Priestland, *Stalinism and the Politics of Mobilization*, esp. 21–34.

[76] David-Fox, *Revolution of the Mind*, 107–8.

helped shape identity.[77] In the Soviet context, the idea of the 'new person' (*novyi chelovek*) has been tied to official readings of the 'new way of life', the 'new life', and 'cultural revolution'. Indeed, in many respects the urban communes can be read as attempts to produce exemplary revolutionaries in keeping with official visions of the 'new person'. The internal rules of the urban commune were thought to produce the ideal individuals who would go on to make socialism. But, at the same time, the urban communes and communards reveal some of the conflicts between modern state ideals and activist appropriation. Where some have said that control of language and the press 'created a world for its users', I would stress that the relationship between state and society was often more complicated.[78] Propaganda is not an exact science. And the popular imagination was both framed and fired by the forces of modernity. After all, people do not just conceive ideas through external frameworks, they transfer onto them their own idiosyncrasies and that with which they feel familiar.

In this sense, the present book should be viewed in line with the work of Mark D. Steinberg and Diane P. Koenker, each of whom have focused on popular receptions of Russian modernization, showing that even in a world of authoritarian politics, there was some room for debate, dissent, and accommodation.[79] It is surely true, even as repressive regimes were forming, that identities, and the field of ideas that created them, developed 'along axes other than those determined' by state.[80] This is History in the light of everyday realities and the accumulation of influences.[81]

What is more, the theme of utopia is clearly visible within the urban communes. Scholars of utopian studies and intentional communities will see that the urban communards of revolutionary Russia share many characteristics with similar groups from across the globe. After all, on some level, all communal movements and shared communities seek the simplification and/or rationalization of life, intimacy, brotherhood, self-awareness, and personal growth. They try to enact schemes of social improvement or visions of social unity that reject established norms.[82] Indeed, living differently and trying to make an alternative future can be seen as a common feature of rebellious thinkers and modern dreamers. But there will be few

---

[77] Stephen Kotkin, *Magnetic Mountain. Stalinism as a Civilization* (Berkeley: University of California Press, 1997); Jochen Hellbeck, *Revolution on My Mind: Writing a Diary Under Stalin* (Cambridge, MA: Harvard University Press, 2006); Igal Halfin, *Stalinist Confessions. Messianism and Terror at the Leningrad Communist University* (Pittsburgh, PA: University of Pittsburgh Press, 2009); Halfin, *Intimate Enemies. Demonizing the Bolshevik Opposition, 1918–1928* (Pittsburgh, PA: University of Pittsburgh Press, 2007); Halfin, *Terror in my Soul: Communist Autobiographies on Trial* (Cambridge, MA: Harvard University Press, 2003); Halfin, *From Darkness to Light*.

[78] Cf. Halfin, *Stalinist Confessions*, 16.

[79] Mark D. Steinberg, *Proletarian Imagination. Self, Modernity, and the Sacred in Russia, 1910–1925* (Ithaca, NY: Cornell University Press, 2002); Steinberg, *Moral Communities: The Culture of Class Relations in the Russian Printing Industry, 1867–1907* (Berkeley: University of California Press, 1992); Koenker, *Republic of Labor*.

[80] Stephen A. Smith, *Revolution and the People in Russia and China: A Comparative History* (Cambridge: Cambridge University Press, 2008), 234–5.

[81] Henri Lefebvre, *Critique of Everyday Life*, vol. 2, trans. John Moore (London: Verso, 2008), 38.

[82] Cf. Ruth Levitas, *The Concept of Utopia* (Oxford: Peter Lang Ltd, 2011).

direct comparisons to other communal groups here. Communes can share many utopian ideals; nevertheless, it is the different ways in which they implement them that displays what a commune means to its members.[83] We will stick closely to the urban communards' own conception of the world, drawing on their frames of reference directly. Accordingly, the reader should be aware that the term 'utopia' itself presents a few problems in the Soviet context. 'Utopia' became a dirty word among the Russian socialists of the twentieth century. The early French socialists of the nineteenth century could be forgiven for their optimistic fantasies; the Soviets, on the other hand, had to prove their 'scientific' credentials. Unsurprisingly, the urban communards did not refer to themselves as 'utopian'. If the term was applied, it was often viewed and intended as an insult.

In addition, as we proceed, this book will reveal how the urban communes and communards touched upon other themes important to our understanding of the modern world, including—extending on the above—a firm belief in the 'rational' and 'scientific'. While the past was labelled 'dirty' and 'unordered', the reinvention of life attempted by the urban communards was sometimes seen to borrow from the time-management techniques of Henry Ford's factories and the efficiency theories of the American engineer Fredrick Winslow Taylor. Once the preserve of the inconsequential, the management of everyday life was now elevated to a science. Furthermore, the urban communards were very much involved in the reimagining of 'space'. They not only tried to reinvent their everyday residences, many rejected the very idea of private spaces—helping to forever taint the idea of the private within the Soviet domestic setting. And, of course, inherent within all these experiences, the urban communes and communards were tied to the processes of urbanization and industrialization, along with all the uncertainties and change that this entailed.

METHODS, SOURCES, STRUCTURE

My approach has grown from an interest in how people understood and engaged in the changes taking place around them in modern Russia. By writing the urban communes and communards back into Soviet history, this book supports the notion that the revolution was often participatory and expressive in nature, but it challenges the assumption that the party was able to design and monitor all facets of these interactions. It acts as a balance to those studies that have privileged the state's coercive power or its ability to control the minds of the general population. It shows, among other things, where human agency sometimes managed to feed back into official structures, when social opinion offered a form of popular legitimacy

---

[83] See Kanter, *Communes*, 2–6. The sociologist, Kanter, was clearly unaware of the Soviet urban communes when she wrote, in reference to the hippie communes of 1960s America: 'the contemporary urban commune is an entirely new development'. But that is not to say she neglected an obvious comparison. The urban communes of Soviet Russia, unlike the hippie communes, do not represent such an obvious rejection of state values.

for the regime, and how the state was forced, from time to time, to co-opt or codify ideas from below.

In the Soviet circus, the ringmaster had to be prepared to respond to the crowd as the act unfolded. Similarly, in this book the Soviet regime is shown to be responsive as well as repressive. It is worth stressing this point because where the history of 'Great Men' once dominated, we might now be in danger of privileging the power of ideology and methods of governance over everyday practice and *habitus*. The lived experience of enthusiasts such as the urban communards offers ballast to untethered assessments of Soviet ideology, helping to ground revolution in 'the supreme court where wisdom, knowledge and power are brought to judgement': the court of everyday life.[84]

This is not an easy tale to tell, however. Piecing together the experiences of the urban communes and communards has at times been like trying to add substance to shadows. There is no central archival holding on these groups. Their written records remain scattered and incomplete. Surviving documentation often provides only a momentary glimpse of commune life. Lest we forget, the routines and motion of everyday life have never been that well recorded. They are taken for granted at the time, which means they evade the historical record and an obvious place within our repository systems. Even those who participated in radical formations such as the urban communes of the early Soviet Union were often men and women of action: 'doers', less likely to obsess over practices of meticulous self-recording for the purposes of posterity. This has affected the way we tell modern history, which might be said to focus on 'big events' with little real recourse to the backdrops of life. But we should not push aside important and revealing parts of history just because they are hard to tell. To recapture the urban commune and the lived experience of Soviet socialism requires a versatile approach.

The range of materials and holdings consulted in this book are, therefore, necessarily wide and varied. I have mined factory reports and institutional surveys, the local records of those institutes known to house or be connected with commune groups, various contemporary studies into social initiatives, official protocols and discussions, media print sources and correspondence, as well as the available diaries and records of those individuals that were involved with or came into contact with the urban communes.

Looking through the industrial reports of trade union groups, for instance, you can sometimes find comments or information on the urban communes. Among other things, these documents help to reveal the scope and the location of commune activity. And by searching through the worker reports of factories such as the Automobile Society of Moscow plant, you will occasionally stumble across the notes of an urban communard.[85] These reports provided a space for the urban communards and other activists to record their experiences. In addition, a systematic search through the records of the Komsomol tells us much about the political

---

[84] Lefebvre, *Critique of Everyday Life*, vol. 3, 6.
[85] These materials are currently housed within the Central State Archive of the City of Moscow (TsGA Moskvy; until very recently known as TsAGM).

convictions of the urban communards and the impact that they could have on Soviet organs.[86]

Away from the central archives, the museum holdings of St Petersburg's institutes of higher education contain invaluable documentation on the activities, arrangements, and personnel of the student communes.[87] Two of the city's five largest student communes were attached to what was then called the Leningrad State Electro-technical Institute (LETI), while the Leningrad State Herzen Pedagogical Institute and the Leningrad State Polytechnic Institute were also heavily populated with commune groups. The museums of these institutes have retained information on many student groups, including files on notable students, which, in the case of the urban communes and communards, have been supplemented with memoir accounts and further information sent at the request of the institute or in response to the queries of inquisitive archivists. These later additions contain the usual pitfalls and inaccuracies of memory-based sources; in the case of the communards, nostalgia for youth and revolution are clearly evident. However, the blend of contemporaneous and reflective materials within these files enables the historian to pinpoint inconsistencies through cross-referencing. The museums also maintain a back catalogue of institute newspapers, which often reported on the communes and communards in question, providing another source of corroboration.

Added to this, the contemporary studies that arose in response to the Central Committee's May 1930 resolution, calling for further study into genuine workers' movements, and the personal records of travellers and journalists interested in the Soviet experiment, provide another important source of information. Indeed, the academic and cultural commentator Klaus Mehnert, it turns out, managed to stumble upon some of the urban communes during his visits to Soviet Russia. He interviewed some of these groups and even acquired access to their diaries and other records. Mehnert said of the urban communes: 'They are the visible and living example of the general socialization of daily life for which the people are striving.'[88] Plus, one of the advantages of studying this period of Soviet history lies in the relative freedom and liveliness of the contemporary press. A detailed and prolonged search of the contemporary print media provides not only a wealth of information on the urban commune, but a valuable insight into the discourses and dialogues in which they were involved. Publications such as *Krasnoe studenchestvo* (*The Red Student Body*), *Krasnyi student* (*Red Student*), and one of the leading Soviet newspapers, *Komsomol'skaia pravda* (*Komsomol Truth*), each produced articles on the urban communes throughout the 1920s. They sent correspondents to interview these groups, and occasionally to stay with them. Furthermore, they encouraged the communards to write in to them, thereby developing a channel of communication

---

[86] See the youth division of the Russian State Archive of Socio-Political History (RGASPI, M.1).

[87] The potential of this archival base was first hinted at by A. E. Bezzubtsev-Kondakov, 'Kommuny Leningrada', *Klio*, no. 3 (2004), 158–63.

[88] Originally published in German in 1932: Klaus Mehnert, *Die Jugend in Sowjetrussland* (Berlin, 1932). Quotation taken from the English translation, *Youth in Soviet Russia*, trans. Michael Davidson (London: George Allen & Unwin, 1933), 162. Also see the travel journal of Anna Louis Strong, *The Soviets Conquer Wheat. The Drama of Collective Farming* (New York: Henry Holt and Company, 1931).

and another source of information on these groups. At the same time, journals such as *Partiinoe stroitel'stvo* (*Party Construction*) conducted small numerical studies and published opinion pieces on the urban communes, while the youth journal *Iunyi kommunist* (*Young Communist*) found itself acting as the unofficial recorder and minute-keeper of an inter-commune meeting in 1930.

By delving into untapped repositories and collating a range of materials, we can, for the first time, explore the thoughts, actions, and daily encounters of the urban communards.

This account opens with an assessment of commune origins. Chapter 1 shows how the urban communes drew on pre-revolutionary sources, including the work of Nikolai Chernyshevsky, alongside modern conceptions of Marxism, as they sought to make their contribution to the 'new dawn'. The urban commune impulse is presented as a construct of activist interpretation and Russian revolutionary traditions. Chapters 2 to 4 are broadly chronological, following the urban communes across the first decade of the Soviet Union, while highlighting the different types of commune groups that developed during this period. Chapter 2 charts the formation and activities of the student communes. Like the circles and discussion groups (*kruzhki*) of pre-revolutionary student radicals, the communes attached to Soviet institutes of higher education are shown to present young activists with a means of political expression. Chapter 3 follows those groups that established themselves outside these institutes, in the apartments and working communities of Soviet Russia. As they became ever more involved in the pursuit of the 'new way of life' and 'cultural revolution', these groups earned the prefix *byt(ovoi)* from the press. This chapter assesses their attempts to remake life and their negative reaction to some of the cultural problems associated with NEP.

Chapter 4 turns our attention to the end of the 1920s, as the urban communes and communards became increasingly concerned with the development of new working practices and Soviet industrialization. This was the time of the 'production commune' (*proizvodstvennaia kommuna*); a period of refreshed zeal and the alluring promise that socialism could be built through hard work. Examining the urban commune in the context of a burgeoning shock-work movement and the rapid mobilization of revolutionary activists, this chapter offers new insights into the labour history of the period. Among other things, it reveals how the production commune was able to influence the working culture of the shop floor, and how the Komsomol and other bodies came to co-opt commune undertakings into official campaigns.

Finally, Chapter 5 explores the consequences of the urban communes' increasing popularity during the First Five-Year Plan (1928–32). Many commune activities were co-opted and absorbed into an increasingly professionalized state apparatus during this time. And, with a number of copycat developments, as well as increased attention from official sources, the fragile cogency of the urban commune phenomenon was gradually eroded. In many ways, the original ideals of the communards are shown to have run their course by 1932. In keeping with the rest of the book, however, this chapter seeks to leave room for the inherent indeterminacies of revolution. The urban communard is not treated as a victim of Stalin and Stalinism.

After all, no blood was shed as a consequence of belonging to a commune. While there was a developing distrust of 'excessive equalitarianism', the official response to the urban communes remained far from hostile—mixed and undetermined would be a fairer assessment. As a result, the urban commune is shown to gradually find itself outside the boundaries of revolutionary debate, leaving the communards to reflect on proceedings, occasionally reforming themselves into lesser 'cost-accounting brigades' (*khozraschetnye brigady*) in order to comply with new factory management regulations. To the end, the urban communes and communards are shown to embrace and engage the ideological concerns of their day. Through their construction, outlook, and demise, the reader can see the everyday formation of Soviet socialism.

As the title suggests, *Living the Revolution* seeks to shed new light on how activists, especially youthful supporters and enthusiasts of revolution, interpreted and acted on their understandings of October at the crucial juncture where ideology and everyday life met. This is a history of the revolution—broadly defined as extending from 1917 through the Stalinist 'Great Break' (or 'Great Turn')—from the ground up, as a story of civic agency and the creation of meaning in social life; a story of how the 'new life,' especially the 'new way of life', was actually built and lived. In many respects, this is a story from below, though not presented in a simple or dichotomizing way, but as practices and discourses in dialogue with institutionalized and centralized political power. This is politics as the tangible and prosaic; a story of big theory experienced but also used in local, small-scale, and living (hence complex) settings. I refuse to romanticize the urban communes as cases of unrealistic and marginal utopianism or as cases of heroic resistance to the increasingly powerful party-state and its ideology. What I present, instead, is a history of Soviet socialism through trial and error, presenting what Trotsky famously called 'problems of everyday life' as the most central site for building revolution.

1

Revolutionary Beginnings

The October Revolution stimulated a range of social activism, from the agitation campaigns of the Communist Youth League (Komsomol) to the movement of local groups, workers' clubs, and revolutionary societies that formed the Proletarian Cultural–Educational Association (Proletkul't).[1] Here young, idealistic men and women would gather to promote socialism. Keen to display their political identity, some sported the latest in revolutionary trends: the leather jacket. Others adopted a rough-and-ready, working-class look, wearing crumpled clothing and eschewing overly decorative items, revelling in the opportunity to defy traditional conventions.[2] But all came to discuss and debate the prospects that lay before them.

The thing that distinguished the urban communes and communards—many of whom functioned within Komsomol and Proletkul't circles—was their added determination to enact a code of collectivism in their everyday lives: to share all possessions, to form cohabitative-housing units, and to undertake everything, including work and leisure activities, as part of a domestic group. They were obsessed with the concept of collectivism and how it might change social relations; they saw it as one aspect of ideological discussion that they could actually construct in the here and now. So they sought to be the future they envisioned. They looked to create a collective bond that would form the basis of a new socialist society. By the end of the 1920s, seeing that the urban communes were engaging with some of the core ideological principles of the October Revolution, the Soviet press reported that articles on collectivism and the reorganization of everyday life could not afford to ignore the lessons of these groups or the voices of their inhabitants.[3]

Of course, the idea of living cheek by jowl was not new to Russia. For centuries a limited and inefficient agrarian economy had tied the majority of its people to the land, where extended families worked and lived in closer proximity than they might otherwise have chosen. Early attempts at industrialization and modernization did little to change the situation, with many urban migrants transporting the shared habits of the village to the city—pooling resources, renting rooms together, and bargaining for collective employment. Inspired by these deeply ingrained community

---

[1] See Lynn Mally, *Culture of the Future: The Proletkult Movement in Revolutionary Russia* (Berkeley: University of California Press, 1990); Christopher Read, *Culture and Power in Revolutionary Russia: The Intelligentsia and the Transition from Tsarism to Communism* (London: Macmillan, 1990), esp. 111–33.

[2] See Anne E. Gorsuch, *Youth in Revolutionary Russia: Enthusiasts, Bohemians, Delinquents* (Bloomington, IN: Indiana University Press, 2000), esp. 89–93, 111–13.

[3] 'Kak dolzhen byt' organizovan studencheskii byt', *Krasnoe studenchestvo*, no. 3–4 (1928), 16–17.

structures and the sheer resilience of their countrymen, a growing number of nineteenth-century Russian intellectuals of varying political persuasions—from Herzen to Dostoevsky—observed an underlying sense of 'brotherhood' and 'collective unity' within their nation and its people. It was suggested that Russia's harsh and sparsely populated land encouraged cooperative forms of survival, in striking contrast to the gladiatorial competition of western social Darwinism, which pitted all against all. The notion that there was a fundamental or exemplary bond exhibited among its people became a core preoccupation of Russian thought, penetrating all manner of theses and radical visions. The agrarian socialist movement known as Populism (*narodnichestvo*) even viewed the peasant village as a prototype model for the future society. By the turn of the twentieth century, the concept of 'collectivism' (*kollektivizm*) came to form a crucial part of Russian public, intellectual, and revolutionary discourses. It was often seen as the thing that made Russia distinct from the West; it informed early syndicalist aspirations; and, according to a popular dictionary originally published in 1895, the word itself even became a synonym for socialism.[4]

The Bolsheviks were very much influenced by this cultural and intellectual preoccupation with collectivism. The October Revolution initiated a renewed and much-radicalized impetus for collective living. Soviet agitation presented the image of a new 'comradely society' in which the individual 'I' would be replaced by the collective 'We'. Collective housing, collective dining, and collective recreation were understood as transformative activities that would help mould a new type of people and a new civilization. Collectivism and Marxism were combined to create a picture of the ideal Soviet society. Incorporating the notion of class warfare, collective pursuits at home and collegial practices at work were presented as the antithesis of 'bourgeois individualism'. Socialized childcare, it was argued, would free women for the labour market and help to instil a sense of community within the next generation.[5] Teamwork and mutual cooperation in industry would unite society's efforts, promote a working-class consciousness, and increase efficiency. This was believed to be the most rational means of organizing society. Only through the pursuit of common goals and shared understandings could the full potential of humanity be achieved.

For those young idealists eager to throw their lot in with the revolution, discussions and debates about socialism instinctively drew on this long-standing and newly re-energized discourse. Collectivism provided the most immediate picture of the new world promised to them in 1917. The first urban communes, more often than not, were founded expressly on the principle of 'revolutionary collectivism'. Understandings of what this actually meant were by no means uniform, but these visions certainly gave young activists something in which they could invest their revolutionary energies.

---

[4] Robert C. Williams, 'Collective Immortality: The Syndicalist Origins of Proletarian Culture, 1905–1910', *Slavic Review*, no. 3 (1980), 389–402; Oleg Kharkhordin, *The Collective and the Individual in Russia. A Study of Practices* (Berkeley: University of California Press, 1999), 76.

[5] Lisa A. Kirschenbaum, *Small Comrades: Revolutionizing Childhood in Soviet Russia, 1917–1932* (New York: Routledge-Falmer, 2001).

In the fevered atmosphere of 1917–18—as civil war unfolded and as previously disenfranchised sections of society threw off their sense of 'rightlessness' (*bespravie*)—'collectivism' was often viewed, in its broadest sense, as the triumphant system that would replace the old social order. This appealed to those activists most alive with the sense of revolutionary opportunity and empowerment. In areas such as the Basmannyi district of Moscow, for instance, nascent commune groups reportedly looked upon the requisitioning of private homes as an act of 'collective takeover'. They were symbolically destroying the hearth of the former elite.[6] Here collective association offered people the opportunity to stick it to their old masters; not only were they attempting to establish a new way of life, they were taking the property of the elite as they did so. Necessity and conviction combined to create a vehemently anti-private egalitarianism—something that would come to rear its head again under Stalin and at various other points throughout the life of the Soviet Union.[7]

At the same time, many urban communes and communards, particularly those attached to institutes of higher education, became engrossed with a youth press that was awash with articles and opinion pieces on collectivism and collective pursuits. Here 'collectivism' was presented as a cohesive or universal social system—an image of the socialist future—but also, with more immediate developments in mind, as the bond already exhibited by small groups engaged in a common task—invoking the example of pre-revolutionary *arteli* (worker teams), student *kruzhki* (discussion circles), and clandestine *iacheiki* (party cells). These were identified as the basic building blocks of revolution and the collective future. As a result, collectivism became increasingly associated with disciplined self-regulation, group obligation, hard-nosed shared-living arrangements, and a commitment to current affairs.[8] As if to highlight the debt owed to their small-scale collective forebears, Nadezhda Krupskaya, leading Bolshevik, Central Committee member, and tireless campaigner for youth education, came to refer to the urban communes as '*kommunki*'—a diminutive of commune, effectively meaning 'little commune', thus emphasizing the associational or syndicalist roots of these groups.[9] Having first encountered the urban communes in the early 1920s, she came to view them as part of a wider organizational impulse to develop collectivism on the land, in the city, and in all aspects of life.[10] Writing later, in 1930, she even placed this activist movement in a somewhat idealistic narrative of collective association stretching back long before 1917; this included the monasteries of the Middle Ages, the early guilds of the industrial period, as

---

[6] I. Gromov, 'Zhilishchnaia nerazberikha', *Kommunar*, 1 November 1918, 3.

[7] Cf. Oleg Kharkhordin, 'Reveal and Dissimulate: A Genealogy of Private Life in Soviet Russia', in Jeff Weintraub and Krishan Kumar (eds), *Public and Private in Thought and Practice. Perspectives on a Grand Dichotomy* (Chicago, IL: University of Chicago Press, 1997), 333–63.

[8] Michael David-Fox, *Revolution of the Mind. Higher Learning among the Bolsheviks, 1918–1929* (Ithaca, NY: Cornell University Press, 1997), 107–8.

[9] N. Krupskaya, *O Bytovykh voprosakh* (Moscow, 1930), esp. 33–6.

[10] *Gosudarstvennyi arkhiv Rossiiskoi Federatsii* (hereafter, GARF), f. A.2313, op. 1, d. 57, l. 138 (Nadezhda Krupskaya's notes and materials from the People's Commissariat of Education, 1921).

well as the cooperative movement and the *arteli* of the nineteenth and early twentieth centuries.[11]

For those that had read their nineteenth-century literature, or those following up common references to radical works, this picture of collectivism was far from alien. Certainly, among the first wave of urban communes these influences were quite apparent, with some groups viewing themselves as Soviet incarnations of the nineteenth-century radicals, the worker *artel'*, or the student *kruzhok*.[12] Meanwhile, the choice of the name '*kommuna*', from French, reflected another key trend in Soviet revolutionary discourse: many of these collective ideals were also associated with that other great totem of revolution—the first example of direct democracy, collective action, and comradely regulation—the Paris Commune of 1871.

*

This chapter will unpack the origins of the urban communes and communards, tracing their engagements with the key revolutionary concept of 'collectivism' and their responses to the unfolding revolution. This serves two purposes: firstly, to highlight the relationship between the discourse on collectivism and the communards' perception of themselves and their actions; and secondly, to foreshadow the full range of post-revolutionary commune activities explored throughout the rest of the book. As we shall see, the fundamental principles of collectivism penetrated every aspect of urban commune life, ultimately determining many of the projects and struggles that these revolutionary enthusiasts decided to involve themselves in. At the same time, as we develop a better understanding of commune activism, it will also become clear that history does not always proceed along straight pathways: sometimes old ideas are given new meaning, while some new ideas are conditioned by the memory and experience that people carry with them. Ultimately, we will see that the actions and beliefs of the urban communes were a product of the Russian experience of modernity and revolution. In this sense, they did not originate in full from one set source; they were created by many minds and with many influences.

SEARCHING FOR SOCIALISM

Each evening after 9 p.m., in a small apartment near the Rubber (*Kauchuk*) Factory, in the southwest of Moscow, the activists of an urban commune sat down together to read and discuss revolutionary literature. Formed by ten young Komsomol members after the October Revolution, this group pooled their income into a 'common pot' (*obshchii kotel*) (see Fig. 1.1), which, after food and other essentials, was used to take out subscriptions to the Soviet press and build a 'small library' of important works.[13] Reading, thinking, and talking about the revolution

---

[11] Krupskaya, *O Bytovykh voprosakh*, 30–3.
[12] Iu. Ber, *Kommuna segodnia, Opyt proizvodstvennykh i bytovykh kommun molodezhi* (Moscow, 1930), 64–5.
[13] G. Levgur, 'Komsomol'skaia kommuna "Kauchuk"', *Iunyi kommunist*, no. 9 (1923), 26–7.

Fig. 1.1. The common pot
Source: 'V nastuplenie!', *Smena*, no. 19 (1929), 3.

gave these youths the chance to digest and appropriate the momentous changes taking place around them. It gave them a window on the future. Modern notions of cleanliness and healthy living seemed to fill the pages of the newspapers and journals that they were reading. Their concern for hygiene and their habit of keeping the windows open for ventilation at night-time certainly bears the hallmark of Soviet advice literature.[14] But alongside these seemingly trite, everyday matters, the communards were also concerned with the bigger question: What would the new socialist world look like? With no single, overarching vision of socialism to hand in the immediate aftermath of 1917, the *Kauchuk* commune, like many others, drew on intellectual sources, developing Soviet discourses, and their own cultural register in order to form a more complete understanding of revolution.[15]

Let us first turn to these intellectual and discursive readings. Of all the books amassed by groups such as the *Kauchuk* commune, none was more influential than Nikolai Chernyshevsky's *What Is to Be Done?* (1863). The *Kauchuk* activists would come to emulate the revolutionary figures in this novel, inspired by their revolutionary deeds and collective world view. It came to be seen almost as a compulsory text for inhabitants new and old. Similarly, a few miles east of *Kauchuk*, at the Automobile Society of Moscow (AMO) plant, the discussion circles and activists that would go on to form some of the most engaged urban communes in the city reported trying to get to grips with the works of Marx. Yet, here too, inspirational characters such as Chernyshevsky's self-denying hero Rakhmetov were what really captured their imagination. His austere and modest lifestyle became a trend among these and many other young revolutionaries. The novel's heroine, Vera Pavlovna, also served as an example of the emancipated woman: rejecting the conventional family in favour of new collective bonds. Many of these themes came to manifest themselves in urban commune life, most obviously with the rejection of luxury, parental authority, and traditional relationship norms.[16] Both the *Kauchuk* and AMO communes went on to cultivate plain ascetic values and new comradely relationships that, like *What Is to Be Done?*, put the 'revolutionary family' before blood ties.

These parallels were not coincidental. At the heart of Chernyshevsky's novel, his protagonists engage in cooperative work and eventually come together to form a 'common apartment'. Here—in what was arguably the first urban commune—this small band of self-sacrificing intellectuals and youths seek to transform themselves and society through modern revolutionary living.[17] Chernyshevsky offered the urban communards a model of revolutionary regeneration, where earnings are divided equally and members help to educate one another. This was the future society as presented in the nightly dreams of Vera Pavlovna: a place where youths 'become people, not dolls'.[18] The old world—depicted as the preserve of wife-beating men, dirt, and vulgarity—was to be swept aside by a new brand of people devoted

---

[14] Cf. Catriona Kelly, *Refining Russia: Advice Literature, Polite Culture, and Gender from Catherine to Yeltsin* (Oxford: Oxford University Press, 2001).

[15] Levgur, 'Komsomol'skaia kommuna "Kauchuk"', 26–7.

[16] *Tsentral'nyi arkhiv goroda Moskvy* (hereafter, TsGA Moskvy; formerly TsAGM), f. 415, op. 16, d. 656, ll. 1–8. (AMO factory, reflections of Komsomol members, 1923–26); TsGA Moskvy, f. 415, op. 16, d. 76, ll. 1–50. (ZiL factory, reflections of A. Bychkov on 'brigades, communes etc.', 1927–30).

[17] Nikolai Chernyshevsky, *What Is to Be Done?*, trans. Michael R. Katz (Ithaca, NY: Cornell University Press, 1989), ch. 3, esp. 188–202.

[18] Chernyshevsky, *What Is to Be Done?*, 187.

to a more equal and rational society. 'Good, strong, honest, capable people', Chernyshevsky declared, 'you have only just begun to appear'.[19]

A story of personal enlightenment and revolutionary struggle, *What Is to Be Done?* became known as the 'handbook of radicalism'. Emerging from the intense intellectual debates induced by the emancipatory reforms of the 1860s, the novel had a profound impact on Russian literature and politics. Like much of the wider intelligentsia, Chernyshevsky thought that Russia, in particular the peasant community, was blessed with a natural sense of brotherhood. But unlike more conservative-minded thinkers, he also believed that the patriarchal structures of elite society inhibited a fuller collective bond. In effect, he widened the rift between reformers and revolutionaries by advocating the wholesale rejection of all tsarist values and institutions. Fyodor Dostoevsky was moved to write his disparaging account of Russia's radicals, *Notes from Underground* (1864), in response to Chernyshevsky's particular vision of 'harmonious living'. But over the coming decades many young revolutionaries and radical sections of society were inspired by Chernyshevsky's novel. As the father of Russian Marxism, Georgi Plekhanov, remarked: 'Who has not read and reread this famous work? Who has not been charmed by it, who has not become cleaner, better, braver, and bolder under its philanthropic influence?' 'We all', he continued, 'draw from it moral strength and faith in a better future.' Profoundly moved by *What Is to Be Done?*, Lenin's praise was equally laudatory. He proclaimed Chernyshevsky 'the greatest and most talented representative of socialism before Marx'.[20]

Groups such as the *Kauchuk* and AMO communes aspired to be the 'Good, strong, honest, capable people' of Chernyshevsky's novel. In contrast to the popular image of the sloth-like Russian elite—best captured in Ivan Goncharov's *Oblomov* (1859)—the 'new people' (*novye liudi*) were men and women of action. The urban communes and communards sought to replicate the voluntarism of Chernyshevsky's characters, believing that by acting as a revolutionary vanguard— by being moral, selfless, and strong—they could transform Russia. They too united together in apartments, met around a 'common table', shared chores and provisions, engaged in cooperative labour, and consciously tried to develop a new, collective 'orientation'. The *Kauchuk* commune was particularly keen to replicate Rakhmetov's simple, utilitarian approach to food. Like him, and in stark contrast to the social world of Oblomov, they proclaimed their tastes to be plain and unfussy, although, at the same time, their nutritional intake, cooking, and eating habits were managed under the 'strictest regulation'. Eating was to become a functional act, regulated and modern. They also saw collective mealtimes as an essential component of comradely living, and, as a result, if members failed to turn up on time they wouldn't get fed.[21] Such uncompromising practices mark out the communards as the children of Chernyshevsky.

[19] Chernyshevsky, *What Is to Be Done?*, 49.
[20] Cited in Michael R. Katz and William G. Wagner, 'Introduction: Chernyshevsky, What Is to Be Done? and the Russian Intelligentsia', in *What Is to Be Done?*, trans. Michael R. Katz (Ithaca, NY: Cornell University Press, 1989), 31–3.
[21] Levgur, 'Komsomol'skaia kommuna "Kauchuk"', 26–7.

Moreover, as a foundational text of the Russian socialist movement, the revolutionary aesthetic and optimism of Chernyshevsky's *What Is to Be Done?* became ingrained within the October Revolution. The Bolsheviks were deeply influenced by Chernyshevsky's imagining of the 'new person', as well as the journey of self-discovery undertaken by his main protagonists. This fed into their writings on 'cultural revolution' (*kul'turnaia revoliutsiia*) and the idea that the individual could be refashioned politically and morally into a collective being. For the urban communards, then, *What Is to Be Done?* served as a source of direct and indirect influence—both through the text itself and through its wider impact on the Soviet revolutionary discourse. Indeed, the AMO activists picked out similar themes of interest in their wider reading, including Fyodor Gladkov's *Cement* (1925) and Panteleimon Romanov's *Without Cherry Blossom* (1927), which, like Chernyshevsky, focused on the ideal socialist citizen—the 'new person'—and new relations between man and woman as the catalyst for revolutionary advance.[22] Books such as Aleksandr Bogdanov's Martian utopia, *Red Star* (1908)—wildly popular after the October Revolution; reprinted in 1918, 1922, and 1928, and selling in the hundreds of thousands—were also seen to continue in the Chernyshevsky tradition, extolling the virtues of rational collective living, school-colonies, and 'new people'.[23] At the same time, the newspapers and journals to which the urban communes subscribed were usually full of articles about a 'new life' (*novaia zhizn'*) that can be traced back to the 'Good, strong, honest, capable people' envisioned by Chernyshevsky. These were the works and the topics that fuelled communard discussions each evening. Such pieces were eagerly consumed and discussed in the 'red corners' that many urban communes established for reading and political enlightenment (see Fig. 1.2). More than the work of Karl Marx, *What Is to Be Done?* and its cast of characters provided the emotional appeal that would galvanize Russian socialism and the forces of revolution.[24]

Nodding his head to Chernyshevsky, Lenin had long argued that revolution could only be achieved through an exemplary 'vanguard'. In his famous 1902 pamphlet, which borrowed its title from Chernyshevsky's nineteenth-century novel, Lenin argued that the working class would never achieve power without guidance from a body of dedicated revolutionaries. In keeping with Chernyshevsky's 'new people', the affirmative action of a small, conscious vanguard became a cornerstone of Bolshevik revolutionary theory.[25] As Russia was still behind the rest of Europe in Marxist terms—having yet to pass through the capitalist stage of development—such pockets of enlightened persons were seen as a crucial component of the revolutionary cause. For prominent Bolsheviks, including Lev Trotsky, Nikolai Bukharin, and Aleksandra Kollontai, as well as the urban communes and communards, the ascetic-vanguard model put forth by Chernyshevsky offered a

[22] TsGA Moskvy, f. 415, op. 16, d. 656, ll. 1–8.
[23] A. Bogdanov, *Red Star. The First Bolshevik Utopia*, ed. and trans. L. R. Graham and R. Stites (Bloomington, IN: Indiana University Press, 1984). For an assessment of the circulation of the text, see ix–x, 12–16.
[24] Cf. Joseph Frank, 'N. G. Chernyshevsky: A Russian Utopia', *Southern Review*, no. 3 (1967), 68.
[25] Kharkhordin, *The Collective and the Individual*, 57–9.

Fig. 1.2. Communards show off their 'red corner'—a space dedicated to study, reading, and political enlightenment

Source: 'Pervaia komsomol'skaia bytovaia kommuna', *Komsomol'skaia pravda*, 3 April 1930, 4.

way to advance the social and cultural front of revolution. In the press and in public speeches, activists, in particular young Komsomol members, were encouraged to act as the nuclei communities—the bearers of a new collectivity—that would transform Russian society as a whole.[26] As the *Kauchuk* and AMO communes sat down to discuss the meaning of collective organization and their wider revolutionary readings, they talked about creating the ideal environment to raise the 'new person', and they looked to establish themselves as the vanguard of everyday revolution. Chernyshevsky and pre-1917 revolutionary discourses bequeathed to the Soviet world and the first urban communards an understanding of *kollektivizm* that went beyond merely restructuring society: it came to define a bond and a way of life capable of remaking human relations.

KOLLEKTIV FOUNDATIONS

The urban communes and communards of the early Soviet state, however, were not the first people to draw Chernyshevsky's 'common apartment' into life. In the 1870s, for instance, just a few years after the publication of *What Is to Be Done?*, as

---

[26] See for example L. Trotsky, *Problems of Everyday Life and Other Writings on Culture & Science* (New York: Monad Press, 1973) and N. Bukharin and E. Preobrazhensky, *The ABC of Communism*, ed. and intro. Edward. H. Carr (Harmondsworth: Penguin Books, 1969).

the Populist movement reached its peak, St Petersburg was awash with stories of a 'commune' tempting young people from the upper echelons of society to live in a state of total collectivism. The memoirs of mathematician Sofia Kovalevskaia tell of the horror induced in the elite by stories of noble boys and girls 'scrubbing the floors' and 'polishing the samovars' of this commune. Rumour suggested that this was an 'immoral environment' where, shockingly, all servants had been banned! Inhabitants, it was said, were treated as equals and expected to share domestic duties between themselves. Probably based on the escapades of the *Znamenskaia* discussion circle (*kruzhok*), which was formed around the same time, St Petersburg society gossip secured for this establishment a mythical status. Founded by the radical writer Vasilii Sleptsov, it was run by a group of young men and women who, like a growing number of their generation, rejected the life of their parents in the spirit of nihilism. Reflected in the panic they stirred, this group challenged the social and political norms of imperial Russia.[27]

By the 1890s more and more radicalized young people were becoming embroiled in discussion circles across St Petersburg. Members of the intelligentsia and the workers' movement united in a common cause. The textile worker Vera Karelina was one of those swept up in this revolutionary tide. She would look back at these years fondly, remembering it as a time when activists came together to discuss radical literature, contemplate the latest sociological theories, and challenge the status quo. The groups she became involved with were particularly keen to spread socialist 'consciousness' among the workers and in the factories. Karelina found herself a member of a *kruzhok* that also went on to form its own 'common apartment' in the Vyborg district (the industrial quarter) of Russia's imperial capital. Like the *Znamenskaia*, this group embraced Chernyshevsky's attitude toward autocracy's social norms. 'We lived as a commune: money was paid into a common fund, we shared a common table, laundry and library', recalled Karelina. Everyone was expected to share in the housework and break down the traditional family structure. Here they could engage in 'serious conversations', promote socialist propaganda, and seek collective self-improvement.[28] Not all of Karelina's radical peers came together in such idealistic arrangements, but most were interested in agitating for alternative living, revolution, camaraderie, and collective solidarity.

Hand in hand with the intellectual and utopian visions of Chernyshevsky, the example of revolutionary forebears such as the *Znamenskaia* group and the Karelina

---

[27] Sofia Kovalevskaia, *A Russian Childhood*, trans. B. Stillman (New York: Spinger-Verlag, 1978), 147.

[28] V. M. Karelina, 'Na zare rabochego dvizheniia v S-Peterburge', *Krasnaia letopis'*, no. 4 (1922), 12–21; V. M. Karelina, 'Vospominaniia o podpol'nykh rabochikh kruzhkakh brusnevskoi organizatsii', in E. A. Korol'chuk (ed.), *V nachale puti. Vospominaniia peterburgskikh rabochikh, 1872–1897* (Leningrad, 1975), 269–91. Cited in Rose L. Glickman, *Russian Factory Women: Workplace and Society, 1880–1914* (Berkeley: University of California Press, 1986), 173–83. Also see Jane McDermid and Anna Hillyer (eds), *Women and Work in Russia, 1880–1930: A Study in Continuity Through Change* (London: Routledge, 1998), 107–9; Gerald D. Surh, *1905 in St. Petersburg: Labor, Society, and Revolution* (Stanford, CA: Stanford University Press, 1989), 116–25; Deborah Pearl, *Creating a Culture of Revolution: Workers and the Revolutionary Movement in Late Imperial Russia* (Bloomington, IN: Slavica, 2015), esp. 27–32.

apartment would have a bearing on the urban communes and communards. These were but two of many discussion circles and debating assemblies (*skhodky*) that arose from the 1870s onwards—some displaying their debt to Chernyshevsky quite openly. With few other means of political organization or expression available to them, radical and discontented sections of educated society came together in these groups to contemplate political reform. An expanding student population toward the end of the century only served as a breeding ground for underground association and subversive activity of this sort.[29] And the revolutionary legacy of these groups permeated early Soviet culture, particularly in the newly requisitioned institutes of higher education, where many young activists and nascent urban communards came to equate their own actions with that of the radical *kruzhki*.[30] At the same time, the revolutionary tales and memoirs of figures such as Karelina formed an important part of activist reading, appearing in early Soviet publications. These accounts offered a practical and a romantic example of revolutionary organization to the next generation of would-be radicals.[31] Indeed, some of the student communes attached to the Electro-technical Institute (LETI) in the early 1920s initially modelled themselves on the *kruzhki*, coming together to debate university life and to read revolutionary journals. One future urban commune started out discussing the practical measures necessary to instil socialism among their fellow students and across the institute. This was an obvious way to bring revolution into their immediate surroundings. Concerned that their efforts were developing into nothing more than a 'cosy tea-drinking session', however, they eventually followed in Karelina's footsteps, deciding to expand their 'collective experience' in the form a 'full commune'. Their choice of name was simple and utilitarian—taking the number of their dormitory room, this group became Commune 133—but, as they came together in this form, they also drew on a much more romantic and imaginative history of collective organization. As with many other commune groups at this time, it all started with the example of the *kruzhki* and the revolutionary traditions of the previous generation.[32]

Over the coming years, many Soviet commentators came to highlight the parallels between these two developments; the radical *kruzhki* were seen as an example of common association and youth mobilization.[33] Strictly speaking, however, the urban commune was not actually a natural continuation of imperial Russia's student movement or, indeed, its rebellious politics. We are not dealing with the same individuals or the same cause. In the wake of 1905, the student population (*studenchestvo*) became politically fractured, while the institutes of higher education under Soviet rule never stimulated the same level of radicalism

[29] See Susan K. Morrissey, *Heralds of Revolution. Russian Students and the Mythologies of Radicalism* (Oxford: Oxford University Press, 1998), chs 1–2; Peter Konecny, *Builders and Deserters: Students, State, and Community in Leningrad, 1917–1941* (Montreal & Kingston: McGill-Queen's University Press, 1999), ch. 1; David Saunders, *Russia in the Age of Reaction and Reform, 1801–1881* (London: Longman, 1992), ch. 8.
[30] M. Iankovskii, *Kommuna sta tridtsati trekh* (Leningrad, 1929), 28–9.
[31] Karelina, 'Vospominaniia', 12–21.   [32] Iankovskii, *Kommuna sta tridtsati trekh*, 28–31.
[33] Ber, *Kommuna segodnia*, 64–5.

as their nineteenth-century counterparts.[34] But for party representatives and those activists inclined to support the October Revolution, the constructs of the old student movement and the imagined virtues of the nineteenth-century radical became a common point of reference within revolutionary vocabulary.

This was also the case with the pre-revolutionary *artel'*. The earliest urban communes and communards took on many different titles and identified with many different contingents of revolution, but few popular developments held as much sway within these groups as the much-romanticized 'worker artels' (*trudovye arteli*).[35] Among revolutionaries, the worker artels and first labour associations of late tsarist Russia had long been held up as higher forms of comradely organization. They were even seen as the precursors of working-class authority.[36] At the AMO plant, in the years immediately following the October Revolution, urban commune groups were praised for exhibiting 'artel-like qualities'. Working together as a team and challenging the production norms of their factory, they were seen as harbingers of better relations between workers, as well as a means of overcoming the inefficiencies of the Russian workplace.[37] For young communards such as Stepan Afanas'evich Balezin, who, as we will see in Chapter 2, helped form some of the early Petrograd student communes after 1917, the artel held connotations of proletarian resistance and worker solidarity. Indeed, one of the first commune groups that Balezin helped to form originally went by the name 'Red Artel'. Living together in the *Mytninskaia* dormitory, in the heart of Petrograd, and working alongside one another at the city port, they seemed to associate the artel with teamwork and working-class companionship.[38] Also, during the opening years of the revolution, when the party was in disagreement over how best to run Soviet factories, the communards' touting of the artel reflected their support for collegial techniques and workers' control of industry. This was in contrast to Lenin's proposal for one-person management (*edinonachalie*), which looked to hand over labour and productivity responsibility to sector heads and old-fashioned bosses.[39]

Picking up these readings from the revolutionary literature and political zeitgeist of early Soviet Russia, the urban communes and communards came to view the artels and discussion circles as part of a broader pattern of actions carried out by pre-revolutionary groups, spontaneous gatherings, and radical associations. This was, after all, how political, social, and industrial resistance was organized in opposition

---

[34] Morrissey, *Heralds of Revolution*, 231 ff.

[35] 'Rabochie i kommuny', *Kommunar*, 24 December 1918, 3; 'Gorodskie kommuny', *Kommunar*, 27 December 1918, 3.

[36] Cf. Kharkhordin, *The Collective and the Individual in Russia*, 76; Mark D. Steinberg, *Proletarian Imagination: Self, Modernity, and the Sacred in Russia, 1910–1925* (Ithaca, NY: Cornell University Press, 2002), 64–5, 102–6; and Stephen A. Smith, *Red Petrograd. Revolution in the Factories, 1917–1918* (Cambridge: Cambridge University Press, 1985), 1–55.

[37] TsGA Moskvy, f. 415, op. 16, d. 590, ll. 51–55 (AMO factory, reflections of Komsomol, 1920–28); first cited in Simon Pirani, *The Russian Revolution in Retreat, 1920–24* (Oxford: Routledge, 2008), 53. Also see 'Gorodskie kommuny', 3.

[38] *Muzei istorii Rossiiskii gosudarstvennyi pedagogicheskii universitet im. A. I. Gertsena* (hereafter, MRGPU im. Herzen), d. B-5, ll. 20–16 (Personal file on Stepan Afanas'evich Balezin, 1904–82).

[39] MRGPU im. Herzen, d. B-5, ll. 20–16.

to the established order of late tsarist Russia. Falling under the category of *kollektiv* (collective)—a noun that seems to have become rooted within professional and revolutionary jargon in the wake of 1905—the small, concentrated unit of campaigners became something of a political and revolutionary phenomenon in the years leading up to 1917.[40] In St Petersburg, for instance, small groups of printing workers organized their own political *kruzhki* and *arteli*, some of which became active in the Assembly of Russian Factory Workers—a workers' organization, led by the politically active priest Father Georgii Gapon, that sought better conditions for its members and came to play an instrumental role in the revolution of 1905. Some of these groups also helped to form a lithographers' trade union in 1905. They were part of what Mark Steinberg has called a 'moral vanguard' calling for better working conditions and rejecting the inequalities of industrial Russia.[41] They formed the nexus from which the revolution of 1905 and subsequent protests emerged. With few other sources of public representation, these troops of activists were seen, by revolutionaries and moderates alike, as the building blocks of social and political transformation. This was reflective of a time when groups, leagues, and societies were formed so that the marginalized and the disaffected could take action into their own hands, press forth their demands, and try to forge political change.

Alongside the illegal underground 'cells' (*iacheiki*) and local networks of revolutionary parties, including those of the Bolsheviks, the 'moral vanguard' were discussing issues such as working norms, urban community, and social hierarchy.[42] In the eyes of urban communards such as Balezin, these close-knit alliances and select companies were the primary medium or strategy through which workers and revolutionaries changed the world.[43] They became a source of reverence and offered them something to emulate.

Adopting the terms 'cell' and 'collective' when describing their own association of activism, the *Kauchuk* commune also tapped into a revolutionary lexicon that privileged small groupings and cooperative alliances.[44] Like many other urban communes and communards, they arose from the political and cultural traditions of the Russian *kollektiv*. This was not a revolutionary unit or method prescribed by Marx. To the urban communards, the *kruzhok*, *artel'*, *iacheika*, and *kollektiv* were symbols of political consciousness, working-class affiliation, and revolutionary intent.[45] Within their example, early Soviet activists found cause for inspiration. In 1918, one young Petrograd student named Arkady Kulikov formed his own '*artel'*'—in this instance a collective, cohabitative arrangement—to help his peers find the income and employment necessary to continue their studies. He was eager

[40] Kharkhordin, *The Collective and the Individual in Russia*, 76.
[41] Mark D. Steinberg, *Moral Communities: The Culture of Class Relations in the Russian Printing Industry 1867–1907* (Berkeley: University of California Press, 1992), 89–91. Also see Steinberg, *Proletarian Imagination*, esp. ch. 2, and Diane P. Koenker, *Republic of Labor: Russian Printers and Soviet Socialism, 1918–1930* (Ithaca, NY: Cornell University Press, 2005), ch. 1.
[42] Steinberg, *Proletarian Imagination*, 38–9.   [43] MRGPU im. Herzen, d. B-5, ll. 20–16.
[44] Levgur, 'Komsomol'skaia kommuna "Kauchuk"', 26–7.
[45] MRGPU im. Herzen, d. B-5, ll. 20–16.

to align their humble actions with this example of proletarian organization. It offered a sense of legitimacy and it spoke to this young dreamer's understanding of revolutionary activity.[46] At the same time, reports suggest that some urban communes channelled the worker alliances and petitions of 1905, canvassing local Soviet authorities for better industrial facilities and domestic conditions throughout the 1920s.[47] In many respects, the legacy of the *kollektiv* encapsulated the spirit of grassroots democracy and self-activity that came to fuel the early years of the October Revolution and the urban commune movement itself. The *kollektiv* was, in other words, firmly rooted in Russia's revolutionary culture.

BECOMING SOCIALIST, AVOIDING PIGS

Russia's revolutionary culture and its predominant strategy of protest were not the only predisposing sources to influence the first wave of urban communes. Following the seizure of power on 24–25 October 1917, the Bolsheviks opened up new horizons and possibilities for the politically conscious labourer. After all, despite the undeniable ruthlessness that accompanied Bolshevik politics, the October Revolution did genuinely open up opportunities for some sections of society—it is not to endorse the Bolsheviks to acknowledge this fact. Initiatives such as the implementation of worker faculties (*rabfaki*) in 1919 provided greater access to higher education for Russia's poor and dispossessed. But it was one of the contradictions of Bolshevik ideology that it aspired to build a vision of unrelenting modernity while promoting the rights of a social base that, in the case of Russia, barely had both feet out of the village. Taking the example of the worker faculties, they functioned as foundation schools, preparing workers and peasants to enter higher education. And it was within these institutes that many young idealists, eager to make the most of new opportunities, first encountered serious revolutionary debate and the prospect of the urban commune. Some went on to participate in Komsomol discussion groups; others joined the first worker communes, pooling their income and sharing resources inside vacated apartments and dormitory rooms.[48] But as this newly enfranchised demographic came to claim their new rights, they also brought with them a little bit of their old communities.

In areas such as the Kaluzhskaia district of southern Moscow, not far from the *Kauchuk* and AMO factories, there were reports of some urban commune groups and worker faculty students using garden plots and any free patch of soil they could find to plant their own beet and potato seeds. They utilized old courtyards

---

[46] K. I. Kochergii, 'Bor'ba za reformu universiteta', *Na shturm nauki. Vospominaniia byvshikh studentov fakul'teta obshchestvennykh nauk leningradskogo universiteta*, ed. V. V. Mavrodin (Leningrad, 1971), 16–23.

[47] *Rossiiskii gosudarstvennyi arkhiv sotsial'no-politicheskii istorii* (hereafter, RGASPI), f. M.1. op. 23, d. 584, ll. 1–47 (Discussion on 'Mass culture and domestic work', Seventh Congress of the Komsomol, 11–22 March 1926).

[48] 'Rabochaia zhizn'', *Pravda*, 11 April 1919, 4; 'Pervaia rabochaia domovaia kommuna', *Pravda*, 12 August 1919, 2.

or the spaces outside their workplace.[49] These were undoubtedly sensible and, for some, necessary measures to undertake during a time of reduced agricultural output. Lenin was in favour of such practical thinking when it came to dealing with the realities of a war-torn economy. However, there was also at play here an element of 'You can take the boy from the village, but you can't take the village from the boy'. This was certainly the case with Kolia Silin, a would-be activist who, just a couple of years after the Bolsheviks seized power, left his parents' farm and joined one of the student commune groups based at the Electro-technical Institute in Petrograd. Once resident in the commune, Silin participated in all the modern undertakings expected of an urban communard, including progressive discussions about sexual equality and support for women in the workforce. But some habits are hard to shake off. Presumably getting carried away by what he thought was a good price, one day Silin decided to purchase a pig and persuaded his fellow communards to let it stay with them in their cramped city dwelling. He told them that this particular sow was a good investment and that it would provide them with lots of piglets that they could sell on. But after just one week—having endured constant squealing and snorting from their newest member—the commune concurred that Silin's 'theory [had] suffered a miserable, practical defeat'.[50]

The punishment for Silin's foolhardiness was a few months of relentless teasing, gleefully doled out by his fellow communards. On at least one occasion this proved too much for the young man. Sitting down to dinner with the group, Silin was passed a plate with a boiled egg in the middle. Taking a spoon to the top of his egg, the shell offered little resistance, crumbling under the force of Silin's blow to reveal nothing but air inside. The rest of the room immediately released a burst of laughter, leaving Silin to admire the latest prank. Some of the communards had carefully emptied the egg in advance and were now proudly admiring their handiwork. But it did not end there. Handed what turned out to be a second dummy-egg, and subjected to a second round of anticipatory laughter, Silin finally snapped, screaming 'What bastard did this?', before grabbing the nearest egg and launching it across the room in a fit of frustration. Unfortunately for one of the other communards, this egg had not been drained, and the yoke was left dripping down the side of his face. This only served to reinforce Silin's embarrassment. It was an incident that he would never be allowed to forget—the rest of the commune saw to that.[51]

While not all early communards followed Silin's particular example, quite a few were the product of Russia's rural poor. Even those with experience of urban life had often grown up or still had family members in the village—figures from just before the October Revolution suggest that barely 10 per cent of Moscow's population were permanent residents, born and raised in the city.[52] Indeed, an advocate of the worker artel, Balezin was nevertheless from peasant stock. Born near the

[49] 'Den' rabotnits', *Kommunar*, 9 March 1919, 3; 'Rabochie kommuny', *Kommunar*, 27 March 1919, 3.

[50] Iankovskii, *Kommuna sta tridtsati trekh*, 32–5.

[51] Iankovskii, *Kommuna sta tridtsati trekh*, 36–8.

[52] Diane P. Koenker, 'Urbanization and Deurbanization in the Russian Revolution and Civil War', *Journal of Modern History*, no. 3 (1985), 424–50, esp. 430.

central Russian city of Perm in 1904, Balezin spent much of his childhood helping his parents work the land. His eyes were only opened to new opportunities after he joined the Red Army in 1918.[53] Likewise, Ali Ianbulat, who became a lynch-pin of the student communes at the Electro-technical Institute, grew up just outside Saratov in central Russia, where his father was a longshoreman on the Volga, while most of his family was tied to seasonal agricultural work. Before moving to Petrograd to pursue an education that just a few years earlier had seemed out of reach, Ianbulat helped his parents to form an 'agricultural collective', seizing the land in the name of the people.[54] Balezin and Ianbulat were part of a generation of rural youths emboldened by revolution. They moved to Petrograd with optimism and a sense of possibility. This revealed itself in many of their actions. But so did aspects of their background. As they came to form their own urban communes within the institute dormitories of Petrograd, experience of small-scale association on the land taught them the virtues of autarky and gave them an idea of what mutual cooperation might look like. And seeing the Bolsheviks celebrate peasant alliances as a means of reclaiming the land in the immediate aftermath of 1917, they felt encouraged to initiate similar unions among their fellow students.[55]

Whether or not the Russian countryside was, in reality, the source of egalitarianism that much of the nineteenth-century intelligentsia imagined it to be, peasant life and the predominant form of agricultural management certainly did accent community, equality, and sharing.[56] Growing up surrounded by the legacy of the Russian *mir* (a traditional self-governing, rural body with elected peasant elders, usually, if not ideally, translated as 'village commune'), activists such as Silin, Balezin, and Ianbulat were minded to support the small, cooperative unit as a base of proletarian organization. They were receptive to the notion of collective association and community partnership. This form of living was familiar to them in many respects. From a background that taught its young that joint action was the standard form of labour, and that land and property were not really subject to private ownership, the advance of 'revolutionary collectivism' seemed to add weight to the idea that this was their world now. Indeed, Balezin and Ianbulat were not above presenting themselves as the 'elders' of their own urban communes, taking the lead when it came to setting the agenda for collective discussions and asking fellow communards to formally elect them as group leaders.[57]

More to the point, many rural youths were influenced by the local Komsomol, party cell, and Red Army portrayals of peasant association, which—as part of the Bolsheviks' attempt to appease the rural population after 1917—often looked to

[53] MRGPU im. Herzen, d. B-5, ll. 20–16.

[54] *Muzei istorii Sankt-Peterburgskogo gosudarstvennogo elektrotekhnicheskogo universiteta, 'LETI'* (hereafter, Muzei istorii SPbETU), KP. osn. 4712, d. 2025, ll. 1–11 (Personal file of Ali Ianbulat).

[55] MRGPU im. Herzen, d. B-5, ll. 20–16; and Muzei istorii SPbETU, KP. osn. 4712, d. 2025, ll. 1–11.

[56] See Andy Willimott, 'The Kommuna Impulse: Collective Mechanisms and Commune-ists in the Early Soviet State', *Revolutionary Russia*, no. 1 (June 2011), esp. 60–2.

[57] MRGPU im. Herzen, d. B-5, ll. 20–16; and Muzei istorii SPbETU, KP. osn. 4712, d. 2025, ll. 1–11.

write revolutionary goals into existing social structures. Aaron Retish has referred to this as a period of 'big tent Bolshevism', when, instead of riding roughshod over the rural community, the party tried to incorporate peasant life into the revolution.[58] In 1918, the Council of People's Commissars (*Sovnarkom*) even allocated 10 million roubles to encourage existing peasant communities to register themselves as 'agricultural collectives' or 'communes' with the People's Commissariat of Agriculture. 'Model Rules for Agricultural-Labour Communes' were released so that these associations might gradually begin to adhere to Soviet ideals. 'Let's live as a Commune!' (*Davaite zhit' kommunoi!*), a propaganda pamphlet advocating collective practice and revolutionary goals, contained one such model, complete with blanks where the rural association could write its name, location, and elected representatives. This model was designed to be detached from the pamphlet and to serve as a means of expanding basic revolutionary principles, such as equality, shared work, efficient management, and cooperation with the local soviet.[59] One thing it did not prescribe—and something that the Bolsheviks certainly did not expect—was for young idealists to transport such models to the city. Yet this seems to be what happened in the case of individuals such as Silin, Balezin, and Ianbulat. The idealizing of their own collective credentials helped to fuel their desire to create similar associations in the city.

This brings us full circle, with the community structures of Russia's poor helping to augment the rose-tinted views of Chernyshevsky and the wider collective revolutionary discourse. But this is not to suggest that the urban communes were a continuation of peasant life. Not all communards had such strong ties to the village. Nor is it to say that the urban communes and communards endorsed peasant culture. Once in Petrograd, activists such as Silin, Balezin, and Ianbulat affiliated themselves with all things modern, urban, and revolutionary. For them, the new socialist world was certainly to be made of metal and glass, not wood and straw bales. They aligned themselves with industrial workers and rejected the superstition, mob justice, and patriarchal norms of country life. The hammer was mightier than the sickle in this respect. Meeting other activists and communards with greater experience of the city only accelerated their modern aspirations. Indeed, it is telling that after the pig fiasco, Silin was forever known as the 'peasant ideologue' (*krest'ianskii ideolog*); in this Petrograd commune the ideology of the old peasant was associated with narrow-mindedness and irrational behaviour. In debates and discussions, the phrase 'peasant ideologue' was levelled at those with ideas that were deemed insufficiently modern or fundamentally 'unscientific'. In effect, then, Silin was teased for having failed to shed certain old habits and undesirable aspects of his background.[60] Despite idealizing aspects of the peasant *mir* as a source for their new collectivism, communes and communards also sought to cast off the inhibitions of the village.

---

[58] Aaron B. Retish, *Russia's Peasants in Revolution and Civil War: Citizenship, Identity, and the Creation of the Soviet State, 1914–1922* (Cambridge: Cambridge University Press, 2008), ch. 7.
[59] M. Sumatokhin, *Davaite zhit' kommunoi!* (Moscow, 1918).
[60] Iankovskii, *Kommuna sta tridtsati trekh*, 36.

Nevertheless, it seems clear that the Bolshevik discourse on collectivism struck a practical chord with the early communards and many other Soviet citizens. These ideas were not alien to would-be revolutionaries. In fact, in some cases the European idea of socialism seems to have been grounded through the medium of Russian collectivism and traditional collective association. Familiar institutions helped bring a certain idea of socialism to life for many activists. At the very least, they made some individuals more amenable to core revolutionary principles, including mutual cooperation and collective ownership. This further explains why the *kollektiv*—a revolutionary mechanism that was neither proposed nor endorsed by Marx—came to form such a crucial part of the early Soviet experience. The *mir* had proven remarkably resilient in the face of numerous attempts to reform Russian society over the years. Physically and culturally, it continued to shape Russia beyond 1917. Thanks in part to the legacy of this institution, the activists that went on to form some of the first urban communes were already versed in the practice of commonality. The *kollektiv* was, therefore, a revolutionary extension of certain established cultural norms. In this sense, we can see that concepts initially delimited within a pre-revolutionary context continued to inform and orientate Soviet cultural perceptions, but they also acquired new meanings and functions along the way.[61] Here, in other words, we can see the urban commune as the layering of cultural systems, new and old, providing young activists with a natural and accessible means of revolutionary participation.

(RE)INVENTING THE COMMUNE

As the revolution developed, the young activists at the heart of this book began, ever more earnestly, to conflate their understanding of collective organization, and the wider discourse on collectivism, with early Soviet visions of the *kommuna*—as inspired by the French revolutionary conception of a self-governing body. Alongside the example of the *kollektiv* and Chernyshevsky's radicals, the Paris Commune of 1871 became a primary signifier of joint action and revolutionary companionship. The *Kauchuk* group, for one, wanted it to be noted that, while there were many collections of people living together and sharing resources, they were different: they wanted to be distinguished as 'a commune'.[62] Placing a banner that read 'commune' above the door was a statement of intent for this group. Traditional Russian words, such as *obshchina* or *mir*—each denoting certain shades of 'community'—might have sufficed, but 'commune' came to encapsulate the full ambition of the *Kauchuk*. Once described by Marx as 'the first dictatorship of the proletariat', the Paris Commune was seen as a model of direct democracy, mutual cooperation, and collective reorganization. This was an event that saw the Left and

---

[61] A similar point has been made about the impact of religion on Russian secular developments. For example, see Susan K. Morrissey, *Suicide and the Body Politic in Imperial Russia* (Cambridge: Cambridge University Press, 2006), esp. intro.
[62] Levgur, 'Komsomol'skaia kommuna "Kauchuk"', 26.

the laymen of Paris throw off the shackles of French autocracy, briefly declaring the formation of a municipal government with what might be described as the first example of a socialist or, at least, a social democratic agenda. Embracing the title as their own, groups such as the *Kauchuk* were presenting themselves as a collective force for modern revolutionary socialism in Russia.

As we proceed, it is worth stressing that it was the Soviet imagining of 1871, not the historic realities of these events, that came to fuel the urban communes and communards. The *Kauchuk* and many others were inspired by the story of the Commune as it was told after 1917.[63] Indeed, the early Soviet state celebrated the insurrectionary events of 1871 as a beacon of socialism. Lenin's *State and Revolution* (1918), which has been described as the Gettysburg Address of the October Revolution, referred to the Paris Commune as the precursor to the soviets.[64] Like many Bolsheviks, Lenin thought of the Paris Commune as a model of socialist statehood. In one of his more utopian moments, Lenin said that replicating the Commune's governmental structure was a task 'immediately fulfillable' upon the seizure of power. While this proved far from true, *Pravda* often compared Soviet Russia to the Paris Commune, the new revolutionary state even acquiring the title of the 'Russian' or 'Soviet Commune' from time to time.[65] In addition, streets were named in honour of the Commune; every March a public holiday marked the start of the uprising; grand street performances re-enacted the events of 1871; leading figurers had memorabilia shipped over from France—Lenin's body was famously adorned by the red flag of the Paris Commune on the occasion of his death in 1924; and the 'lessons of the Commune' became an entrenched topic of discussion in Soviet publications.[66] Narrating the history of the Paris Commune through writings and celebrations, the Bolsheviks created socialism's first martyr story and portrayed themselves as the successors of 1871.[67]

Furthermore, the early Soviet state hosted its own attempts at the municipality commune. One of the most famous examples was in Baku, where an emergency city government formed amid the ethnic, religious, and political tensions sweeping across Transcaucasia. In April 1918, fearing that the October Revolution would degenerate into war between Armenians and Azerbaijanis, Stephan Shaumian led a bloc of Bolsheviks and Socialist Revolutionaries in a short-lived experiment of maximalist socialist administration.[68] It was reported at the time that Baku was the

---

[63] Cf. Eric Aunoble, *'Le Communisme, tout de suite!' Le mouvement des Communes en Ukraine soviétique, 1919–1920* (Paris: Les Nuits Rouges, 2008), esp. 19–21.

[64] Marian Sawer, 'The Soviet Image of the Commune: Lenin and Beyond', in James A. Leith (ed.), *Images of the Commune. Images de la Commune* (Montreal: McGill-Queen's University Press, 1978), 245–63.

[65] See *Pravda*, 1 May and 1 July 1919, 18 March 1920; cited in Robert Wesson, *Soviet Communes* (New Brunswick, NJ: Rutgers University Press, 1963), 5.

[66] For more on Soviet celebrations and festivals, see James von Geldern, *Bolshevik Festivals, 1917–1920* (Berkeley: University of California Press, 1993), esp. ch. 6.

[67] For example A. Slutskii, *Parizhskaia Kommuna 1871 goda* (Moscow, 1925), esp. 117 ff.; M. N. Pokrovskii, *Brief History of Russia*, 2 Vols (New York, 1933), 184–6. Also see I. S. Galkin, *I Internatsional. Parizhskaia Kommuna* (Moscow: Akademia nauk SSSR, 1963). Many of these and later writings rely heavily, if not entirely, on Lenin's assessment of the Paris Commune.

[68] Ronald G. Suny, *The Baku Commune 1917–1918. Class and Nationality in the Russian Revolution* (Princeton, NJ: Princeton University Press, 1972), 214–15, 234–5.

'reincarnation' of the Paris Commune. Quoting Lenin, Shaumian even called for Russia to be turned into 'a republic of communes'.[69] When the Baku Commune collapsed in July 1918, Shaumian and his fellow revolutionaries were immediately portrayed, like the Communards of 1871, as martyrs—glorified as 'The Twenty-six Baku Commissars'.[70]

Accounts from urban commune diaries reveal that, for these activists, the anniversary of the Paris Commune remained a celebration of heroism and martyrdom throughout the 1920s. They viewed the original Communards of 1871 as figures to emulate.[71] Indeed, one group named Spark (*Iskra*), an urban commune group based in one of the worker barracks of the Stalingrad Tractor Factory, proclaimed that it was their ambition to replicate the 'selflessness and devotion' of 1871. To carry the name of these heroes, they insisted, was a 'great responsibility'.[72] Towards the latter half of the 1920s, as the shock-work movement gained a head of steam, admiration for the Communards only grew within this group. The heroes of 1871 seemed to offer a template for the 'new person'—the individual willing to sacrifice him or herself for a greater cause. The group's own sense of martyrdom was likely exacerbated by the fact that they unsettled their neighbours, often attracting 'sidelong glances' or outright 'taunting' as they returned home to the barracks each evening. The older workers, in particular, were suspicious of these young people. They didn't take kindly to what was perceived as the commune's sense of righteousness. But as Spark grew from the original five inhabitants to include, as they put it, '6 Komsomol members, a Jew, and workers of Tatar and German origin', the commune felt increasingly confident in their revolutionary conceit. They boasted that they were the face of the new world. Their diversity became a sign of their revolutionary standing and another marker distinguishing them from the forces of resistance.[73] For them, to be a 'Soviet communard' meant ploughing all their energies into group work, industrial construction, anti-racism, and other revolutionary tasks, even when confronted with obstacles and opposition.

Beyond the notion of individual heroism, the urban communes and communards also came to associate the Paris Commune with shared domestic arrangements and revolutionary living. In the immediate aftermath of 1917, publications such as *Kommunar* (*The Communard*) helped to ground grand revolutionary visions and the imagined principles of 1871 in concrete, even prosaic form, attaching the word *kommuna* to any grassroots body that orientated itself around collective principles. Amid the relics of the old way of life—just as the Paris Commune was surrounded by hostile forces in imperial France—such 'communes' represented a pocket of collective revolutionary success. In print between October 1918 and June 1919, the pages of the daily newspaper *Kommunar* eagerly reported on collective units of farming, accommodation, and labour as examples of 'spontaneous commune

[69] *Bakinskii rabochii*, no. 103, 3 June 1918; no. 104, 5 June 1918; cited in Suny, *The Baku Commune*, 267.
[70] John M. Thompson, *A Vision Unfulfilled: Russia and the Soviet Union in the Twentieth Century* (Toronto: University of Toronto Press, 1996), 171.
[71] 'Dnevnik odnoi kommuny', *Komsomol'skaia pravda*, 9 July 1930, 5.
[72] 'Dnevnik odnoi kommuny', 5.   [73] 'Dnevnik odnoi kommuny', 5.

forms'. As the first self-proclaimed urban communes began to arise, they too received the keen attention of this publication.[74] Reportedly 'growing like mushrooms', these groups were thought to offer a sign of hope in a Soviet cityscape still riddled with bourgeois pretensions.[75] At the same time, while the early trumpeting of the Paris Commune could not be translated into a 'socialist commune state'—not least because of the realities of civil war and the inevitable failure of an international revolution to occur as forecasted—a number of other facilities and institutions adopted the title *kommuna*. Schools, orphanages, juvenile detention centres, and provincial administrations became mini 'communes'. Increasingly, the press and activist groups, including Spark, equated the term 'commune' with spaces or bodies dedicated to collective development. Mentioned in the same breath as the *artel'* and the *kollektiv*, the Soviet understanding of the 'commune' extended to cooperative organization and mutual aid. But indicative of more than just group association, it also implied an environment, system, or lifestyle devoted to instilling collective values. As a political label, therefore, it symbolized a broader commitment to creating collectivism within socialist society.

The opening years of the October Revolution also witnessed the transformation of a number of luxury hotels, such as the Astoria and the Hotel de l'Europe of Petrograd, into specialized residences for party officials. Known as 'Houses of the Soviets' (*Doma Sovetov*), they contained collective services, including general catering and shared facilities designed to free the inhabitants from domestic chores and introduce new socialist environments.[76] The designs for non-party variations became known as 'house-communes' (*doma-kommuny*). Building on Lenin's citation of Friedrich Engels's *The Housing Question* (1872), which stated that the Paris Commune had shown how the proletariat could benefit from 'the rational utilization of...buildings',[77] the renovation of domestic and interior life became identified with socialism itself.[78] As early as October 1918, a certain Professor G. D. Dubelirov announced a model 'house-commune' architectural competition to cater for '100–200 people', with the added stipulation that 'besides living quarters', the complex had to provide: 'a) communal kitchen, b) dining-hall, c) bathroom, d) kindergarten and school, e) library and study-room'. These were the essentials for a microcosm of socialism: a self-contained community that would

---

[74] 'Po kvartiram rabochikh', *Kommunar,* 9 October 1918, 3. *Kommunar* was published in Moscow under the auspices of the Central Committee of the All-Union Communist Party (Bolsheviks). Between October 1918 and June 1919 the vast majority of its pages were concerned with collective agricultural practices, but it included numerous articles on worker communes and urban, collective housing. It was suggested that the stories covered under this title should subsequently be added to the remit of *Pravda* and *Bednota*. On the print run of *Kommunar*, see RGASPI, f. M.1 op. 3, d. 1, ll. 4–4ob. (The minutes of the meetings of the Bureau of the Central Committee of the Komsomol, 1919).

[75] 'Pereselenie v burzhuaznye doma', *Kommunar,* 17 October 1918, 2.

[76] N. B. Lebina, *Povsednevnaia zhizn' sovetskogo goroda: normy i anomalii, 1920–1930 gody* (St Petersburg: Letnii sad, 1999), 161.

[77] V. I. Lenin, *State and Revolution*, intro. and trans. Robert Service (London: Penguin Books, 1992), 52–3, 53. Cf. Robert Service, *Lenin, A Political Life*, Vol. 3: *The Iron Ring* (Macmillan: London, 1995), 34–7.

[78] Michael David-Fox, 'What Is Cultural Revolution?', *Russian Review*, vol. 58, no. 2 (1999), 181–201, 199.

break down the barriers of the old life, introduce new companionate relations between man and woman, and develop new collective habits.[79] While a lack of stability and finite resources prevented the standardization of the house-commune at this time, a formative discourse on home planning and daily life (*byt*) was firmly established.[80] This was a discourse imbued with the confidence of modernity and bolstered by the Marxist conviction that matter determines consciousness.[81] It was also a discourse that inadvertently influenced the evolving definition of 'commune', elevating the importance of new domestic arrangements and revolutionary forms of residence.

As their calling card suggests, the activists that formed the urban communes were actively responding to this developing discourse. For them, the 'commune' was a revolutionary space with domestic materialism at its heart. That is, they took from their wider readings the belief that they could mould the individual into the ideal collective being through changes made to the basic design of daily life. As early as 1920 and 1921, at their third and fourth congresses, Komsomol delegates highlighted the connection between these activists and the broader discourse on the 'new way of life' (*novyi byt*), when they referred to the urban communes as places where youths could develop their revolutionary identities away from the corrupting influence of the family and bourgeois life.[82] Among the many varied examples of the urban commune impulse, from those based in the student dormitories to those housed inside factory barracks, and, as we shall see, from those groups inclined to support Trotsky during the early 1920s to those convinced of his treachery come 1927, one thing that remained constant was the idea that they might create the ideal conditions from which the 'new person' and a new collective community would emerge. They thought that by regulating themselves and their surroundings they could advance socialism. This, above all, is what *kommuna* came to signify for them. And, in the early 1920s, as the dream of the *dom-kommuna* and new housing facilities started to fall short of their original collectivist ideals, the necessity of the urban commune only increased in the mind of its creators.[83]

*

Urging tomorrow to come today, the urban communes and communards embarked upon a form of collective experimentation that was meant to unleash the harmonious

---

[79] 'Iz primery programmy dlya sostavlenaya proekta pokazatel'nogo, razrabotannoi', 16 October 1918; reproduced in K. N. Afanas'ev (ed.), *Iz istorii sovetskoi arkhitektury 1917–1925 gg. Dokumenty i materialy* (Moscow: Akademiia nauk SSSR, 1963), 17.

[80] Richard Stites, *Revolutionary Dreams, Utopian Vision and Experimental Life in the Russian Revolution* (New York: Oxford University Press, 1989), 201.

[81] See David Crowley and Susan E. Reid (eds), *Socialist Spaces. Sites of Everyday Life in the Eastern Bloc* (Oxford: Berg, 2002), 11. Also see Victor Buchli, *An Archaeology of Socialism* (New York: Berg, 1999), esp. ch. 2; and Caroline Humphrey, 'Ideology in Infrastructure: Architecture and Soviet Imagination', *Journal of the Royal Anthropological Institute*, no. 1 (2005), 39–58.

[82] *Tovarishch komsomol. Dokumenty s"ezdov, konferentsii i TsK VLKSM, 1918–1968* (Moscow, 1969), vol. 1, 34, 63.

[83] On the collectivist ideals of the Soviet housing project, see Steven E. Harris, *Communism on Tomorrow Street: Mass Housing and Everyday Life after Stalin* (Baltimore, MD: Johns Hopkins University Press, 2013), 55–8; and Mark B. Smith, *Property of Communists: The Urban Housing Program from Stalin to Khrushchev* (DeKalb: Northern Illinois University Press, 2010), intro.

potential of humanity. Their ambitions were grand. Embracing a Soviet vision of the Paris Commune—an image not necessarily rooted in historical reality—connected them with a supposed example of socialist heroism; a guide to the eradication of state institutions; a form of direct democracy; a formula for mass participation; a rough sketch of revolutionary organization; and, crucially, a lively discourse on housing and the reorganization of everyday life. Viewing themselves in this light emboldened these young activists, giving them the confidence to engage in local revolutionary projects and major ideological debates. The name 'commune' acted as an authenticating label, allowing them to display an affinity with the latest revolutionary and discursive developments of the early Soviet state.

But, as we have seen, the identity of the urban communes and communards was woven from many strands. While they adopted the term 'commune', they were also the product of a revolutionary culture that saw the small, collective unit as the basic building block of socialism. They consciously built on the legacy, mythology, and practices of the *artel'* and the *kollektiv*; they were inspired by Chernyshevsky's revolutionary saga and the promise of the 'new person'; and some brought with them a practical knowledge of common association from a society with a celebrated tradition of kinship. In this sense, their understanding of the *kommuna* was predicated on a broad reverence for collectivism and small-scale alliances. The urban commune was, in other words, a revolutionary phenomenon quite specific to Russia in its form and culture. Or, from another perspective, it can be said that the group dynamics of the Soviet communards offered a variation on traditional *kollektiv* precursors.

Yet it was only after 1917, with 'the collectivization of the means of production', as Krupskaya would later profess, that *kollektiv* forms could develop and work towards the 'socialization of life'. It was only in the wake of October, she believed, that they could advance a world in which all would 'live with dignity' (*zhit' po-chelovecheski*).[84] Where 'monastic communism' had been 'bound by austerity' and pre-revolutionary guilds, cooperatives, and other associations were limited to a world of 'consumerism', the *kommunki*—small social experiments in 'the practice of life'—would flourish as 'applications of science' in a new, consciously modern world. October, she insisted, had released these groups to explore the Marxist principle of 'everything according to one's need'. Wherever and however their collective practices were deployed, they would now be involved in the 'dissipation of the old way of life' and the conscious construction of the 'new life'.[85] Like the communes and communards themselves, Krupskaya saw this as the dawn of a new age for collective association. And, exaggerated though her claims might be, they do speak to the mentality and self-identification of the urban commune impulse. They reveal the reflexivity of the urban communards' collectivism. New revolutionary paradigms renewed and shaped the urban communards' interest in collective association as they began to form their own connections with the Soviet world and its ideological messages.

---

[84] Krupskaya, *O Bytovykh voprosakh*, 3–4. [85] Krupskaya, *O Bytovykh voprosakh*, 30–6.

As much as anything, the urban commune was a modish revolutionary development among young activists and would-be revolutionaries keen to feel part of the historic events unfolding before them. Whether they arose in the student dormitory after prolonged ideological discussion, within 'bourgeois' apartments seized in the name of the proletariat, or inside factory complexes abounding with a renewed sense of comradeship, the urban communes and communards pulled together revolutionary trends, new and old, as they sought to make the October Revolution part of them. They synthesized the pre-revolutionary struggle for dignity, active solidarity, and collective action with the latest understandings of a forceful collective discourse and the Soviet imagining of 1871. The *kommunki*, as Krupskaya described them, extended revolutionary readings on collectivism and the collective body into their daily attempts to be socialist.

While control commissions and the Soviet leadership came to view collectivism as the necessary subjugation of the individual to the interests of the party, the experience of the urban communes and communards was much richer. They were involved in an attempt to enact a collectivism of more immediate significance. Reading and debating the meaning of this ideological concept led them to adopt a number of traits associated with established forms of group alliance, certain living arrangements and habits understood to instil a sense of comradeship, and, as we shall explore in the coming chapters, a firm commitment to social and educational work (*obshchestvennost'*) in their wider communities. Inspired by nineteenth-century radicalism, some modelled themselves on the exploits of Chernyshevsky's Rakhmetov, equating collectivism and revolution with self-regulation and plain asceticism. Others embraced the notion of the *kollektiv* and group protest as the main force for historical change. From the Soviet discourse on domesticity and everyday life (*byt*), many took socialism to mean shared-living space and the overhaul of familial customs, some reasoning that internal walls were a bourgeois creation. Commitment to the party and a sense of party-mindedness (*partiinost'*) remained important to many of these young activists, but collectivism acquired a number of other connotations and compulsions that would come to define the urban communes.[86] The manner in which these collective impulses and convictions played out in the hands of the urban communes and communards marked the next important step in their development.

---

[86] Cf. David-Fox, *Revolution of the Mind*, 107–10.

2
Socialism in One Dormitory
Student Communes

'The commune... forged the education of youth in the spirit of human dignity, morality, hard work, social duty, and responsibility.'

'The commune... there our youth blossomed.'

Ali Ianbulat, student communard.

Reflecting on his experience of dormitory life in post-revolutionary Russia, Ali Ianbulat reveals the affinity between the urban commune and the activist student.[1] Born in 1905, Ianbulat was part of a generation of students entering higher education under the new Soviet system. Partly educated in a parish school, near the Volga valley city of Saratov, where teachers employed a liberal use of the whip, he came to welcome the October Revolution as a dawning opportunity. A bright boy, who was encouraged to read from a young age by his literate and doting grandmother, Ianbulat was frustrated by what he later called the 'nineteenth-century mores' of his pre-revolutionary schooling. And despite the fact he and his family had to retreat into the countryside to escape the worst of the civil war, by 1919 the rapidly maturing Ianbulat was urging all those around him to embrace the socialist cause. Over the coming years, in a whirlwind of activity, he would join the Communist Youth League (Komsomol), start working for the local revolutionary press, and pick up his education in the evening classes of a worker faculty (*rabfak*).

It seemed that History was on Ianbulat's side. Allowing this revolutionary wave to take him to Moscow, he and some fellow youths attended a Komsomol event where Ianbulat met with Lenin's sister, Mariia Il'inichna Ul'ianova. It so happened that she took a liking to Ianbulat, particularly impressed by his revolutionary activities and by his desire to pursue further education.[2] It may also be that this young man reminded Mariia of her own time in Saratov, where, between 1909 and 1912, she helped turn the local branch of the Russian Social Democratic Labour Party (RSDRP) into a Bolshevik stronghold.[3] Whatever it was that first drew Mariia to his story, this encounter proved most fortuitous for Ianbulat. Mariia was moved

---

[1] *Muzei istorii Sankt-Peterburgskogo gosudarstvennogo elektrotekhnicheskogo universiteta, 'LETI'* (hereafter, Muzei istorii SPbETU), KP. osn. 4711, d. 2025, ll. 1–11, quotation 3 (Personal file of Ali Ianbulat).

[2] Muzei istorii SPbETU, KP. osn. 4711, d. 2025, ll. 1–11.

[3] See Katy Turton, *Forgotten Lives: The Role of Lenin's Sisters in the Russian Revolution, 1864–1937* (London: Palgrave Macmillan, 2007), ch. 3.

to inform the Commissar of Enlightenment, Anatolii Lunacharskii, all about Ianbulat. She insisted that Lunacharskii himself immediately provide the young man with an admission statement and reference for higher education. Armed with this formidable backing, and under the advice of Mariia, Ianbulat put himself forward for the entrance exam of what was by that time the Leningrad State Electro-technical Institute (LETI). Upon clearing this final hurdle, Ianbulat found himself admitted to the exciting world of higher education, where the student body was feverishly discussing the prospects of socialism. He immediately became embroiled in long conversations about collectivism and internationalism, the impact of the 'imperialist war', global revolution, as well as racism and xenophobia. Most importantly, however, he was introduced to an idea that would affect the rest of his educational experience: the student commune.

The student commune presented Ianbulat with what he referred to as his 'second revolutionary awakening'.[4] Here he was shown how student activists had started to put ideological theory into practice, attempting to live the socialist life. He saw groups coming together to share all their possessions, putting their stipends and earnings into a common pot (*obshchii kotel*), and invoking the reformation of domestic norms. Communes, he noticed, would eat, drink, work, and play as a cohesive unit. Among other things, they undertook collective trips to the theatre, the cinema, the Hermitage, and the Russian Museum. They were looking to define the lifestyle of a socialist. He also saw these groups put themselves forward as the social, political, and cultural 'guardians' (*opekuny*) of their dormitories and the wider institute. Their domestic concerns were matched by their determination to help promote the revolutionary cause within the educational institute more broadly.[5]

Aligning himself with the new wave of 'proletarian' and 'labouring' students entering university—himself a product of the rural poor—Ianbulat was keen to engage in all the revolutionary pursuits he could. He was astutely aware of the possibilities presented to him by the October Revolution, and he intended to make the most of each and every one of them. He eventually became an effective propagandist, the head of Komsomol schools in the Leningrad district, a member of the local Komsomol Committee, and an editor of the factory newspaper, *Krasnyi elektrik* (*Red Electric*). But, crucially, he became a member and vocal advocate of the LETI communes. If all else failed, Ianbulat soon realized, it was the commune that would provide him and his fellow students with a means of developing revolution both within themselves and in their wider environment.[6]

*

It has become a bit of a cliché to speak of student politics as 'radical', but clichés often have their roots in a truth. In many respects the youthful optimism and

---

[4] Muzei istorii SPbETU, KP. osn. 4711, d. 2025, l. 4.
[5] Muzei istorii SPbETU, KP. osn. 4712, d. 2026, ll. 1–5 (Ali Ianbulat, experiences of LETI communes in the 1920s).
[6] Muzei istorii SPbETU, KP. osn. 4711, d. 2025, ll. 3–4.

openness to radical change present within the student population after 1917 provided fertile soil for the urban communes.[7] The introduction of workers' faculties (*rabfaki*) in 1919 and the influx of students with a greater vested interest in revolution certainly accelerated a change in the political face of these institutes.[8] As Ianbulat was entering Soviet higher education, in the mid-1920s, these changes were already quite apparent. There was a contingent of socialist discussion circles (*kruzhki*) and debating assemblies (*skhodki*), a number of ongoing Komsomol and party agitation campaigns, and a certain air of vibrancy.[9] At the same time, there was a degree of freedom granted by the political upheaval in higher education. As Leningrad botany professor Vladimir Nikolaevich Sukhachev reflected, this was a time when Soviet students were encouraged to 'recognize themselves as active builders of socialism'.[10] The youth press was urging students to take part in revolution', promoting a 'literal perception' of socialism. After all, they were seen as the next generation of revolutionary leaders; the Bolsheviks wanted to encourage their potential. Catching wind of the urban commune phenomenon, some sections of the press even felt encouraged to suggest that its readers 'do away' with the bourgeois and 'be collective'. The 'best conductors of collectivism', enthusiastic reporters proclaimed, 'can be found in a dormitory commune'.[11] In this environment the student commune offered a means of participating in the construction of revolution. It became an instrument through which Ianbulat and other would-be radicals could attempt to fashion their revolutionary ambition and aspiration.

Inspired to form his own commune alliance with a group of fellow students shortly after arriving in Leningrad, Ianbulat took custody of a simple dormitory room and looked to create a new revolutionary bond through a strict code of shared living. No inhabitant was allowed to accumulate their own wealth or possessions, and each one of them had to take their turn as 'duty officer' in charge of the daily wake-up call, as well as monitoring domestic life in general. He and the other students involved in this enterprise found themselves seeking entertainment and revolutionary enlightenment, as many other such groups had before them, through regular trips to local museums, the cinema, and attending public lectures by the likes of Vladimir Mayakovsky. They also encouraged the wider student community to join them in their weekly discussion of the newspapers, journals, and local issues, such as the plight of their institutes.[12] Beyond this, noted Ianbulat, a degree of coordination developed between this group and the student communes attached to the Medical Institute, the Institute of Civil Engineers, and many other Leningrad university departments. Once or twice a year 'meetings were arranged between the communes of the Leningrad universities and the technical colleges'.

[7] N. B. Lebina, *Povsednevnaia zhizn' sovetskogo goroda: normy i anomalii, 1920/1930 gody* (St Petersburg: Letnii Sad, 1999), 164–5.

[8] Susan K. Morrissey, *Herald of Revolution. Russian Students and the Mythologies of Radicalism* (Oxford: Oxford University Press, 1998), 231 ff.

[9] See Filimonov, *Po novomu ruslu, vospominaniia*, 9–11.

[10] *Leningradskii Universitet*, 19 November 1935, 4; cited in P. Konecny, *Builders and Deserters, Students, State, and Community in Leningrad, 1917–1941* (Montreal: McGill-Queen's Press, 1999), 3.

[11] *Severnyi komsomolets*, 2 March 1924; cited in Lebina, *Povsednevnaia zhizn' sovetskogo goroda*, 166.

[12] Muzei istorii SPbETU, KP. osn. 4712, d. 2026, ll. 1–3

Two to three times a year they 'attended an evening party hosted by one of the other communes of Leningrad'. As a result of the ties made at these events it was not uncommon for members of different communes to meet, exchange views on literature, attend lectures together, and discuss the grander 'political developments' of their time.[13] The commune rapidly became the nexus of Ianbulat's student activism.

It is clear that students such as Ianbulat saw the commune as a crucial part of their educational experience and revolutionary growth. It offered a way to comment on and press the socialist agenda within their respective institutes. Recent studies into student life in the early Soviet state have revealed that a growing number of discussion circles, political gatherings, and cell meetings were providing young believers with a platform for political expression at this time. But these studies have also suggested that party representatives were able to use these associations to mould young minds in line with official Bolshevik thinking. This extends the notion that censorship is often 'less pervasive than self-censorship' to argue that revolutionary views acceptable to the party were carefully 'disseminated' through officially endorsed political rituals.[14] The example of the student commune seems to corroborate this argument insofar as it supports the claim that revolution was not just coercive but expressive and participatory in nature.[15] Yet the student commune challenges the determinacy present within the notion that the party was able to construct, monitor, and lead revolutionary expression at ground level. In reality, the student communes were often sympathetic to official ideology but not necessarily submissive to its local rendering or established practices—such as they were during the turbulent years following the October Revolution. As we will see in this chapter, the student communes were the product of a dialogue between youthful enthusiasm, ideological imperatives, and dormitory life. As we take a tour through some of these groups, highlighting key aspects of their development and self-perception, we will see the results of a proactive engagement with party views and revolutionary ideology.

BEGINNING IN THE DORMITORY

The first student communes emerged in the birthplace of the revolution, Petrograd, between 1918 and 1919, before then sprouting up in Moscow and other cities.[16] At the Petrograd Peter the Great Polytechnical Institute around this time, Nikolai Aleksandrovich Filimonov, a member of the three-person commune described at

---

[13] Muzei istorii SPbETU, KP. osn. 4712, d. 2026, l. 2.

[14] Igal Halfin, *Stalinist Confessions. Messianism and Terror at the Leningrad Communist University* (Pittsburgh, PA: University of Pittsburgh Press, 2009).

[15] I. Halfin, *Stalinist Confessions*, esp. 17. The notion that self-censorship was more effective than official censorship is extended from Michael David-Fox, *Revolution of the Mind. Higher Learning Among the Bolsheviks, 1918–1929* (Ithaca, NY: Cornell University Press, 1997), 100.

[16] V. S. Izmozik and N. B. Lebina, *Peterburg sovetskii, 'novyi chelovek' v starom prostranstve, 1920–1930-e gody* (St Petersburg: Kriga, 2010), 142–4.

the beginning of this book, noted how these units of collective cohabitation arose with a sense of purpose and a way of life that was in juxtaposition with the stale surroundings of the old student life.[17] Inherent within the formation of these early communes was the struggle for better conditions, comradely equality, and an alternative way of life. They established 'common pots', systems of mutual subsistence, and ultimately a range of new domestic and ideological arrangements by which to live.[18] From humble beginnings such groups developed systems of internal regulation, complete with shared resources designed to facilitate socialist visions in the dormitory and institute. Systems of necessity, such as the pooling of money for food and materials, combined with wider political and ideological convictions. The most active communards went on to campaign for the spread of revolutionary practices, citing their own actions by way of example.

M. A. Rom, a student of the Third Pedagogical Institute from 1919, insisted that Soviet institutes of higher education did not constitute socialist bodies at this time. Some professors even continued to 'preach anti-Bolshevik and anti-revolutionary messages', he remarked with alarm.[19] At the same time, explained Rom, he and his classmates were buoyed by 'military victories in the civil war' and the growing sense of hope that came with these advances. At long last, it was just about possible to envisage an end to all the fighting that had dominated Russian life in recent years. They felt encouraged 'to move to a new stage of revolution', remarked Rom, a stage of 'socialist construction' and 'new creative forces'. Consequently, Rom and some fellow would-be activists took it upon themselves to form a number of political agitation teams and discussion circles to promote the socialist cause within their institute. They met to coordinate their messages, posted numerous announcements on the walls of their institute, and organized open forums for students and professors. They also encouraged students to attend study sessions where together they would try to get to grips with *Das Kapital*.[20] Likewise, another young idealist, K. I. Kochergii, picking up his education after a stint in the Red Army, was moved to take the revolutionary initiative. He organized what was referred to as an 'alliance of proletarian labour students'. Based out of a small dormitory room, this self-proclaimed revolutionary 'faction' consisted of seven student members. By night they would 'merrily boil potatoes on the stove', remembered Kochergii, but by day they sought to engage in political discussions, press the merits of socialism upon their peers, and participate in as many local revolutionary

---

[17] Filimonov, *Po novomu ruslu, vospominania*, 3–12. NB. Founded in 1899 as the Saint-Petersburg Polytechnical Institute, this educational establishment underwent many name changes. It was known as the Saint-Petersburg Peter the Great Polytechnical Institute from 1910–14; the Petrograd Peter the Great Polytechnical Institute from 1914–22; the First Petrograd Polytechnical Institute from 1922–23; the Petrograd Polytechnical Institute from 1923–24; and the Leningrad Polytechnical Institute from 1924–30.

[18] Filimonov, *Po novomu ruslu, vospominania*, 11–12.

[19] M. A. Rom, 'V bor'be za sovetizatsiu universiteta', in V. V. Mavrodin (ed.), *Na shturm nauki, vospominaniia byvshikh studentov fakul'teta obshchestvennykh nauk leningradskogo universiteta* (Leningrad, 1971), 7–16. N.B. In 1925 the First, Second, and Third Pedagogical Institutes were united to form the State Leningrad Herzen Pedagogical Institute.

[20] Rom, 'V bor'be za sovetizatsiu universiteta', 7–8.

campaigns as possible. Kochergii, in particular, was looking to extend the collective camaraderie of his Red Army experience into student life, channelling his energy into improving dormitory and institute politics.[21]

This was the improvised and agitated 'canon' from which the home-grown student communes first emerged. The conditions of the student dormitory, explained Kochergii, helped bring his alliance together. Group bonds and political convictions were set in opposition to the material scarcity that surrounded them all. The battle against the material and ideological shortfalls of student life became part and parcel of their struggle for socialism. Kochergii and his 'alliance of proletarian labour students' developed connections with other activists and student commune groups, who would help them find extra income when needed, and would then stand next to them when it came to pressing the socialist agenda in and around the university or institute.[22] Together, revolutionary activists and the earliest student communes were helping to create the local parameters of revolution. Urging greater change, recalled one student, these revolutionary enthusiasts even began to concern themselves with the 'composition of the student body', challenging anyone not deemed to be sufficiently proletarian—perhaps a precursor to the first *chistka*, or 'cleansing' (non-violent evictions at this stage), of politically unsatisfactory persons in higher education which would unfold in 1924.[23]

It is hard to say precisely how many student communes and cohabiting units were formed in this way. The record-keeping infrastructure of the new Soviet state was in its infancy through much of the 1920s. This is reflected in the data emanating from the Soviet institutes of higher education. One set of institutional figures suggests that as few as two student communes were formally registered in Petrograd by 1923. According to the same figures, this number swelled to twenty-five communes with a recorded membership of 2,500 in 1929, growing to sixty communes with 7,700 members the following year.[24] While marking a significant growth at the end of the 1920s—coinciding with a reinvigorated interest in collectivism and collective association—these records do more to reflect the voluntary and elusive nature of these groups. Even these latter numbers are limited in their scope, only accounting for the very largest student groups and dormitory formations. But one only need turn to local and national print sources to note a much greater number of commune developments across Petrograd/Leningrad, Moscow, and other Soviet cities.

Indeed, as the Herzen Pedagogical Institute student newspaper, *Pedvuzovets*, subsequently revealed in great detail, the student commune could take a multitude of forms. The paper reported on a series of 'room-communes' (*komnaty-kommuny*),

---

[21] K. I. Kochergii, 'Bor'ba za reformu universiteta', in V. V. Mavrodin (ed.), *Na shturm nauki, vospominaniia byvshikh studentov fakul'teta obshchestvennykh nauk leningradskogo universiteta* (Leningrad, 1971), 16–23.

[22] Kochergii, 'Bor'ba za reformu universiteta', 17–19.

[23] K. G. Sharikov, 'Kandidat istoricheskikh nauk, universitet na pod'eme', *Na shturm nauki*, 23–40.

[24] A. Andropov, *Na novykh putiakh studencheskogo byta* (Moscow, 1930), 7; *Otchet Leningradskogo proletarskogo studenchestva za 1928/29*, 87; first cited in Konecny, *Builders and Deserters*, 3.

with as few as three to six members, arising within the student dormitory. It suggested that there were, in fact, hundreds of commune groups by the mid-1920s. Those that survived the initial burst of enthusiasm spread across dormitory floors and entire buildings, to form what were called 'floor-communes' (*etazhi-kommuny*) and 'dormitory-communes' (*obshchezhitiia-kommuny*).[25] Others found themselves migrating to ever-larger buildings in search of space, potential, and the fulfillment of their collective visions. Added to this, the urban and student commune took on many different titles and identified with many different aspects of revolution, including the much-romanticized, pre-revolutionary 'worker artels' (*trudovye arteli*). By their very nature, these groups were often beyond institutional management and formulaic statistics. They were based on personal bonds and transitory structures. Some were able to attain financial support within their respective institutional systems; some even acquired the backing of local Komsomol representatives. But they received no official attention from the upper echelons of the party apparatus. Their interaction with officialdom came, intermittently, through lower-level representatives and secondary bodies, such as institute staff and select Komsomol cells.

CULTURAL REVOLUTION IN THE DORMITORY

Irrespective of the support they may or may not have received, or the number of communes officially registered, it is not at all hard to understand the demand for change that ran through the communes. The activists that assembled the student communes looked to enact the promise of socialism where they thought it was lacking. This led them to comment on a number of different issues. As the revolution unfolded, however, it was noticeable that these groups were becoming increasingly concerned with what might be categorized as the broader 'cultural failings' of their institutes. From their time in the Red Army, figures such as Rom and Kochergii had been introduced to the idea of a 'third front', promoting the virtues of new social and cultural practices in accordance with Bolshevik visions of socialist modernity. After all, the Red Army was about more than securing the borders of revolution; it was charged with advancing what was termed 'political' and 'cultural enlightenment'. When they entered higher education, Rom and Kochergii would, in many ways, seek to continue this mission. They became embroiled in what contemporaries came to know as the struggle for 'cultural revolution' (*kul'turnaia revoliutsiia*). Alongside other activists and the student communes, they constituted a voluntary or social contingent of the 'cultural front'. For these young activists, in the context of the post-1917 institute of higher education, cultural revolution would include not just learning and the arts, but the development of a way of life marked by modern, socialist practice. It was measured in terms of cleanliness, dedication to study and society, reading, knowledge of Marx, financial competence,

[25] See 'Za kommunu', *Pedvuzovets*, 28 November 1929, 4; 'Za perestroiku byta', *Pedvuzovets*, 13 January 1930, 3.

domestic management, social and personal discipline, collective pursuits, political consciousness, and a general progression from 'pre-revolutionary' or 'bourgeois' habits to modern, socialist living. A key aspect of Bolshevik and Russian socialist theory before 1917, cultural revolution was essentially founded upon the principle that it was possible to build the foundations of a socialist civilization through the cultivation of new revolutionary values, goals, and practices in everyday life.[26] This was, therefore, a revolution that encouraged social participation and popular ideological engagement.

In their most basic form, the earliest student communes sought to develop comradely and cooperative forms of residence within the dormitory. As they did so, they increasingly began to promote the idea of domestic renovation and the restructuring of everyday life (*byt*). Commune groups cast aspersions not only on the state of their dormitory buildings, but on the disorder of their peers and the student lifestyle in general. For some, the commune offered a means of escaping and combating what they considered the 'filthy', unkempt surroundings of student life. As contemporaries noted, for the activists of this period, when faced with residences filled with 'dirty dishes, dead cigarette butts sitting in water, and bread crumbs spread across the table', it was clear that a determined cultural struggle was needed.[27]

The idea of cultural revolution as the domestic reformation of dormitory life was given further credence by the introduction of the first 'inspection teams' and 'cultural-life commissions' in the early 1920s. These teams and commissions would eventually report on dormitory conditions and student life for the Komsomol and other bodies within the institutes of higher education.[28] But, much like the self-proclaimed 'factory deputies' that would appear in Soviet industry during the Five-Year Plan, the dormitory 'inspection teams' and 'cultural-life commissions' were initially formed by pro-party forces and activists, including some communards, keen to promote new rational and socialist practices.[29] Their concern for cleanliness and the general cultural level of student dormitories subsequently gained them the attention of both the student and national press. For example, in a clever play on the name of the Leningrad Medical Institute dormitory—whose acronym, *Medved*, reads 'Bear' in Russian—the student paper *Pedvuzovets* noted a decline in conditions, declaring that cultural activism in this residence had gone

[26] Cf. Michael David-Fox, *Crossing Borders: Modernity, Ideology, and Culture* (Pittsburgh, PA: University of Pittsburgh Press, 2015), ch. 4. For a debate on how the term 'cultural revolution' has been used and interpreted by historians of modern Russia and the Soviet Union, see Michael David-Fox, 'What is Cultural Revolution?', *Russian Review*, no. 2 (April 1999), 181–201; Sheila Fitzpatrick, 'Cultural Revolution Revisited', *Russian Review*, no. 2 (April 1999), 202–9; Michael David-Fox, 'Mentalité or Cultural System: A Reply to Sheila Fitzpatrick', *Russian Review*, no. 2 (April 1999), 210–11.

[27] *Muzei istorii Rossiiskii gosudarstvennyi pedagogicheskii universitet im. A. I. Gertsena* (hereafter, MRGPU im. Herzen), d. B-5, ll. 20–16 (Personal file on Stepan Afanas'evich Balezin, 1904–82).

[28] On sanitary inspections and hygiene observation in the 1920s, see Tricia Starks, *The Body Soviet. Propaganda, Hygiene, and the Revolutionary State* (Madison, WI: University of Wisconsin Press, 2008), esp. ch. 2.

[29] S. Sheftel', *Deputaty na zavode. O sovetskom aktive zavode 'Kauchuk'* (Moscow, 1932).

'into hibernation'.[30] The ups and downs of this institute dormitory, and its room-communes, became a key feature within this and other student newspapers. Indeed, the struggle for the 'cultural hearth of the dormitory' became a key slogan of inspectors and the student press into the 1930s.[31]

Far from simply creating an environment of vigilance and fuelling press articles, the 'inspection teams' and 'cultural-life commissions' attached to this and other institute dormitories organized a series of domestic cleanliness competitions. Results could vary from one visit to the next. And reports surviving from later years reveal the uncompromising, unequivocal approach of the inspectors. In 1928, it was recorded that of the sixty rooms in the *Medved* dormitory, four were of a 'good' standard and four 'bad'; the rest were deemed 'satisfactory'. Based on cleanliness, management, and suitability for study throughout the year, room number 328 was cited as the best performer. But 404 was awarded the winner's prize in consideration of the greater number of students (ten in total) living within this dormitory room, which, it was explained, required greater management and planning on the part of the inhabitants. In turn, room numbers 225 and 316 were named and shamed as the worst performers, and it was claimed, rather optimistically, that these results helped to foster purpose and competition, with everyone looking 'forward to the next contest!'[32]

In this particular case, inspections could not prevent further dips in the 'cultural level'. 'Dirt and disorder', 'individualism', and 'drunkenness' seem to have taken hold in the *Medved* dormitory, wrote *Pedvuzovets* shortly after this last inspection. In fact, it was now thought that the dormitory was performing at a lower standard than it had during the inspections of 1925 to 1926. In the worst cases, the student paper reported with horror, the mess in some rooms was now such that 'the floors and beds became indistinguishable'; inhabitants 'stopped eating collectively'; '184 empty [alcohol] bottles' had been found strewn across the hallway after a student party; and 'sexual exploitation' or 'unsavory favours' were being used to gain access to the largest rooms.[33] Proposing the arrival of a hypothetical 'naive girl'—someone in search of socialism and a good example, it was suggested—*Pedvuzovets* asked the persistent offenders of this dormitory: 'What could you offer such a girl other than cigarette butts, disorder, and empty [alcohol] bottles?'[34]

Despite the annoyance and tacit resistance of some students, the nascent cultural inspections and dormitory competitions of the early 1920s spurred many communes into action, seemingly developing a second wave of collective activists. A deepening concern for the 'cultural hearth' of student life led to the creation of groups such as Commune 133, which emerged from the dormitory room of the same number on Krasnyi Rassvet Ulitsa in Petrograd during the 1922–23 academic year. Starting as a group of fourteen young hopefuls, they embraced cultural competition and vied to establish themselves as a bastion of socialist enlightenment within

[30] 'V medvede', *Pedvuzovets,* 12 February 1928, 4.
[31] B. K., 'Za kul'turnoe obshchezhitie', *Pedvuzovets,* 5 September 1931, 2.
[32] Konkursnaia kommissiia, 'Itogi konkursa', *Pedvuzovets,* 28 April 1928, 3.
[33] A. Lezhin, 'Medved' v deistvitel'nosti', *Pedvuzovets,* 28 April 1928, 3.
[34] A. Petanova, 'Devushka s fabriki i paren' iz "Medvedia"', *Pedvuzovets,* 7 March 1930, 4.

their dormitory—the importance of these roots and their dormitory activities is highlighted by the fact they retained their title, Commune 133, even after moving on to larger quarters.[35] Similarly, the local student press reported on cases of communes eagerly scrubbing the floor, clearing rooms and corridors of debris, and seeking prominent positions to display their collection of revolutionary literature in anticipation of the cultural inspections.[36]

From these rooms of revolutionary aspiration and competition evolved a deepening desire to hasten the development of socialist practices and socialist community within higher education. The cultural mission would become a significant and dynamic aspect of student life. If a basic understanding of collectivism provided the student commune with form and structure, then the various components that made up cultural revolution helped provide content. By acting on and embracing the idea of cultural revolution within the dormitory, the student communes and communards sought to establish themselves among a vanguard of revolutionary activists. At the same time, the relish and fervour that they displayed for cleanliness competitions and the like only served to heighten the importance of cultural revolution in dormitory life. In an attempt to answer the 'cultural question' and offer themselves as an exemplary model to both 'naive girls' and the 'cultural-life commissions', more students formed collective pacts and put new ideals into practice. As the meanings and methods of cultural revolution continued to be debated within the Soviet press, especially during the early 1920s, the student communes were turning this important ideological and discursive category into a series of tangible exercises and set habits.

Viewed from this angle, the student communes and communards can be seen to gain their sense of agency and revolutionary selfhood, in large part, from the internalization and enactment of cultural revolution. In the years following 1917, the Bolsheviks struggled to secure control of higher education, and the activists that formed the student communes were well aware of this fact. Peter Konecny, whose work charts the development of Soviet higher education through to 1941, has quite rightly suggested that the old pre-revolutionary student movement would eventually be replaced by a number of state-sponsored organizations. He is also right to say that these organizations would come to 'professionalize' student politics.[37] But the student dormitory of the 1920s, it must be said, was still a curious mix of the autonomous and the official. It was a place where student activists could still exercise their own interpretations of socialism. And while a growing number of grassroots-level circles and cells fell under the purview of state institutions, they, like the student communes, often remained too particular and uneven to function as official auxiliaries.[38] Within the dormitory, the student communes and communards

---

[35] For reflections on the formation of this commune, see 'Kak zhivem kommunoiu', *Krasnoe studenchestvo*, no. 9 (1928), 16–17.

[36] Nabliudatel', 'Organizuem zhizn' "Medvedia"', *Pedvuzovets*, 18 March 1928, 3.

[37] Konecny, *Builders and Deserters*, 9.

[38] A similar assessment is made about Soviet grassroots-level developments in David Brandenberger, *Propaganda State in Crisis. Soviet Ideology, Indoctrination, and Terror under Stalin, 1927–1941* (New Haven, CT: Yale University Press, 2011), 176.

absorbed socialist visions by osmosis, acting like the next generation of leaders that the Bolsheviks expected them to be, but they also rebelled insofar as they noted the insufficiencies of revolutionary practice and sought to rectify the gap between promise and reality. Above all else, the thing that united and galvanized these student communes was their willingness to act on the physical, political, and cultural limitations of the institute dormitory. Extending beyond the party's centralized propaganda mechanisms, they put themselves forth as a new political-cultural enlightening force.

ARCHITECTURE OF THE STUDENT COMMUNE

Clearly, given their spontaneous nature, not all student communes followed the same trajectory or shared exactly the same goals. Some proved more successful than others in terms of size and longevity. Many room-communes did not extend beyond the four walls of their original founding. Some proved to be little more than temporary products of youthful enthusiasm, dispersing at the end of the semester or term, never to reform. And occasionally, communes would collapse as personal animosity weakened group cohesion. This was certainly the case with one of the student communes based at Moscow State University. Formed alongside a number of other communes that had sprung up in 1923, this particular group got bogged down in a series of arguments from the get go. They argued about their daily routine, cleaning the dormitory room, and personal sleeping habits. They just could not agree on how to live together, let alone how best to enact cultural revolution. As tends to happen in such situations, those involved felt personally invested in their own proposals. For instance, some of the communards felt that they were being accused of laziness when the others turned down their suggestion for a relaxation in the daily routine and the agreed wake-up time.[39] In other instances, group unity was compromised when female communards noticed that they were vulnerable to accusations of frivolity from male counterparts who thought they knew best—when Venus and Mars come together, even in a willingly progressive commune, some habits will always die hard.[40] In a final attempt to reconcile their differences, the commune held a collective meeting and talked long into the night. Everyone was given the opportunity to share their grievances and discuss the prospects for the commune. But it was futile. Too many clashes and slights had come to pass. Eventually, they agreed to disagree: by a show of fifteen hands to one, they voted to disband the commune and go their separate ways. Their collective alliance had lasted little over a month.[41]

All the same, throughout the 1920s, numerous small groups of committed students and activists experimented with the idea of the commune. Many tried repeatedly to form the ideal collective unit. For some, failure and starting over became

---

[39] [Student communard], 'Gibel' odnogo kollektiva', *Krasnoe studenchestvo*, no. 11 (1926), 26–7.
[40] G. Ts., 'O kommunakh II MGU', *Krasnoe studenchestvo*, no. 11 (1926), 24–6.
[41] [Student communard], 'Gibel' odnogo kollektiva', 26–7.

a much-repeated cycle. If one attempt fell apart, often the leading figures—those that had invested their revolutionary identity into the idea of the commune—would go on to form another alliance. As Ianbulat explained, the most ambitious student communards were never bound to 'internal concerns'. They were always on the look out to amplify the commune message and spread their revolutionary conviction. Indeed, there were always more ideological imperatives to experiment with, and more solutions to everyday shortfalls.[42] For the believer, these early years were exciting times. And troubling for their neighbours though they could be, those bitten by the commune bug did not sit still. They tended to look for new ways to reform and to advance themselves and their communes.

A path of progression and constant self-assessment was at the core of the communard vision of revolution. This can be seen in the example of the straight-forwardly titled Commune of the Student Water-Transport Workers (*Kommuna studentov-vodnikov*), which formed in one of the dormitories attached to the Polytechnic Institute in October 1923. Aware of the animosity that other student groups had allowed to develop, this twelve-person commune started out by organizing a 'committee' in charge of 'accounting...their strengths, capabilities and needs'.[43] Essentially, this was a gathering of founding members that set the rules of commune life and ensured that any new members would be compatible with the group—conducting interviews with potential recruits. Without such a rational structure, one of the communards insisted, 'every commune is doomed to failure'. '[T]he commune, being very cohesive and organized', they continued, 'offers the best means to influence everyday life'. As the commune started to attract more members, the 'committee' moved to ensure that internal regulations were tightened and domestic developments continued to promote the 'restructuring of everyday life'. Any spatial expansion of the commune had to be matched, even surpassed, by domestic revolutionary advancements. It was decided that they had to make sure all communards were well versed in the expanding discourse on collective and domestic organization. They moved to establish their own 'collective library', subscribing to leading Soviet newspapers and youth journals. This was achieved by implementing a proportional membership charge set at 30 per cent of an individual's monthly income or stipend. Writing to the youth journal *Krasnyi student* (*Red Student*), the commune somewhat immodestly said that these developments 'brought enormous moral benefit' to the group and even 'attracted the attention of other communes [at the institute]'. They presented their arrangements as a wholehearted attempt to eradicate the 'rudiments of private instinct' from members new and old.[44]

Like many other student communes around this time, this group increasingly found itself discussing and experimenting with the principles of what became known as the 'Scientific Organization of Labour' (Nauchnaia Organizatsiia Truda),

[42] Muzei LETI, KP. osn. 4711, d. 2025, l. 1.
[43] [Signed: 'Member of the commune'], 'Kommuna studentov-vodnikov', *Krasnyi student*, no. 4–5 (1924), 44–5.
[44] [Signed: 'Member of the commune'], 'Kommuna studentov-vodnikov', 44–5.

commonly referred to as NOT. This was a system of time-discipline and daily regulation very much influenced by the industrial efficiency theories of the American engineer and manufacturing consultant Frederick Winslow Taylor. But while Taylor extended the 'time-sheet' and 'clocking-in' of the Victorian Wedgwood factory—pursuing an invasive system of precision management to regulate employees like mechanical parts—the variation presented in the Soviet Union offered a more complete view of human management and encompassed a broader range of activities, including leisure time, entertainment, domestic life, and social duty.[45] Platon Mikhailovich Kerzhentsev, the main exponent of NOT, went as far as to establish a body known as the 'League of Time' (Liga Vremeni) to implement systems of time management and rational reorganization in factories, schools, and universities.[46] The efforts of this body were eagerly reported within the youth press, further helping to disseminate the notion that daily life could be rationalized.

In the Polytechnic commune—possibly following the example of other student communes reported in the press at this time—NOT manifested itself in things such as detailed 'duty boards', which allocated domestic and cultural chores to each communard, setting precisely the structure of the day. The communards increasingly embraced the rhetoric of 'time management' and seemingly started to think of themselves as agents of 'rational management'. They introduced a system of 'careful calculation and prudent spending', ensuring equal consumption of breakfast, lunch, and dinner at the precise cost of seven roubles and eighty kopeks per communard. Each meal, moreover, was scheduled for the same time each day.[47] Of all the discursive themes and cultural visions they embraced, NOT stimulated the most discussion and experimentation among the group. These rather prescriptive attempts at 'scientific management' reveal a tension at the heart of this commune: with the promise of modern socialism came the belief that these youths could change the world at will—everyday life itself was presented as a battleground—but as daily actions were given new meaning and everyday habit acquired added significance, a degree of rigid self-righteousness also started to set in.

Just over one year on, in 1925, as membership grew to seventy-six, one of the Polytechnic communards, a young woman named Mai, wrote again to *Krasnyi student* to inform the journal of the group's progress in the area of 'time management'. She proudly regaled them with the tale of how the commune had adapted their internal structure to meet the challenge of replacing 'the old, obsolete...family'

---

[45] Edward P. Thompson, 'Time, Work-Discipline, and Industrial Capitalism', *Past & Present*, vol. 38, no. 1 (December 1967), 56–97, esp. 81–3. These were known as 'tell-tale' clocks and were accompanied by regular patrols of watchmen. Thompson shrewdly noted that such industrial discipline, whether it came in the form of Puritan ethics, Stalinism, or nationalism, would be seen in every developing nation. For a discussion of the impact of Taylorism in the Soviet Union, see Charles Maier, 'Between Taylorism and Technocracy: European Ideology and the Vision of Industrial Production in the 1920s', *Journal of Contemporary History*, vol. 5, no. 2 (1970), 27–61; L. A. Pamilla and V. M. Chukovich, *NOT—velenie vremeni* (Minsk: Belarus, 1973); Kendall Bailes, 'Alexei Gastev and the Soviet Controversy over Taylorism, 1918–1924', *Soviet Studies*, no. 29 (1977), 373–94; Stephen A. Smith, 'Taylorism Rules OK?', *Radical Science Journal*, no. 13 (1983), 3–27.
[46] P. M. Kerzhentsev, *Bor'ba za vremia* (Moscow, 1923).
[47] [Signed: 'Member of the commune'], 'Kommuna studentov-vodnikov', 44–5.

with disciplined routine. A rotation system now allocated two communards each day, whose job it was to 'prepare food', 'maintain cleanliness', and keep 'order in the commune', she explained. Those on duty, it was noted, had to ensure that their fellow communards used their time efficiently and effectively. Their budget, managed with a similar level of care, Mai revealed, was adapted to allocate extra funds to expand the library, which now housed all 'the latest books of modern literature'. They also scheduled regular trips to the cinema, theatre, and concert halls, which were designed to advance the cultural level of the collective.[48] All these developments were couched in the language of 'rational time management', 'time savings', and modern 'efficiencies'. Thanks to these 'scientific' advancements, Mai insisted, the commune had also been able to buy chess and checkers sets, create their own 'red corner' dedicated to study, and form a separate fund to facilitate political and cultural campaigns across their institute. In summary, Mai rallied, their 'cultural mission was now proceeding at full speed'.[49]

THE EVERYDAY HOUSING COMMUNE

With the end of civil war in 1920–1, more and more student activists and communes had been minded to engage in the developing cultural front and experiment with new ideologically driven theories like NOT. Based on their attempts to implement such ideas, one student commune even went on to claim that they had designed a system of potential 'national significance'. Developing over the mid-1920s, this group experimented with new domestic habits, cultural and political campaigning, and—labelling themselves the 'Everyday Housing Commune' (*Zhilishchno-Bytovaia Kommuna*; acronym ZhBK)—they came to argue that 'all dormitories should follow our methods' and arrangements.[50] Galvanized around an insistent and determined young man by the name of Stepan Afanas'evich Balezin, they would look to present their commune as an exemplary structure designed to help advance the revolutionary project within all institutes of higher education.

Despite these subsequent pretentions, however, Balezin's journey to this point is a familiar and humble one. The commune became an important part of his life because it could offer him a revolutionary voice on issues that he cared about—a voice otherwise denied him. It is worth spending some time looking at how he came to commune life and ZhBK, for his journey down this road speaks to the broader development of the student commune and the early Soviet institutes of higher education in general.

Born on 4 January 1904 (old calendar: 22 December 1903) in Volodinsk, a small village in Perm Oblast', Balezin, like Ianbulat, Rom, and Kochergii, was keen to enact the promise of revolution. The fifth of seven surviving children, he remembered how tough life was in Volodinsk. The region's poor soil, plus the ill

---

[48] Kommunar Mai, 'God raboty kommuny Studentov-vodnikov', *Krasnyi student*, no. 1 (1925), 22.
[49] Mai, 'God raboty kommuny Studentov-vodnikov', 22.
[50] MRGPU im. Herzen, d. B–5, ll. 4–1.

health suffered by his father as a result of his service during the Russo-Japanese War (1904–05), severely limited the family income.[51] One of the fortunate few, however, Balezin was given a place in the parish school. His father tried to initiate his son's return on more than one occasion, keen to benefit from an extra pair of hands in and around the home. But one of Balezin's teachers, Paisa Pavlovna Belozerova, persuaded him to let the boy continue his education. Eventually, with assistance from the local *zemstvo*, Balezin entered a secondary school (later classified as a gymnasium) in Birsk, where an arrangement was made so that he could live in the house of one of his tutors. This economic support was a lifeline for Balezin, but it did shine a light on his family's impoverishment, opening him up to a great deal of teasing and bullying from fellow pupils. Balezin remained sensitive about the ordeals he suffered at the hands of his classmates and about his place within the school for many years.

He was still in Birsk when the February Revolution broke out in 1917. The first signs of his revolutionary spirit appeared when, along with a small group of friends, he organized an anti-authority 'student committee'—mimicking contemporary political developments. Balezin and his friends watched as the world around them changed irrevocably over the course of 1917. Their aspirational 'committee' served as a means of digesting this change. And come the spring of 1918, at just fourteen years old, Balezin would step out upon his own revolutionary path. Returning to his native village, he immediately sought out his old teacher, Belozerova. By this time she had acquired Bolshevik party membership. She provided Balezin with a series of revolutionary books and an expansive reading list, encouraging him to embrace the Bolshevik cause. Feeling a growing sense of 'class identity', Balezin joined a desperate Red Army and found himself in the Kazan regiment before the year was out. It would be another year, during which time he would endure the loss of many revolutionary friends, before he returned home again. But he returned more determined than ever. With his seven years of education and Red Army experience, he managed to get appointed as a teaching assistant in the nearby village of Pavlovsk. Dismayed at the lack of Komsomol or party representation here, he quickly set up a youth circle (*kruzhok*) to discuss the war, civil war, and the meaning of socialism. He also set about turning the school building into a workers' club come evening time. By 1920, when he was still only sixteen, Balezin succeeded in formally organizing a Komsomol cell in Pavlovsk. He led this twenty-person cell on numerous political-enlightenment campaigns and anti-religion marches throughout the surrounding area.[52]

Unsurprisingly, Balezin attracted the attention of the Komsomol district committee and soon found that doors started to open for him. In March 1921, he was moved to a school in Ufa, in the Bashkirian region, central Russia, where he was asked to participate in the Komsomol's political and cultural-enlightenment campaigns. By the start of 1923, at nineteen years old, he was called back into the Red Army

---

[51] A. S. Balezin, F. B. Glinkina, E. G. Zak, and I. A. Podol'nyi, *Stepan Afanas'evich Balezin, 1904–1982* (Moscow: Nauka, 1988), 9–10.

[52] Balezin et al., *Stepan Afanas'evich Balezin*, 10–12.

to participate in its regional propaganda missions. Then, before the year was over, he was granted his main wish. Reward and good favour was bestowed upon him by Komsomol officials, as he was given the opportunity to pursue his education and teacher training at the Social Education Institute in Petrograd (soon to become absorbed within the Herzen University). At last, he had made it to the peak of the education tree, and he was excited by the prospects that lay before him.

But a hard reality awaited the young man in Petrograd. Upon entry to the institute, Balezin was to be as dismayed as he had been in Pavlovsk a few years early. For, even here, in the crucible of the October Revolution, he found that Komsomol and party forces were weak and ineffective. He was shocked to discover that people 'were still openly hostile' to the Bolshevik cause, and some professors and institute staff appeared to be deeply unsettled by the new type of student entering their institute. Balezin recalled the dismissive remarks of his anatomy professor, Matuschka: 'You are all the same, you workers, you do not understand the school of science, and, I wonder, do you even need it?' More surprising to Balezin, the Komsomol representatives appeared unorganized and unprofessional. The more studious individuals and the most academically gifted alike were often given the contemptuous nickname '*akademist*' (academic) or '*akademiata*' (academic fledglings), thereby implying that they were too soft and that they were not putting enough time and effort into the Komsomol's public activities.[53] Balezin, much like Ianbulat, Rom, and Kochergii, soon realized that he had to continue his struggle for revolution. And, having made it this far, he was not going to be bullied anymore—be it at the hands of academic staff or certain Komsomol representatives. He was determined to bend the institute to his revolutionary will.

Joining the Komsomol cell at his institute, Balezin attempted to rectify what he saw as the 'misguided views of all sides'. He argued that student newspapers should become 'militant organs' in the battle against people like his anatomy professor, and he introduced a new slogan that jarred with the incumbent views of Komsomol representatives: 'One hundred percent toward study and one hundred percent toward social duty'. His vision was not without its supporters. Apparently, the party representative, R. Savchenko, was in favour of Balezin's slogan, and it would soon be reproduced on the pages of student wall-newspapers as: 'Give us one hundred percent in all areas—study and social work'. But, Balezin claimed, the fact that party and trade union stipends were paid regardless of achievement rendered the slogan empty.[54] In the end, the answer to all of Balezin's concerns was to present itself in the form of the student commune.

It was within the student commune that Balezin felt able to fulfil his revolutionary visions. His first experience of commune life came in 1923, with a group named Artel 'Red Student' (*Artel' 'Krasnyi student'*; sometimes just *Krasnaia artel'*). This small, six-person association was originally formed, with Balezin's assistance,

---

[53] MRGPU im. Herzen, d. B-5, ll. 19–17.
[54] MRGPU im. Herzen, d. B-5, ll. 20–16. These stipends were paid based on class background (positive discrimination toward the 'labouring classes'). Party stipends included not only monetary reward but also two free train tickets per year. Trade union stipends included up to 75 per cent discount on food in public canteens.

to help students who did not have an adequate stipend. They got jobs at the port and pooled their resources inside the confines of a single dormitory room. Noting the lack of support for such students, the constructs of the commune seemed to offer a logical and ideologically acceptable solution to their troubles.[55] It did not stop there, however. Once admitted, members were required to manage their resources strictly and combat monetary wastefulness. This was another issue that Balezin felt the authorities were failing to resolve. Even students with a stipend were 'unable to manage their money to the end of the month', he noted.

Tellingly, the commune also looked to enact Balezin's slogan, 'Give us one hundred percent', organizing a system of shared note-taking to ensure that their work at the port did not detract from their studies. Then they realized that many other students could benefit from this practice. Securing the assistance of some pro-Bolshevik teachers, they reproduced notes, copied out lecture manuals, and even formed rudimentary textbooks, which, by all accounts, were eagerly acquired by their fellow students. In this instance, the commune was helping to bridge the material gap of higher education—not a unique occurrence, according to reports suggesting that the Petrograd/Leningrad Komsomol organization was heavily reliant on small, voluntary groups assisting them in their duties at this time.[56]

Balezin felt vindicated. 'Members of the commune', he explained with pride, had shown 'an aptitude for both study and voluntary work'. They had undertaken actions that would benefit their own education and that of their follow students.[57]

AFTER THE FLOOD

In the autumn of 1924, voluntary work would take on a new impetus and expand the scope of Balezin's commune visions. Earlier in the year, the great leader of the October Revolution, Lenin, had passed away after a series of debilitating strokes. And now, as if to symbolize the sense of uncertainty felt in some quarters, a raging storm sent heavy winds, driving rain, and a swollen tide along the Baltic coast and into the Gulf of Finland. Seawater was driven into the Neva river, which duly burst its banks and flooded basements, shops, canteens, and numerous buildings along Nevsky Prospekt and the surrounding streets. 'Red Student' launched itself into action, immediately joining forces with fellow activists to form an emergency relief team. They recovered the property of locals, housed and fed sailors helping with the operation, arranged collective meetings to plan the clear-up, and pressed their institute to mobilize more student helpers. Balezin remembered that they 'showed great diligence in these tasks', although he had to admit they were not beyond occasionally helping themselves to the beer they discovered on basement salvage operations along Nevsky Prospekt.[58]

After this formative experience, the group doubled its membership, growing to twelve. Into the fold came figures such as Z. Bal'tsev and N. Ivanov. A series of cartoons produced by the communards themselves present Bal'tsev as an earnest

55 MRGPU im. Herzen, d. B-5, l. 16.   56 MRGPU im. Herzen, d. B-5, l. 16.
57 MRGPU im. Herzen, d. B-5, l. 16.   58 MRGPU im. Herzen, d. B-5, l. 15.

Fig. 2.1. Communard caricature: Bal'tsev
Source: 'ZhBK', *Krasnoe studenchestvo*, no. 11 (1928), 54.

Fig. 2.2. Communard caricature: Ivanov
Source: 'ZhBK', *Krasnoe studenchestvo*, no. 11 (1928), 54.

young man, keenly marching around the university with petitions for revolutionary change (see Fig. 2.1). Ivanov, on the other hand, another activist with Red Army experience, is imaginatively depicted in armour, clearly contemplating his revolutionary duty (see Fig. 2.2).[59] At the same time, Balezin—who is ironically depicted as the princely mastermind of the group in these drawings (see Fig. 2.3)—also saw to it that Ol'ga Komova, Ninka Larionova, Marusia Tropina, Nadiusha Borodina, Anechka Semenova, and a certain Zhemchuzhnikova all joined the commune, too. All fellow students of the Social Education Institute, Balezin had first come across this impressive group of women in their capacity as 'illustrative designers' for the Komsomol. Together they formed the gloriously titled 'Women's Poster Army' (*Plakatzhenarmiia*), which was responsible for making many of the propaganda posters that came to adorn the institute from 1924 (see Fig. 2.4).[60]

This was the moment that Balezin decided to bestow upon this collection of activists the title of 'Everyday Housing Commune' (*Zhilishchno-bytovaia kommuna*). No longer going by the name 'Red Student' or 'Red Artel', they commonly referred to the group by its new acronym, ZhBK, while individual members were collectively known as *Zhe-Be-Kovtsy*. And it was now that Balezin decided to throw his

---

[59] Later recounted in 'ZhBK', *Krasnoe studenchestvo*, no. 11 (1928), 52–5.
[60] MRGPU im. Herzen, d. K-38, ll. 25–18 (Personal file of Ol'ga Sergeevna Komova).

Fig. 2.3. Communard caricature: Balezin
Source: 'ZhBK', *Krasnoe studenchestvo*, no. 11 (1928), 54.

Fig. 2.4. 'Women's Poster Army' (*Plakatzhenarmiia*), with Balezin (centre) and Komsomol representatives present, *c.*1924
Source: MRGPU im. Herzen, d. K-38.

full lot in with the student commune; all his revolutionary passions and energies would be channelled through the group from this point on. Incorporating the Women's Poster Army into the commune, Balezin planned for the group to develop its own wall-newspaper (*stengazeta*) and life-newspaper (*zhivgazeta*) performances. Furthermore, acquiring a vacant apartment from one of the professors with the aid of some Komsomol friends, Balezin also sought to advance the commune's attempt to reform domestic and cultural life. As they moved into the Moika-side apartment, just opposite the main courtyard of what was about to become the Herzen University, the commune started to formulate their plan of action. They agreed that to achieve the 'socialization of higher education', first they had to enact a system of domestic equality. It was made clear that in this commune of six men and six women, the cooking duties and various household chores were to be shared.[61] Balezin saw this as a practical attempt to standardize sexual equality and to eradicate the misogynistic habits that were still evident across the institute. Only by moulding themselves into exemplary revolutionaries could they spearhead the cause of socialism, he explained.[62]

The commune even established an internal competition for the best breakfast and dinner. All communards were expected to take part. It was thought that the competition would encourage everybody to take meal preparation and domestic chores seriously. Judged on cost, taste, and sustenance, Komova recalled, it was also hoped that it would instil a sense of collective awareness and responsibility within the group.[63] In addition, it was agreed that each communard should contribute fifteen roubles a month toward the common pot. This was then allocated towards the daily upkeep of the commune and the basic needs of each communard. Any money left over was used to buy group tickets to the theatre and museums. Occasionally they managed to save up enough money to buy other treats, such as new shoes and even watches. Considered luxury items, these watches were nonetheless justified as instruments of modern efficiency. In the spirit of NOT and 'time management', it was hoped that these purchases would help to regulate the group.[64]

A system of writing 'open and frank letters' was introduced after a few weeks. The rationale behind this idea was that it would provide an outlet for personal grievances, while ultimately helping to develop the revolutionary consciousness and self-awareness of each member. Communards were expected to write these letters and post them on an internal noticeboard that had been put up in the hallway of the apartment. Komova received one of these letters from fellow communard Ninka Larionova. To her surprise, she was accused of 'showing off'. Komova admitted to feeling angry at first. But, grudgingly, after the initial ill feeling had passed, these comments were 'taken into account' and Komova accepted that her 'showing off' was, as Larionova had put it, a 'shortcoming' unbecoming of a communard. The language of 'shortcoming' seems to have been employed to

61 MRGPU im. Herzen, d. K-38, ll. 23–22.   62 MRGPU im. Herzen, d. B-5, l. 14.
63 MRGPU im. Herzen, d. K-38, l. 23.   64 MRGPU im. Herzen, d. B-5, l. 14.

soften the blow, while also implying that all had the potential and obligation to improve themselves. This type of communication remained an important aspect of commune life, explained Komova. After all, they had explicitly agreed to 'help each other learn and develop . . . [socialist] identities'.[65] Through these rituals they were attempting to gradually nudge each other into line—as they understood it, into a new socialist line of behaviour. Such practices became a mainstay of Soviet education and Soviet workplaces in the years to come, with Soviet citizens calling out the faults of their peers in wall-newspapers and public forums. As ZhBK shows, the groundwork for such exchanges was laid early.

These internal rituals did not seem to hinder the popularity of ZhBK. By the start of the 1925 term, the commune had expanded to thirty live-in members. Clearly mastering the art of self-promotion, Balezin was presenting ZhBK as the solution to what he called the 'turmoil of the institute'. He also scouted out potential new recruits from the latest intake of students. And, if we are to accept Komova's assessment at face value, despite a few tense moments and the inevitable argument or two, the commune was seen as a 'joyful and witty' alliance by many of their peers.[66] More and more activist students became aware of the group through their political campaigning and propaganda work across the institute. Organizing political forums, both inside and outside the commune, they also provided activists with a space in which to discuss the latest party news. Occasionally, they found themselves debating the developing power struggle and speculating over who would replace Lenin. Opinion was far from uniform at this stage, but nurturing a continued sense of indignation over the state of higher education, Balezin and ZhBK seemed to be relatively receptive to the concept of 'socialism in one country' put forth by Stalin—they wanted to get their own house in order before contemplating Trotsky's global vision of revolution. The issue of 'who you were with', in terms of the future of the party, would become an increasingly important topic of conversation in the months and years ahead.[67]

Before the academic year was over, however, it was decided that the commune had outgrown the five small rooms of their Moika-side apartment. Again, managing to pull some strings with his friends inside the local Komsomol cell, Balezin secured a number of rooms within a student dormitory on Roshal' Embankment (now Admiralty Embankment). Here Balezin and the original core of ZhBK started by encouraging some of the existing residents to join them. Then they got everyone, *zhebekovtsy* new and old, to keep a diary of their daily actions. Inspired by the craze for NOT, they struck upon the idea of using 'diary data' to better assess how members spent their time. Some forgot to keep a record of their actions over the weekends—suggesting that we are still dealing with a group of people susceptible to the various pleasures of student life—but on the whole it was thought to have been a helpful exercise. After a few weeks, the commune introduced a new

[65] MRGPU im. Herzen, d. K-38, l. 23.   [66] MRGPU im. Herzen, d. K-38, l. 22.
[67] MRGPU im. Herzen, d. B-5, ll. 10–9.

schedule, which allocated set times for washing, studying, eating, revolutionary campaigning, and recreation. In a bid to improve the health of commune members and to manage their budget, they also placed restrictions on alcohol consumption and smoking. Over the coming months they enjoyed some success on the alcohol front, but the 'struggle against smoking' ended in failure, with many of the non-smokers instead managing to pick up the habit.[68] We should remember, however, that they were in good company. As John Reed noted of the revolutionary gatherings in 1917: 'A foul blue cloud of cigarette smoke rose from the mass and hung in the thick air. Occasionally someone in authority mounted the tribune and asked the comrades not to smoke; then everybody, smokers and all, took up the cry, "Don't smoke, comrades!" and went on smoking.'[69]

By 1926, after two years of collective experimentation, Balezin and the commune were convinced they were making good headway. 'There should be more of us', they urged the institute and party representatives. They were certain that their actions were having a positive impact on university life. And while the priority of the local authorities seemed to lie elsewhere, Balezin and the *zhebekovtsy* were typically undeterred. Throughout the rest of the year they continued a full-frontal campaign to expand the commune. Converting more of their existing neighbours, encouraging smaller communes to join them, and bringing in new students, they soon came to occupy nearly two full floors of the Roshal' dormitory, with a total of 125 members.[70] They slept two to three people per room, and managed to turn some of the other rooms into spaces for collective study and recreation. On top of this they organized their own canteen, which was modelled on the collective canteens attached to the Soviet factories (see Fig. 2.5). And, at all times, members were expected to maintain their wider revolutionary activities: assisting the Women's Poster Army, holding political debates across the university, and so on. A formal committee, headed by Balezin, was arranged to oversee commune practices and to ensure that the group remained true to its collective ideals. If new members did not come up to scratch, they were expelled. Indeed, on at least one occasion a young would-be activist approached Balezin to complain that the commune was more demanding than anticipated. Such figures were 'freed' before the day was out, remarked Balezin.[71]

Returning from the summer break of 1926, having had time to reflect, Balezin felt frustrated that the commune had not received greater support from the local authorities. He decided to try a new tack, expressly designed to win the group official support. This was the young lad at his boldest. He started to present ZhBK as an exemplary facility, an 'organized dormitory' (*organizovanoe obshchezhitie*), that the authorities or the institute leadership could replicate. Insisting that ZhBK was a system of living that could be 'rolled out across the Soviet Union', Balezin even persuaded the local Komsomol to conduct a study comparing their 'organized

[68] MRGPU im. Herzen, d. B-5, l. 2.
[69] John Reed, *Ten Days that Shook the World* (London: Penguin Books, 1977), 98.
[70] MRGPU im. Herzen, d. K-38, l. 22. Also see 'ZhBK', 52–5.
[71] MRGPU im. Herzen, d. B-5, l. 12.

ЖБК. 1 — Рабочая комната. 2 — Кухня. 3—Столовая. 4 — Делают стенгазету. 5 —Читальня.
6 — Клуб.

5 Красное студенчество

Fig. 2.5. Dormitory rooms reimagined and reappropriated by the student commune, ZhBK. 1) Workers' room. 2) Kitchen. 3) Canteen. 4) Making the wall-newspaper. 5) Reading room. 6) Club

Source: *Krasnoe studenchestvo*, no. 16 (1927), 65.

dormitory' to that of a 'normal dormitory'. And upon surveying monthly budgets, time management, incidents of drunkenness, cleanliness, commitment to wider causes, and educational resources, this Komsomol study concluded with one line: 'The results are all too obvious.'[72] In other words, ZhBK was better on every conceivable level. Still, no official support or funding was forthcoming. ZhBK and the other commune groups that had spread across the institute were not an unwelcome development; the Komsomol and university leadership just did not know what to do with them at this point in time. They needed to see more from them before they could act. Yet, despite these continued reservations, the study did help ZhBK in one respect. It helped them garner more attention from the press and increased the group's popularity among local activists. Indeed, off the back of this added publicity, membership expanded to over 200, and ultimately the group was forced, again, to find new accommodation.[73] Clearly, Balezin was the sort of person that channelled his frustrations into his work and into his constructive energies, always determined to prove his ideas. His hard-fought activism, and his ambitions for ZhBK, seemingly knew no bounds.

EXTRACURRICULAR ACTIVISM

Balezin was still fighting to see the promise of revolution enacted around him. Having established a firm foothold within Soviet institutes of higher education by the mid-1920s, a select number of student communes, like those involved with ZhBK, looked to structural advance as a means of progressing their revolutionary visions. In these, the most ambitious and extreme cases, leading communards wanted to see how far they could take the collective ideals of the commune. They wondered if they could extend the ideas of 'scientific management' and the 'reformation of domestic habit' still further. A few found themselves, like Balezin, flirting with the idea of presenting their domestic arrangements as new 'modern facilities'. In these cases, it was argued that Taylorist efficiencies could be applied to the total redesign of human domestic spaces—an idea also seen in the West at the turn of the century, both in the form of new, liberal ergonomic designs for the home and more radical, socialist visions of centralized domestic services.[74] Forming as they did in the dormitories of higher education, some communes thought they had the option to proceed with their cultural mission through room-to-room expansion and peer pressure. Many thought they could rationalize the dormitory as a modern unit of domestic residence. By 1928–29, Herzen dormitory no. 3, for instance, would be all but overrun by a collection of smaller room-communes, with their own specific regulations, which then together tried to govern the dormitory and whose members

---

[72] MRGPU im. Herzen, d. B-5, l. 2 (Komsomol survey included in Balezin's file).
[73] See 'ZhBK', 52–5.
[74] See Lillian Gilbreth, *The Psychology of Management: The Function of the Mind in Determining, Teaching and Installing Methods of Least Waste* (New York: The Macmillan Company, 1921); Jill Lepore, *The Mansion of Happiness: A History of Life and Death* (New York: Vintage Books, 2012), ch. 4; Sheila Rowbotham, *Dreamers of a New Day: Women Who Invented the Twentieth Century* (London: Verso, 2011), esp. chs 6 and 7.

talked about turning the whole building into a larger commune facility—'a total commune'. With their own wall-newspaper, *Kommunar* (*Communard*), and a system of collective decision-making, they wanted to unite these 'student cells' to act as a formative force for the 'collective everyday life'. Here students discussed not only time management, but the complete elimination of private areas and the rational redesign of space with the aim of promoting modern living and socialist consciousness.[75]

Pedvuzovets reported on a 'floor-commune' attached to the third floor of another Herzen dormitory, which, expanding through the mid-1920s, reached a peak of 170 members by the end of the decade. This student commune asked its members to give twenty roubles a month from their stipend, the majority of which was spent on food because they would eat in public canteens. They elected a collective decision-making body with a chairperson in charge of the agenda—a system that mimicked Soviet governmental structures, while also ensuring that all issues went to the group vote. Like the early votes in district soviets, these were cast openly and were vulnerable to personal pressure and strong characters. This commune also had ambitions to spread across 'not only one floor, but all of the dormitory', explained *Pedvuzovets*.[76] The student communards here believed that this was the only way to 'create the necessary conditions' for socialism among the student body. In time they hoped to establish their own collective canteen, cultural recreation centre, and dedicated study area. As membership began to increase they, like ZhBK, made a public appeal, insisting that they needed support from official sources or the trade union if they were to succeed in transforming the dormitory as a whole.[77]

Building on the collective activism that emerged in the immediate wake of October 1917, these grander dormitory visions represent the peak of commune ambition with regard to domestic design. These visions were the product of those groups that had best managed to secure themselves a place within the institute dormitories and the activist communities of higher education, putting them in a position to make the most of a growing student population come the mid-1920s.

In one sense, looking across the opening years of the revolution, the actions and sheer bloody-mindedness of these larger groups, and of individuals such as Balezin, was not typical of the student commune. Few managed to expand into such numbers or to convince their neighbours to join the collective cause. Fewer still came close to actually achieving control of whole or even large sections of the student dormitories. Most remained limited to smaller alliances. But in another sense, insofar as they represented a body of activists running ahead of local revolutionary forces, Balezin and company were quite typical. For, in essence, the student commune was the product of the most revolutionary contingent of the new student body: an impatient contingent eager to press for the promises of socialism, prepared to put their ideas into practice, and willing to demand more than political

[75] D. Chezhin, 'Za perestroiku byta', *Pedvuzovets*, January 1930, 2.
[76] S. Vodovol, 'Za kommunu', *Pedvuzovets,* November 1929, 4.
[77] Vodovol, 'Za kommunu', 4.

rhetoric from the local revolutionary leadership. In many ways, the room-commune, floor-commune, and dormitory-commune—the actual spaces they occupied—were but the physical manifestations or the architecture of activism. Even these larger variants never wanted to limit themselves to being 'islets of socialism', as some have seen them.[78] Rather, they sought to function as engaged activists, helping to enact socialism among themselves and in those around them. They lived socialism at home and they campaigned for it outside their rooms, too. They employed popular images of NOT and other examples of the 'cultural struggle', thus subjecting themselves and the world around them to an active and practical engagement with the revolutionary discourses of the early Soviet period.

Indeed, from his base in LETI, Ali Ianbulat criticized the press reports of the mid- to late 1920s for focusing on the physical structure of the commune but ignoring the core—what he called the 'traditions' (*traditsii*)—of these groups: the shared experience, activism, conversations, and group bonds of the communards. The student commune was not confined to the dormitory, he insisted, but emerged from it as a collective agreement and a form of voluntary campaigning.[79] One of the most important 'traditions' of the LETI student communes, explained Ianbulat, was the 'communication' between communards and 'all areas' of university life. They sought to play a role in all areas of life, 'in school, at home, in public and private affairs', he proclaimed.[80]

Emerging as they did, as a contingent of collective organization and cultural revolution, the activists of the student communes can be seen to have embraced a modern, socialist revolutionary outlook that did not distinguish between public and private affairs. After October 1917, the early Soviet citizen was encouraged to revolutionize both public and private realms simultaneously. While narrow-minded, private concerns had to be combated, a proletarian consciousness was seen as a precursor to collective society.[81] The morally redeemed individual, reborn as the 'New Soviet Person' (*novyi sovetskii chelovek*), was inexorably tied to early Soviet visions of society.[82] This was a vision formed around Marx's tenet on society: 'The individual is a social being.'[83] Everyday life and domestic issues could never be merely private affairs. For the student commune, therefore, personal and social

---

[78] Richard Stites, *Revolutionary Dreams: Utopian Vision and Experimental Life in the Russian Revolution* (New York: Oxford University Press, 1989), 205.

[79] Muzei istorii SPbETU, KP. osn. 4711, d. 2025, l. 1.

[80] Muzei istorii SPbETU, KP. osn. 4711, d. 2025, l. 1.

[81] Here the limitations of Jürgen Habermas's famous liberal framework—the universalist assumption that all individuals cultivate a private realm—becomes most apparent. Jürgen Habermas, *The Structural Transformation of the Public Sphere. An Inquiry into a Category of Bourgeois Society*, trans. Thomas Berger (Cambridge: Polity Press, 1989). Cf. Jochen Hellbeck, *Revolution on My Mind: Writing a Diary Under Stalin* (Cambridge, MA: Harvard University Press, 2006), 86–98; Oleg Kharkhordin, 'Reveal and Dissimulate: A Genealogy of Private Life in Soviet Russia', in Jeff Weintraub and Krishan Kumar (eds), *Public and Private in Thought and Practice: Perspectives on a Grand Dichotomy* (Chicago: University of Chicago Press, 1997), 333–63; Kharkhordin, *The Collective and the Individual in Russia: A Study of Practices* (Berkeley: University of California Press, 1999).

[82] Kharkhordin, *The Collective and the Individual*, 335.

[83] Karl Marx, *Economic and Philosophical Manuscripts of 1844* (Moscow: Progress Publishers, 1959), 104. Cf. Hellbeck, *Revolution on My Mind*, 85–6.

development was not only the revolutionary 'duty' of every member, but the expression of an equation whose units had to act as a whole in order to balance revolutionary theory. They were part of a revolutionary culture that saw the transformation of self and the enlightenment of others as part of the same, intertwined goal.[84] Establishing themselves as a vanguard—the commune representing a revolutionary advance on the traditional Russian *kruzhok*—communards could then seek to extend socialist revolution in the wider environment.

Come 1927, even as ZhBK was beginning to struggle with a series of internal conflicts—the result of the inevitable problem of 'quantity over quality', as some of the original members put it—Balezin was still pressing on as hard as ever, encouraging his fellow communards to engage in revolutionary campaigns and to organize political discussions across the university.[85] Hardened by their experience of trying to promote ZhBK, Balezin, Bal'tsev, Ivanov, Komova, and some of the other founding members started to direct their frustrations towards the old head of the Leningrad Central Committee, Grigorii Zinoviev, or, more specifically, his supporters. Zinoviev was once a potential successor to Lenin, but as he fell from power after 1926, this particular group of communards was only too ready to act. When one teacher was subsequently observed recommending Zinoviev's writings to her students, they went to 'press her on the issue'. 'You were still able to walk under tables [*peshkom pod stol*] when I first met with Lenin', she retorted dismissively when they came to challenge her. She also told them not to be so taken with the latest developments and machinations of party politics, warning that 'things could change at any time'.[86] But it appears that Balezin and this assembly of communards was undeterred. With the derogatory remarks of his old anatomy professor still fresh in his mind, Balezin was always keen to enter into such confrontations. Zeal always has the potential to turn into zealotry, especially when political visions appear to be delayed.

Becoming more convinced than ever of the need to concentrate on change at home, and championing the virtues of 'socialism in one country', members of ZhBK increasingly levelled the accusation of 'romanticism' at students and teachers who disagreed with them about the course of the October Revolution during their political debates and discussions.[87] They were, perhaps unwittingly, beginning to embrace the developing concept of 'party-mindedness' (*partiinost*)—the idea that the best way to fulfil the promise of the October Revolution was to support a strong party and help the regime achieve its immediate and primary objectives.[88] They had always been impatient; they just wanted to get things done.

*

[84] See David-Fox, *Crossing Borders*, ch. 4.   [85] MRGPU im. Herzen, d. B-5, l. 11.
[86] MRGPU im. Herzen, d. B-5, l. 8.   [87] MRGPU im. Herzen, d. B-5, ll. 7–6.
[88] See John Barber, 'The Establishment of Intellectual Orthodoxy in the USSR, 1928–1934', *Past and Present*, no. 83 (1979), 141–64, esp. 153–4; David Joravsky, *Soviet Marxism and Natural Science, 1917–1932* (London: Routledge, 1961), esp. ch. 2; and David-Fox, *Revolution of the Mind*, 195, 233–4, 239, 259–60.

Engaging in the political life of the university and pressing the revolutionary agenda had become a fundamental component of student commune life. As Ianbulat explained, it was thought that the communard should carry a 'public burden' (*obshchestvennaia nagruzka*).[89] Employing the terminology of the youth journals and newspapers avidly read by the likes of Ianbulat, commune life became increasingly tied up with the notion of Soviet *obshchestvennost*' (socialist, civic work or duty). Students who are 'not one hundred percent involved' in socialist, civic activities should not be part of higher education, reported *Krasnyi student*.[90] Only the 'sick and weak' were exempt from this 'honourable duty', as Ianbulat came to see it.[91] In 1928, writing in *Krasnoe studenchestvo* (*The Red Student Body*), Balezin came to a similar conclusion. Reflecting on the trials and tribulations of ZhBK, he confirmed that 'the commune and public life were inseparable'.[92] Balezin also discussed the activities of the student communards in terms of a commitment to *shefstvo*, the 'sponsorship' or 'guardianship' of local revolutionary undertakings. In this account, the communard is represented as an exemplary figure, a revolutionary 'guide'.[93] In Balezin's mind, these were most definitely communes of the *aktiv* (activists).

Indeed, ultimately the expansion of ZhBK weakened the original resolve of the commune. This was the point when such groups found themselves 'compromised', reflected *Komsomol'skaia pravda*.[94] Many of the later recruits would leave the commune in 1928. But the activism of Balezin and the founding members persisted, as they rallied together and decided to 'start afresh' in the new academic year. The core of the group remained. If Balezin's assessment of these later incarnations is anything to go by, then, the *zhebekovtsy* continued to make their mark, demanding revolutionary change and promoting their vision of the socialist lifestyle within the dormitory and institute.[95]

Domestically, the student commune was a creation that encouraged self-assessment and new cultural habits. Ianbulat even recalled some cases where communards were told to write an autobiography to help them reflect upon their own revolutionary development.[96] Just as Soviet schools promoted diary writing to develop revolutionary consciousness, so these autobiographies were a medium through which communards asked questions of themselves and their revolutionary environment. Indeed, it appears that some collective groups and worker-brigades subsequently adopted this practice during the First Five-Year Plan, when diaries and reflections were read aloud and discussed by the group.[97] But for all their domestic experimentation, most communards kept an eye on the revolutionary horizon. As much

---

[89] Muzei istorii SPbETU, KP. osn. 4711, d. 2025, l. 1.
[90] E. Petrov, 'Akademizm i obshchestvennost'', *Krasnyi student*, no. 6 (1925), 12.
[91] Muzei istorii SPbETU, KP. osn. 4711, d. 2025, l. 1.
[92] MRGPU im. Herzen, d. B-5, ll. 4–1 (Draft article included in Balezin's file); S. A. Balezin, 'Istorii ZhBK', *Krasnoe studenchestvo*, no. 16 (1928).
[93] MRGPU im. Herzen, d. B-5, ll. 11, 4–1.
[94] S. Tregub, 'Ne toi storonoi', *Komsomol'skaia pravda*, 2 April 1930, 3.
[95] MRGPU im. Herzen, d. B-5, ll. 11.   [96] Muzei istorii SPbETU, KP. osn. 4712, d. 2026, l. 1.
[97] See Hellbeck, *Revolution on My Mind*, ch. 2, esp. 44–5; 'Working, Struggling, Becoming: Stalin-Era Autobiographical Texts', *Russian Review*, no. 3 (2001), 340–59.

as anything, the commune residence was seen as a means to an end, not an end in itself. It was a space for collective, cultural, and personal re-education. As Ianbulat put it, they were attempting to 'forge the education of youth in the spirit of human dignity, morality, hard work, [and] civic duty'.[98] From these student communes, young activists could set an example for their peers, and then go out into the institute to press for revolutionary change on specific issues.

In the process, as they sought to live and promote their understanding of socialist revolution, the student communes and communards found themselves foregrounding certain aspects of Soviet ideology in an environment that had seen its fair share of revolutionary false starts and delays. As well as helping to stimulate the routine of dormitory and cultural-life inspections, they put pressure on the Komsomol with regard to certain local revolutionary projects. The Herzen student newspaper, *Pedvuzovets*, would come to report that the attention that the student communes paid to collective dining—a staple concern of groups such as ZhBK—helped beckon 'factory-based canteen regulations into the Leningrad institutes of higher education'. By the end of the decade, it was noted, the Komsomol had been persuaded to include canteen regulation and dining experience within their remit. As well as producing a guide on how to behave in the collective canteen, local Komsomol cells also introduced new dormitory guidelines and started to monitor the wider cultural level of student life much more intently.[99]

In their own way, the student communes also acted as a constituency for certain ideological and even political developments. As they experimented with the various components of socialist and Soviet discourse, including NOT and the reformation of everyday life, they helped fuel further discussion of these ideas within the local and, on occasion, the national press. Their influence, therefore, can be seen not only in the practical modifications that they managed to implement within their institutes, but also in the ideas and ideals that they helped to promote.[100] In many respects, groups such as ZhBK opened their educational institutes to the militant, proletarian hegemony and heightened antagonisms that began to emerge in the latter half of the 1920s. In their struggle against non-socialist or undesirable teaching staff, they anticipated and conditioned a developing cultural clash with the old specialists (*spetsy*) and hangers-on of a previous age. Their constant campaigning, alongside their carefully regulated and vigilant lifestyle, helped prepare the ground for more revolutionary assaults and bequeathed an ethos of hard-nosed revolutionary discipline within activist circles.

From their initial struggle to promote socialist practices within the institutes of higher education after 1917, the student communes were ready and eager to embrace change. They provided a generation of would-be radicals and activists

---

[98] Muzei istorii SPbETU, KP. osn. 4712, d. 2026, l. 1.

[99] S. Cherniakh, 'Stolovaia komissiia dolzhna realizovat' predlozhenie studenchestva', *Pedvuzovets*, 18 October 1931, 4.

[100] Cf. Larry E. Holmes, *Stalin's School: Moscow's Model School No. 25, 1931–1937* (Pittsburgh, PA: University of Pittsburgh Press, 1999), esp. 16–20. In a similar vein, Holmes argues that the teachers and pupils of School No. 25 exhibited popular agency both when they resisted and when they embraced certain aspects of Soviet policy.

with a home, an exploratory vision of socialism, and a means of speculating with the latest ideological imperatives. They looked to enact socialist revolution in their daily routine—to show it could be done—to petition local authorities, challenge their peers, and shape the wider revolutionary environment. And, it so happened, along the way they helped to cement the idea of the activist, urban commune within the popular revolutionary imagination.

3

Socialism in One Apartment

Byt Communes

'Instead of disorder, confusion, and *Oblomovshchina*, here we embrace the new life.'

AMO Commune.

'The *byt* commune is the basic unit of the future society.'

Iunyi kommunist, no. 1 (1930).

Beyond the walls of higher education, too, the urban commune would play an important role in the lives of many young activists and aspiring revolutionaries. In the immediate wake of October 1917, a precedent was set by some young workers who, determined to put revolutionary rhetoric into practice, went about seizing apartments and appropriating living space in the name of socialism. Many of these revolutionary youths embraced the term 'commune' (*kommuna*) or came to associate themselves with it in the coming months.[1] Keen to extend collective living outside of, or after, their studies, some early student communards joined forces with these radical workers and formed commune groups in the tenements and various housing blocks of the urban Soviet landscape. Others first encountered the idea of the commune in the evening classes of the workers' faculties (*rabfaki*), where participants came face to face with student activists, early commune visionaries, and advocates of collectivism. In some cases, encouraged to attend other revolutionary gatherings, including the collective summer camps run by the Communist Youth League (Komsomol) at the time, youths came away determined to form their own spontaneous experimental communes.[2] Indeed, having engaged in a number

---

[1] See I. Gromov, 'Zhilishchnaia nerazberikha', *Kommunar*, 1 November 1918, 3; N. Shurygin, 'Rabochaia zhizn'', *Pravda*, 11 August 1919, 4; 'Pervaia rabochaia domovaia kommuna', *Pravda*, 12 August 1919, 2.

[2] Leonid, 'O letnikh koloniakh', *Iunyi kommunist*, no. 3–4 (1921), 12; 'Lager'-kommuna', *Iunyi kommunist*, no. 4 (1923), 30–2; Iu. Steklov, 'Komsomol'skoe leto', *Iunyi kommunist*, no. 15–16 (1928), 60–3. According to subsequent Komsomol reports, these camps were primarily funded in order to provide urban relief for the youths of Soviet cities. But the ideological nature of these camps was captured in the glorious titles adorning their various entrances: 'commune-camp', 'school-commune', 'summer-colony', and 'collective-dacha'. See *Rossiiskii gosudarstvennyi arkhiv sotsial'no-politicheskii istorii* (hereafter, RGASPI), f. M.1, op. 4, d. 39, ll. 130–9 (Meeting of the Komsomol Secretariat, 12 June 1929). For a further insight into the collective summer camps, see A. G. Kagan, *45 dnei sredi molodezhi* (Moscow, 1929) and *Rabochaia molodezh' na otdykhe* (Leningrad, 1927). Kagan, a Soviet doctor who worked in the camps, said that they were spaces where youths discussed the merits of collectivism and were taught how to live a healthy and virtuous life.

of discussions about the merits of collectivism at one Komsomol summer camp in 1921, a group of young Moscow workers, all aged between nineteen and twenty-two years old, went on to form a commune as soon as they returned to the city. Taking the name of the factory where they worked, the Automobile Society of Moscow (AMO) commune, these young enthusiasts sought out an apartment and actively tried to apply the lessons they learned at camp: pooling resources, sharing essential items, and agreeing upon a socialist approach to life.[3]

Although never sanctioned by an official revolutionary body, the urban communes found a receptive forum in the evolving youth movement of the early Soviet state. As early as January 1918, four young men and two women—all leading members of the Socialist League of Young Workers (SSRM), a precursor to the Komsomol—decided to rent an apartment on Dvorianskaia Street (now Grazhdanskaia Street), in the heart of Petrograd. Here, not far from the Mariinskii Palace, they founded a commune with the express aim of providing a living example of socialism for the young workers of the city.[4] While this proved a short-lived alliance, and while its members subsequently found themselves on the losing side of a debate about the role of the pro-Bolshevik youth movement and its relationship with the party, the idea of the urban commune—a total commitment to one's political beliefs—lived on. After October 1918, when the SSRM gave way to the more party-orientated Komsomol, leading figures in the youth movement and vocal youth activists continued to jump at the opportunity to sing the praises of urban communes. Revolution can be about tone as well as policy.

In 1919, noting the emergence of a commune in the north-eastern Basmannyi district of Moscow, the Komsomol delegate, Vladimir Dunaevskii, even declared that such alliances marked a clean break with the past and the corrupting influence of the traditional family home.[5] Somewhat optimistically, he recommended that parents allow their adolescent children to join such groups.[6] Like the SSRM delegates before him, Dunaevskii also believed that the urban communes offered a living example of socialism in a world still beset by old habits. Among other things, Dunaevskii insisted, the Basmannyi commune was helping to promote sexual equality and improve the lot of women. He saw men and women living side by side, each questioning gendered assumptions about the other. This was, he announced, nothing short of 'a socialist revolution in life'.[7] And he was not alone in his opinions. In the eyes of a growing number of young activists, the urban communes were becoming 'exemplary' formations of socialism and socialist life. This, it was argued on the pages of the youth press, was where workers and youths could come together to lead the charge for socialism.[8] The idea of the urban commune as a

---

[3] A. Z. Mar, 'Zelenye pobegi', *Smena*, no. 19 (1929), 2–3.
[4] G. Driazgov, 'Anarkhistskaia kommuna', in P. F. Kudelli (ed.), *Leninskoe pokolenie* (Leningrad, 1926), 81; first cited in Isabel A. Tirado, *Young Guard! The Communist Youth League, Petrograd 1917–1920* (New York: Greenwood Press, 1988), 41–2.
[5] V. I. Dunaevskii, 'Oktiabr' i trud rabochei molodezhi', *Iunyi kommunist*, no. 15 (1919), 2–5.
[6] V. I. Dunaevskii, 'Kommuny molodezhi', *Iunyi kommunist*, no. 16 (1919), 5–6.
[7] Dunaevskii, 'Kommuny molodezhi', 5–6.
[8] Aktivnyi rabotnik, 'Kommuny molodezhi', *Iunyi kommunist*, no. 3–4 (1919), 10–11.

space of revolutionary practice rapidly secured itself a place in the mindset of many young activists.

As the AMO commune came together, then, it built on a growing perception of the urban commune as a mechanism for social change and as a signifier of revolutionary morality. When deciding how to proceed, this budding collective discussed what it meant to be socialist, drawing on some of the examples presented to them both in camp and in the youth press. They embraced the 'common pot' (*obshchii kotel*), initially agreeing to contribute 40 per cent of their earnings, with the intention of increasing this to 100 per cent in the near future. They set a number of rules and regulations designed to foster comradely relations, including stipulations that saw all members renounce the right to private property, private space, and individual pursuits. They also craved the modern: they associated socialist living with clean conditions, electricity, and, perhaps as a reminder of their shared camp experience, the primus cooking stove, around which they would prepare meals together each evening.[9] Through these 'little tactics of the habitat'—conscious attempts to design everyday life to fit ideological visions—this group of young activists sought to become part of the revolution.[10]

Similarly, other activists, at the AMO plant and elsewhere, increasingly came to see the Soviet discourse on the 'way of life' (*byt*) and the modernization of daily routine as part of a commune meme—an imitable revolutionary creation seen to carry the essential characteristics of socialism; that is, a unit, idea, or behaviour that helps pass certain cultural understandings from person to person through mimicry or repetition.[11] In the south-west of Moscow, for instance, the ten young Komsomol members who made up the *Kauchuk* commune (taking their name from the Rubber Factory, where they worked) came to see 'the struggle for cleanliness', the rearrangement of rooms so as to avoid dirt entering the bedrooms or kitchen, sleeping with the windows open to ensure good ventilation, and the regulation of personal hygiene as essential components of commune life. The *Kauchukovskie*, as they called themselves, pooled their earnings and, within the first seven months of their existence, they established a system of buying fresh linen from the local cooperative, implemented a series of strict hygiene rules, and allocated to a single individual each day the job of ensuring all cooking and cleaning duties were undertaken and completed.[12] With these practices the *Kauchukovskie* were attempting to replicate aspects of the modern hygienic discourse that ran through Russian socialist thinking both before and after 1917. This was the idea, repeated in many works, that new scientific and hygiene advances represented the antithesis of the backwardness and material squalor of old Russia. Keen readers of revolutionary

---

[9] Mar, 'Zelenye pobegi', 2–3.

[10] Originally pronounced by Michel Foucault, the phrase 'little tactics of the habitat' refers to the politics behind spatial design and was first used in relation to Soviet socialism by Stephen Kotkin. See Kotkin, *Magnetic Mountain: Stalinism as a Civilization* (Berkeley: University of California Press, 1997), part II, esp. 149–55. Cf. Timothy Johnston, *Being Soviet: Identity, Rumour, and Everyday Life under Stalin* (Oxford: Oxford University Press, 2011), esp. xxxi–xxxiii.

[11] *Tsentral'nyi arkhiv goroda Moskvy* (hereafter, TsGA Moskvy; formerly, TsAGM), f. 415, op. 16, d. 656, ll. 1–8 (AMO factory, reflections of Komsomol members, 1923–26).

[12] G. Levgur, 'Komsomol'skaia kommuna "Kauchuk"', *Iunyi kommunist*, no. 9 (1923), 26–7.

literature and the Soviet youth press, the *Kauchukovskie* also viewed the commune as a space to practice the important revolutionary concept of *samodeiatel'nost'*: the self-activation and self-conscious responsibility necessary for the construction of a modern, socialist society. In a world that kept one foot across the throat of the proletariat, crushing the potential of a higher, socialist consciousness, *samodeiatel'nost'* was the exemplary behaviour, brotherly care, and willingness to take the revolutionary initiative that fuelled characters such as Rakhmetov in Nikolai Chernyshevsky's *What Is to Be Done?* The *Kauchukovskie* were, by their own reckoning, a necessary example showing that it was entirely possible to reorganize life along these lines.[13]

Writing to *Iunyi kommunist* (*Young Communist*), the *Kauchukovskie* proudly declared that by implementing these practices they had created 'not a hostel', or some forced cohabitative arrangement, 'but a commune'.[14] This was the conscious collective environment that was going to help them change the world. They, like a growing number of activist youths and revolutionary commentators, saw within the question *What Is to Be Done?* a crucial sub-question: 'How do you live' (*Kak ty zhivesh*')?[15] In the urban commune these activists found a space to embark upon new approaches to family life, the interaction of the sexes, and personal relationships. They also discovered a space that allowed them to live out, or at least invoke, some of the promises of modern socialism. Here they could seek the rational reorganization of daily habit, implement scientifically approved routines, and modernize. These were the key ideological themes that came to drive Soviet discussions of the 'new way of life' (*novyi byt*), the 'new life' (*novaia zhizn*'), and the 'new person' (*novyi chelovek*). More and more, the activists that formed urban communes came to identify their collective formations with the ideas and ideals that made up these revolutionary concepts.

These activists were desperate to prove that everyday life, set in the average urban dwelling, could be refashioned irrevocably. Inspired by a growing discursive interest in the manner and design of life, and indignant over the lack of practical progress in this area and the potential threat of revolutionary compromise or complacency, they took the arrangements of the commune into the apartment blocks and urban residences of the Soviet city. As we will see in this chapter, situated in the heart of urban society, the communes and communards looked to serve as an example of revolutionary living to the wider world. While there was a great deal of crossover between these groups and the student communes, those positioned within society garnered a more overt reputation for trying to challenge the customs and norms of ordinary life. Through the experimentation of these activists, the '*byt* commune' would enter the Soviet revolutionary consciousness.

---

[13] Levgur, 'Komsomol'skaia kommuna "Kauchuk"', 26–7.
[14] Levgur, 'Komsomol'skaia kommuna "Kauchuk"', 26–7.
[15] This question was an inherent aspect of the Bolshevik vision of the 'new way of life' (*novyi byt*). It became a prominent theme of discussions about urban and domestic planning. See 'Kak ty zhivesh'', *Stroitel'stvo Moskvy*, no. 3 (1927), 25–7.

FROM THE FLOORS OF THE OLD HOUSE

In the context of the years immediately following the October Revolution, the physical realities of the old 'way of life' (*byt*) were all too apparent to many activists. As the first urban commune groups began to requisition living space, it was very much a case of to the victors went the spoiled. The new Soviet state inherited a war-torn economy, and the communards, like many others, found themselves occupying hastily adapted, unsanitary, and unsafe homes. The Bolsheviks would admit as much in March 1919, when, at the second party conference, they declared that the revolution desperately needed to 'strive for the improvement of housing conditions ... for the elimination of ... unsanitary, old housing quarters; for the elimination of unfit housing'.[16] 'The difficulties came in the autumn', remembered one communard, 'when the slanting rain and steely winds of October penetrated cracks in the windows'.[17] Others spoke of dilapidated conditions, wooden panels and door frames ripped out to provide firewood, peeling wallpaper, and the decaying remnants of a former life.[18] It is noticeable that the majority of the first urban communes were exposed to some of the worst conditions and forced to modify residences that were especially unsuitable.[19] In regard to the core contingent of the urban communes, the Soviet youth, it was noted at the time that many had experience of living in converted hostels and barracks. It was estimated, even come the mid-1920s, that up to 95 per cent of all hostel inhabitants were of Komsomol age— that is, fourteen to twenty-eight years old.[20] Komsomol records from the period reveal a sustained level of apprehension about the areas and conditions in which many youths were living. Youths seemed to have been bound to the poorest districts and the most cramped residences since 1917.[21] Concern was expressed that up to half of all urban youths would suffer ill health as a result of inadequate housing.[22]

Faced with these surroundings, the struggle against the old 'way of life' was an ideological mission that clearly resonated with early commune enthusiasts. Deprivation was an obvious obstacle to progress, while the musty, decaying grandeur of some requisitioned homes made many indignant. Here, then, was something immediate and tangible for them to get their teeth into—the dead weight of the past. Visions of modern socialism could be enacted in opposition to the objective realities of urban life in the early Soviet state. In the first instance, the priority was to make sure that their new abodes were fit for purpose, fixing draughts and leaks. Then the communes could get to subdividing unnecessarily large rooms,

---

[16] *KPSS v rezoliutsiiakh i resheniiakh s"ezdov, konferentsii i plenumov tsentral'nogo komiteta*, vol. 2 (Moscow, 1983), 90; cited in Mark B. Smith, *Property of Communists: The Urban Housing Program from Stalin to Khrushchev* (DeKalb: Northern Illinois University Press, 2010), 15.

[17] A. Grinberg, 'Kommuna v puti', *Smena*, no. 30 (1931), 12–13.

[18] 'Rabochaia zhizn'', *Pravda*, 11 April 1919, 4.

[19] Richard Stites, *Revolutionary Dreams, Utopian Vision and Experimental Life in the Russian Revolution* (Oxford: Oxford University Press, 1989), 213.

[20] 'Nash byt—Oskolok novogo byta', *Krasnyi student*, no. 1 (1925), 35.

[21] RGASPI, f. M.1, op. 23, d. 584, ll. 1–5 ('Discussion of mass culture and everyday matters', XII Congress of the Komsomol, 11–22 March 1926).

[22] RGASPI, f. M.1, op. 23, d. 584, ll. 1–5.

removing needless decorations, acquiring modern instruments, and generally repurposing old apartments for their own ends. These were to be socialist spaces now; they had to reflect the modern, collectivist values of the October Revolution. 'From the floors of the old house spring the shoots of the new life', reportedly became a customary phrase of the urban communes.[23]

This remained the case even as Lenin implemented the 'strategic retreat' known as the New Economic Policy (NEP). Launched at the Tenth Party Congress in March 1921, this policy saw the limited restoration of a market economy. Restrictions on private trade were alleviated and the unpopular policy of grain requisitioning was curtailed as part of a desperate attempt by the Bolsheviks to incentivize economic growth and fix the state's broken food supply network. With NEP also came the end of 'revolutionary housing repartition' (*revoliutsionnyi zhilishchnyi peredel*)—the expropriation of housing through official proclamation or local initiative—and, in some rare cases, the return of private landlords, with increased (though still regulated) rents and a different agenda when it came to building management.[24] Yet the urban communes and communards remained committed to the reformation and modernization of day-to-day life. This momentary pause in state policy—the start of a period of economic 'breathing space'—did not necessarily call forth revolutionary compromises in all areas.[25]

If anything, with the coming of NEP, the urban communes and communards became more galvanized in their struggle against the old 'way of life' in the home. Domestic space—through the virtue of attaining it and the act of reforming it—was very much a site of revolution. As Nadezhda Mandelstam later reflected, 'future generations will never understand what "living space" [*zhilploshchad'*] means to us'.[26] Seizing the grandest old apartments in the name of the proletariat was taken as a sign of moral victory and celebrated with great relish. Indeed, the fact that the Russian bourgeoisie and middle classes were less numerous than in the West meant the revolution was often enacted not against a class enemy per se, but against the symbols and the concept of an old cultural hegemony. Hence the home and daily life, places where old cultural hegemonies could be hidden in plain sight, remained a key battleground in the struggle for socialism.

Indeed, coming together shortly after the implementation of NEP in 1921, a group of eleven young men and one woman, all Komsomol activists based in Tomsk, formed a commune with the express aim of revolutionizing what they called 'ordinary life' (*povsednevnaia zhizn'*). They fixed up an old apartment in a matter of days, and made it clear that in their domestic arrangement no one was permitted the old luxury of private property. All members were expected to 'give over their salary' to an allocated individual from among their rank. That person would then

---

[23] L. Alelekov, 'Chekanka novogo cheloveka', *Smena*, no. 5 (1931), 22–3.

[24] Kotkin, *Magnetic Mountain*, 159–60.

[25] See Michael David-Fox, *Revolution of the Mind. Higher Learning among the Bolsheviks, 1918–1929* (Ithaca, NY: Cornell University Press, 1997), esp. 6–7 and Anne E. Gorsuch, 'NEP Be Damned! Young Militants in the 1920s and the Culture of the Civil War', *Russian Review*, no. 4 (1997), 564–80.

[26] N. Mandelstam, *Hope Against Hope*, trans. Max Hayward (London: Harvill Press, 1999), 135.

purchase 'everything on behalf of the commune'. More than this, they declared that 'no single issue concerning a member of the commune can ever be considered private or of no concern to the collective'.[27] The conviction that they displayed for collective living, and the speed at which they established this commune, was reflective of their determination to defend revolutionary values in the face of NEP.

In their small and humble city apartment, they were embracing collectivism as a way to overcome the petty-mindedness and self-interest that they associated with the old order and, certainly, with the previous tenants. In addition to their Komsomol work—undertaking agitation campaigns through workers' clubs and the like—they considered it their duty to try to reform the family and the very nature of the individual. As such, they also sought to replace traditional forms of domesticity with new scientific and rational approaches to life. Leaving nothing to that old force, chance, they, like their student counterparts, would eventually come to implement a daily timetable, allocating a set time each day for breakfast, lunch, and dinner, as well as work and leisure pursuits. Clearly wanting to show that they were up to speed with the latest revolutionary thinking, and echoing a growing contingent of commune groups in the process, they declared that 'the question of life [*zhizn'*]' and the 'many questions concerning the way of life [*byt*]' were fundamental concerns to one and all. As a group, they moved to make modern practices, including collective physical exercise and other 'rational behaviours', an integral part of their daily routine. Reflecting on commune life, they declared: 'Thus, we practise the construction of the new way of life (*novyi byt*)'.[28]

For the Tomsk commune, stubbornly refusing to compromise on their revolutionary ambitions, the 'new way of life' represented a statement of intent: this was the stuff that socialism was made of. That NEP brought with it a potential cultural retreat seemed reason enough to spur this and other communes into action. It also encouraged many to broaden their activism. Peter Gooderham was the first to note that 1921–22 marked the start of an activist reassertion of socialist values.[29] In opposition to the revolutionary compromises associated with NEP, activists called for maximum initiative and energy in the revolution of life. In discussions on *byt*, the term 'NEPification' (*Oneprivanie*) became commonly associated with the return of profiteering and the corrupting influence of exploitative classes in society.[30] The re-establishment of fine dining, cabaret, luxury consumerism, and horse racing—some of the raffish, cultural surpluses of NEP—only seemed to provide visual confirmation of this challenge.[31] One young activist referred to such developments as 'the disgusting offspring of NEP'. In such circles, NEP became a trope for social, cultural, and political degeneracy.[32] It was no coincidence that many youths and

---

[27] Kollektiv, 'Stroiut novyi byt', *Iunyi kommunist*, no. 1 (1924), 45.

[28] Kollektiv, 'Stroiut novyi byt', 45.

[29] Peter Gooderham, 'The Komsomol and the Worker Youth: The Inculcation of "Communist Values" in Leningrad during NEP', *Soviet Studies*, no. 4 (1982), 506–28.

[30] David-Fox, *Revolution of the Mind*, 104.

[31] Horse racing was revived in 1922. See Robert Edelman, *Spartak Moscow: A History of the People's Team in the Worker's State* (Ithaca, NY: Cornell University Press, 2009), 48.

[32] David-Fox, *Revolution of the Mind*, 104.

Komsomol members also felt economically disadvantaged by the 'Damned NEP', which, it was noted, encouraged the employment of adult workers over youth training.[33] NEP seemed counter-intuitive to many of these young activists, not least because it was this section of society that had the most to lose from the return of market forces.[34] To the likes of these young revolutionaries, the 'new way of life' and NEP were diametrically opposed.

In 1923, activist concern was answered in the form of a central directive, urging state organizations and press outlets to become more active in the struggle for the 'new way of life'.[35] This rubber-stamped the actions of many communes and communards, while giving added credence to the notion that everyday life was a central site for building socialism—a theme of growing importance in the revolutionary discourse of the preceding years.[36] The 'new way of life' was now semi-officially proffered as a 'counterweight' to the cultural surplus of NEP, with the Komsomol calling upon its members and cells to strengthen their activities in areas where traditional habits and bourgeois practices were preventing young people from fully participating in socialism.[37]

In turn, this secured the urban communes and communards more attention in the press, helping to spread the good news of this collectivist phenomenon. Drawn into the cultural politics and ideological debates surrounding NEP, the urban communes became ever more associated with the broader battle for *byt*. Hitherto given all sorts of names and descriptions in the press, including 'youth communes' (*kommuny molodezhi*), 'worker communes' (*rabochie kommuny*), and 'artel-communes' (*arteli-kommuny*), after 1921 the urban commune increasingly acquired the prefix *byt*. '*Byt(ovaia) kommuna*' connected these groups with a revolution in daily routine, social practice, and domestic life.[38] By virtue of their engagement with the revolutionary discourse on socialist life, the name seemed to stick—even becoming the standard description of commune formations in some publications.[39] Sent to stay with a commune for a number of nights, Z. Karpenko, a reporter for *Smena*,

---

[33] On the reflections of contemporary activist Komsomol members, see Klaus Mehnert, *Youth in Soviet Russia*, trans. Michael Davidson (London: George Allen & Unwin, 1933), 61. Cf. Gorsuch, *Youth in Revolutionary Russia: Enthusiasts, Bohemians, Delinquents* (Bloomington, IN: Indiana University Press, 2000), esp. chs 3–4.

[34] Gorsuch, 'NEP be Damned!', 564–80.

[35] The directive and the ensuing revolutionary drive was detailed in a series of articles in the Leningrad Komsomol journal *Iunyi proletarii*, no. 5 (1923) and no. 6–7 (1923). First cited in Gooderham, 'The Komsomol and the Worker Youth', 508–9.

[36] For example, see N. Bukharin and E. Preobrazhensky, *The ABC of Communism*, ed. and intro. Edward H. Carr (1922; Harmondsworth: Penguin Books, 1969) and L. Trotsky, *Problems of Everyday Life and Other Writings on Culture & Science* (1923; New York: Monad Press, 1973).

[37] Gooderham, 'The Komsomol and the Worker Youth', 508–9. Later reports also show the Komsomol discussing the 'new way of life' and the example of the urban commune together. For example, see RGASPI, f. M.1, op. 4, d. 45, ll. 36–7 ('Restructuring the way of life', Secretariat of the Komsomol, 15 July 1930).

[38] For the sake of clarity and conformity the prefix '*bytovaia*' is shortened to *byt*. This avoids confusion over case endings and highlights the connection between the urban commune and the revolutionary perception of the 'way of life' (*byt*).

[39] For an overview of contemporary press reports on the urban communes and communards, see A. Kaishtat, I. Ryvkin, and I. Soschovik, *Kommuny molodezhi. Po materialam obsledovania i pod redaktsiei instituta sanitarnoi kul'tury* (Moscow, 1931).

later confirmed that such groups appeared determined to 'solve the housing problem' and 'ford' (*brod*) the gap to the 'new way of life'.[40] Indeed, from this moment on, the press periodically encouraged communes and communards to write into them on the issue of *byt*.[41]

Meanwhile, caught up in what was fast becoming a moral panic about the cultural surplus of NEP and the remnants of the old 'way of life' still in existence, the AMO commune drew upon a classic Russian literary reference, declaring that they were opposed to the return of slovenly decadence and social decay, as depicted in Ivan Goncharov's tale of old Russia, *Oblomov* (1859). 'Instead of disorder, confusion, and *Oblomovshchina*', they insisted, 'here we embrace the new life.'[42] The term *Oblomovshchina*, coined by the nineteenth-century literary critic Nikolai Dobroliubov, referred to the damaging idleness that afflicted the book's protagonist, Oblomov, and his ilk.[43] It was also a term used by Lenin, who, in 1922, concerned about the residual old 'way of life', stated: 'Oblomov still lives … it will be necessary to give him a good washing and cleaning, a good rubbing and scouring to make a man of him.'[44] In the commune itself, this meant a renewed effort to live the socialist lifestyle: allocating funds towards those activities deemed necessary for an assault on Oblomov, including collective exercise and shared domestic cleaning; abstaining from socially irresponsible acts, such as excessive consumption of alcohol or attending 'bourgeois' drinking establishments; purchasing hygiene products; maintaining study areas and bathing them in electric light; and tuning their 'ham' radio to the new socialist airwaves.[45] As much as anything, the commune was functioning in opposition to a set of values and habits that they deemed to be non-socialist and un-modern—the things that NEP threatened to maintain.

Similarly, another self-identified '*byt* commune', formed in 1921, would consciously renounce bourgeois behaviour and traditional domesticity, likening such things to the dandy habits and arrogant indifference exhibited by the old order of Alexander Pushkin's *Eugene Onegin* (1833). Mourning the death of Lenin a few years later, in 1924, the same commune memorialized the great leader as the antithesis of the old 'way of life' and the superfluous traits personified by Pushkin's protagonist. They moved to model themselves on a seemingly ascetic yet modern imagining of Lenin: aspiring to create a commune of simple surroundings, 'minus unnecessary ornamentation', but rationally organized, with space for study and 'electric light by which to read'.[46] To reject the world of Oblomov and Onegin was

---

[40] Z. Karpenko, 'V kommunakh rabochei molodezhi', *Smena*, no. 3 (1926), 8.

[41] See 'Podelites' opytom kollektivnoj zhizni', *Smena*, no. 19 (1930), 14.

[42] Later reported in L. Bernshtein, 'Kommuna—ne mechta', *Iunyi kommunist*, no. 1 (1930), 31. The dangers of *Oblomovshchina* were also noted by other communes; see M. Afanas'ev, 'Novomu bytu—byt', *Krasnoe studenchestvo*, no. 13 (1928), 20–1.

[43] N. A. Dobroliubov, 'Chto takoe Oblomovshchina?', *Sobranie sochienii*, vol. 2 (Moscow, 1952), 107–41.

[44] V. I. Lenin, 'Speech to a Meeting of the Communist Group at the All-Russian Congress of Metalworkers, 1922', *Collected Works*, vol. 33 (Moscow: Progress Publishing, 1970), 223. Cf. Tricia Starks, *The Body Soviet: Propaganda, Hygiene and the Revolutionary State* (Madison, WI: University of Wisconsin Press, 2008), 23.

[45] Bernshtein, 'Kommuna—ne mechta', 31.

[46] 'Lenin v kommune Vkhutemas', *Molodaia gvardiia*, no. 2–3 (1924), 107–11.

to reject the unwanted consequences of NEP. Oblomov and Onegin, now embodied by the newly emerging NEPmen and kulak exploiters, were viewed as the harbingers of social ill and a roadblock to socialism. The revolutionary virtue of Lenin's approach to life—frequently cited in the press at the time—was, on the other hand, viewed as a source of inspiration by these communards.

In this vein, like the AMO commune, many activists became particularly concerned about alcohol consumption and drunken behaviour among youths. One commune based near the Moscow Electric Factory went as far as banning its members from drinking alcohol altogether.[47] While not quite so strict, the *Kauchukovskie* nevertheless spoke proudly of maintaining a 'vigilant' eye on communard activities. 'If someone went to a party', they declared, 'all would know about it and discuss it.'[48] From 1923, as the Bolsheviks started to expel party members for habitual drinking, the *Kauchukovskie* and other communes began to campaign even more vociferously against alcohol. They now openly equated drunkenness with cultural backwardness, ill health, and the re-emergence of old habits.[49] Seen as the root cause of many other social problems, including crime, street fighting, and poor labour discipline, here was one example of how the pursuit of a 'new way of life' in the commune could advance socialist society in general. Throughout the mid-1920s, alcohol and social delinquency remained a primary concern for the urban communes and communards. Numerous newspapers carried images of scruffy, drunken individuals—all seemingly rendered as being as idle as Oblomov or as devoid of responsibility as Onegin (see Figs 3.1 and 3.2). Fears were raised that alcohol could lay waste to the first generation of Soviets.[50] Such were the dangers of NEP and revolutionary complacency.

In various other cases, urban communes expressed concern about sexual promiscuity, incidences of threatening bravado among young men, disrespect shown to women, and a general un-comradely roughness, often seen to be bound up with a caddish trend for swearing and uncouth behaviour. Again, these developments were equated with the ill-disciplined, irrational, and un-modern world of pre-revolutionary Russia and its exploitative elements. As many communards saw it, this was preventing the advance of comradely cooperation and mutual responsibility.[51]

As they continued on their mission to present a living example of socialism, commune groups and individual communards set themselves in opposition to those afflicted by such social ills. They stood as the mirror image of what the press called the dangers of 'philistine behaviour' (*meshchanstvo*) and the example of 'hooligans' (*khuligany*). As they did so, they cemented a place for the '*byt* commune' among youth circles. And, as Michael David-Fox has argued, *byt* began to serve as

---

[47] Kaishtat et al., *Kommuny molodezhi*, 62.
[48] Levgur, 'Komsomol'skaia kommuna "Kauchuk"', 26–7.
[49] See Kate Transchel, *Under the Influence. Working-Class Drinking, Temperance, and Cultural Revolution in Russia, 1895–1932* (Pittsburgh, PA: University of Pittsburgh Press, 2006), 112–15.
[50] See Gorsuch, *Youth in Revolutionary Russia*, ch. 3, esp. 67–70.
[51] See Karpenko, 'V kommunakh rabochei molodezhi', 8; Slavina, 'Mat i zerkalo', *Komsomol'skaia pravda*, 16 April 1927, 3.

Fig. 3.1. An archetypal drunken 'hooligan'

Source: 'Kak vesti bor'bu s khuliganstvom. (Soveshchanie pri redaktsii "Komsomol'skoi Pravdy" ot 23 sentiabria 1926 goda)', *Komsomol'skaia pravda*, 30 September 1926.

Fig. 3.2. A disreputable Soviet youth

Source: 'Kak vesti bor'bu s khuliganstvom. (Soveshchanie pri redaktsii "Komsomol'skoi Pravdy" ot 23 sentiabria 1926 goda)', *Komsomol'skaia pravda*, 30 September 1926.

'a badge of political affiliation, staking out the boundaries of revolutionary and reactionary'.[52] The young activist and one-time communard M. Tamarkin reflected on the mid-1920s as the period when '*byt* communes' spread across 'Moscow, Leningrad, Dnepropetrovsk, and the remote corners of the USSR'. Each one, he insisted, committed to 'blowing up the old way of life' (*vzorvem staryi byt*).[53] For the revolutionary enthusiasts that formed these groups, the dividing line between the new and the old 'way of life' became the core issue around which their revolutions were based. They did not always agree on what the 'new way of life' should look like, but they were all fundamentally invested in this evolving battle for *byt*.

COMMUNE OF TEN

The importance of this battle was felt nowhere more intensely than at 6 Mokrinskii Lane, in the Kitai-Gorod region of Moscow. It is here that we will now turn our attention, where, up a rickety old staircase, on the second floor of a dilapidated apartment block, with steam rising from the Chinese laundry below, a group

---

[52] David-Fox, *Revolution of the Mind*, 101.
[53] M. Tamarkin, 'Vzorvem staryi byt', *Komsomol'skaia pravda*, 13 September 1929, 4.

of friends, five young women and five young men, had decided to form a commune. This was to be the setting for a prolonged and determined struggle to stake out the boundaries between revolutionary and reactionary. First coming together in the winter of 1924, these wide-eyed enthusiasts stumbled across this residence, in an area that had become notorious for boozing and crime, and tenaciously they declared it to be the perfect place to put up a fight for the 'new way of life'. Above the door to their new home they erected a sign that read 'COMMUNE'. Inside, they littered the walls with revolutionary posters and slogans. With two bedrooms, a kitchen, and a living room (known as 'the club') where all debates and discussions were held, they looked to create their own living example of socialism.[54]

At the heart of the commune, one of the founding members, Andrei, a student with Komsomol membership and experience of collective association in the dormitory, helped recruit suitable candidates to the cause. Writing from the confines of his parental home during the summer break, Andrei implored one activist to join him as he contemplated the future:

> Dear Friend,
> When I think that the petit-bourgeois family atmosphere with which I am now surrounded awaits me when I leave college in a year's time, I get cold shivers down my back. And a deep sorrow seizes me. Is a return to the old family regime really the only way out? Brrr, horrible. I haven't the least desire for that. Sergei! My friend! What do you think of staying together after college too? Staying together even if one of us marries? Lead our lives together? Your money would be my money and my money yours. Everything would be common to us both. Let us proclaim a storm! We will storm all right—if not heaven, anyhow the forms of life! And what is more important? Do you think this is all fantasy? No, my dear fellow, don't say that.
> With a Komsomolite's greetings,
> Your Andrei.[55]

The Mokrinskii Lane commune marked an attempt to realize this comradely vision. Banding together friends from university and the Komsomol, it was agreed that the commune had to live in total equality, and, just as importantly, it had to be composed of both men and women. Only then did they stand a chance of offering a genuine alternative to the old family. It was also said that it would be more fun if the women and men lived together. But it was made abundantly clear at the outset

---

[54] This description of the commune setting is cross-referenced from a range of sources and reflections. See R. Pragera, 'Kommuna desiati', *Smena*, no. 12 (1928), 10–11; A. Revina, 'Zhizn' desiati', *Smena*, no. 19 (1929), 5; Mehnert, *Youth in Soviet Russia*, 159–64; Klaus Mehnert, *The Anatomy of Soviet Man*, trans. Maurice Rosenbaum (London: Robert Cunningham & Sons, 1961), 46–50; Wilhelm Reich, *The Sexual Revolution: Toward a Self-Governing Character Structure*, trans. Theodore P. Wolfe (1945; New York: Farah, Strans and Gironx, 1971).

[55] This letter was copied from the commune's diary and reproduced in Mehnert, *Youth in Soviet Russia*, 171. The original diary and other materials of the commune have since been lost. The conscious effort to record and preserve their own history, which now only survives in parts, nevertheless tells us something about the importance they attributed to their actions.

that everyone was expected to do precisely the same share of the housework and actively challenge traditional gender roles.[56] As they came to write their founding agreement (*ustav*), they expanded on their desire to eradicate traditional, family-based ties and relations: 'We are of the opinion that sexual relationships (love) should not be restricted. Sexual relationships should be open', they declared. This ended up being less a statement about intended sexual conduct between communards—though, as one might expect, some did find themselves spending nights together—than a general endorsement of companionship and new ideological approaches to relations between the sexes. 'Un-comradely relations result in a desire for secrecy and dark corners, flirting, and similar undesirable manifestations', the communards theorized.[57] This was their way of saying that they were willing to contemplate and even experiment with socialist ideas in the most intimate and personal areas of their lives.

Also put on the agenda were issues such as implementing common finances, sharing personal items, modern hygienic practices, the daily routine, and even the growing problem of swearing, the punishment for which, it was agreed, was to be extra chores. Channelling the modern structures of revolutionary government that surrounded them, the communards established a series of 'committees' (*komitety*) tasked with rationally organizing specific aspects of commune life. This included a general 'finance committee' in charge of planning income and overall expenditure; a 'housekeeping committee' responsible for domestic provisions and monitoring housework; a 'political committee' in charge of gathering books and newspapers for the group, as well as being responsible for maintaining relations with the Komsomol and coordinating any revolutionary campaigns that the commune might engage in; a 'clothing committee' that managed clothes, laundry, and shoes; and a 'hygiene committee' responsible for looking after the health of communards, as well as attaining soap and tooth powder. Each individual communard's income flowed into the common pot, which sat on the main table in 'the club'. At the end of the month all communards would meet around this table to ratify the budget allocation of each 'committee' for the following month.[58]

There was something 'naïvely doctrinaire and yet touchingly human' about the way they went about all of this, noted the German traveller Klaus Mehnert, who would stray off the beaten path to visit the commune.[59] These 'committees' were aspirational: with only ten communards, there was clearly no need for such a structure. In effect the commune was splitting its members into pairs and giving them specific responsibilities each month. But to say 'committee' was to speak the language of modernity, science, and rational order.

And yet, modern aspirations did not guarantee ordered debate. In a 'finance committee' meeting, one of the women, Nina, found herself deeply frustrated when a fellow communard failed to see that the group was in need of more warm clothing.

---

[56] Pragera, 'Kommuna desiati', 10–11.   [57] Mehnert, *Youth in Soviet Russia*, 173.
[58] Pragera, 'Kommuna desiati', 10–11; Mehnert, *Youth in Soviet Russia*, 166.
[59] Mehnert, *Youth in Soviet Russia*, 163.

Faced with a choice between domestic renovations or clothing, Nina snapped: 'You must see, fathead, that one can't be without an overcoat in the winter.'[60]

In other areas, too, rational plans and good intentions were not always enough. For instance, the group's diary noted a number of lapses in commune order as they approached the end of their first year together. On 28 October 1925, it was recorded that the 'housekeeping committee' overslept, which meant that there was no breakfast provided and the commune was not properly cleaned that day. On 29 October, things did not improve. Not only was there no breakfast, it now became clear that the larder and lavatory had not been cleaned in a while, and a thick layer of dust had been allowed to build up on most surfaces. In addition, it was logged that the front door was left unlocked and the lights were left burning in two of the rooms—something that had happened on a number of occasions over the course of the year. By 30 October, with unwashed dishes still standing in the kitchen, and nothing left to eat off, the commune called an emergency meeting, initiated a mass tidy up, and looked to hit the reset button.[61] Indeed, after this incident, the commune decided they should recruit another member, who, instead of going out to work or being expected to contribute to the group's finances, would act as primary housekeeper. Luckily for the commune a young woman named Akulina subsequently agreed to join the commune in this capacity, which seemed to improve things considerably—although the group's apparent desire to stress how Akulina was being admitted on an equal footing to everyone else might be seen to belie some unease with the fact they had effectively hired a maid.

At various stages over their first year together, the group also had to deal with communards falling out, moments of selfishness, later referred to as cases of 'self love' or 'primitive egoism', setbacks, doubt, and even walkouts.[62] As a commune, they were certainly still learning through experience, constantly calling meetings to solve problems and to remind themselves of their original goal.

When it came to reiterating their general collective approach to life, the commune members were not above reminding one another of their personal responsibilities to the group. All had pledged to 'subordinate personal desire' to the commune, it was repeated. Losing three members over the course of 1925, some of the remaining communards were quick to label their former companions 'bourgeois'. 'Good riddance!', proclaimed one communard. They were 'not committed fighter[s] for the new way of life'. Certainly, one of the early 'deserters' had said that she simply could not cope without more time to herself. Some of the remaining communards were a little more forgiving and nuanced, however. They suggested that the commune had a responsibility to choose their fellow 'revolutionary fighters' more carefully.[63] Ultimately, the group was united by one assessment: 'Well, in place of each weakling will come [those that are] stronger!' They wanted to bring in new people slowly and prudently. All replacement communards, it was agreed, would be interviewed and asked to state their commitment to both

[60] Mehnert, *Youth in Soviet Russia*, 167.   [61] Mehnert, *Youth in Soviet Russia*, 164–5.
[62] Pragera, 'Kommuna desiati', 10–11; Mehnert, *Youth in Soviet Russia*, 169.
[63] Pragera, 'Kommuna desiati', 11.

Fig. 3.3. Mokrinskii Lane communards pose for a photograph in 1929
Source: 'V nastuplenie!', *Smena*, no. 19 (1929), 2.

collectivism and the 'new way of life'. Implementing a more rigorous entry procedure, with future candidates also asked to provide short biographies—mimicking Soviet higher education and institutional practices—became another example of the communards' belief in the rational perfection of daily matters.[64] Most believed that if they kept pushing at this door, it would eventually yield. And so, in the latter months of 1925, following the unforeseen departures, the commune would bring in new members using just such methods. They were nothing if not persistent.

At the same time, the communards were quick to highlight their successes. They proudly declared that they had established a roster that ensured all communards bathed and changed their clothes weekly. And they were particularly keen to stress that all communards cleaned their teeth daily. Showing awareness of the latest press discussions on hygiene, they pointed to an article, recently published, that suggested that only 61 per cent of young people regularly cleaned their teeth, while only 47.7 per cent of young men and 72.5 per cent of young women changed their underclothes once a week. They believed they were doing rather well by comparison. As Mehnert remarked when presented with these facts, 'one cannot do without statistics in Russia to-day'.[65] As with their 'committees', to look at things through 'statistics', and, on occasion, to produce 'data' and 'tables' on your own everyday affairs, was to show you had embraced a new, rational approach to life. Everyday life, having previously required little thought, was now becoming a science. Backed by the promise of socialist modernity, these activists were still confident that they could set an example for all urban residents, right here, in the middle of Mokrinskii Lane (see Fig. 3.3).

SEX AND LOVE IN THE COMMUNE OF TEN

In their quest for more equal relations between the sexes, as in so many of their revolutionary aims, the communards of 6 Mokrinskii Lane would find themselves

[64] Pragera, 'Kommuna desiati', 11.   [65] Mehnert, *Youth in Soviet Russia*, 169–70.

assessing and reassessing their approach. Many communards had thought that the
course of action in this area would be self-evident, perhaps even easy. At times,
however, they found themselves having to negotiate certain cultural hangovers. In
late 1925, one collective meeting was called by the women communards, who had
become frustrated by their male counterparts' inability to iron properly. 'The boys
aren't suited to ironing', complained Lena. 'The washing must be ironed—not
crushed!', she remarked with a wry smile. Proposing something of a tactical retreat,
Nina even suggested that they could 'give the boys simple things to iron, [such as]
sheets and towels'. Lelia went a step further, arguing that 'We girls [had] better do
the ironing alone'. Akulina agreed, 'The lads will scorch all the washing and strew
the coal about. One ought not to trust them with the ironing.' But this would have
been an unacceptable admission of failure. Besides, ironing was seen as an important
part of personal hygiene, not least because it was known to kill the lice that caused
diseases such as typhus.[66] The men had to take their share of responsibility in these
matters. Vladimir proposed that the 'boys will learn how to iron right enough', if
only the commune was prepared to teach them. Maybe they could be 'given ... things
in succession, first the easy and then the difficult', he suggested gently. Eventually,
it was agreed that all communards must do their share of the ironing (see Figs 3.4
and 3.5). Nina was put in charge of distributing the work and overseeing the men's
progress.[67]

Under Nina's guidance the men redoubled their efforts. Soon they worked their
way up from sheets to more complicated items, including blouses, and it was
remarked that they ironed no worse than the Chinese laundry below their apartment. But, while it should not be used to excuse all actions, the communards still
remained a product of their time as far as 'the chopping and fetching of wood' was
concerned. It was said that the women were not strong enough to undertake these
tasks. They, it seems to have been agreed all too easily, were to take on extra darning
work by way of compensation.[68]

The 'sexual question' also gave rise to a series of problems that had not been
anticipated during the founding of the commune. At first the communards were
free to engage in whatever sexual relations they wanted. As their founding agreement explained, they were of the opinion that to develop a 'new way of life' the
communards had to renounce all personal materials and all private relationships—
private sexual affairs and traditional patterns of coupling were thought to be lacking in 'companionable' attitude. But, after a few amorous encounters between
at least one communard pair, it was soon decided that such connections could not
be so easily dismissed. What is more, the commune came to agree that a certain
amount of privacy in this area was not necessarily 'un-comradely' in nature. They
had learned that you cannot easily regulate desire.[69]

[66] See Donald Filtzer, *The Hazards of Urban Life in Late Stalinist Russia: Health, Hygiene, and Living Standards, 1943–1953* (Cambridge: Cambridge University Press, 2010), 127–32.
[67] Mehnert, *Youth in Soviet Russia*, 172.   [68] Mehnert, *Youth in Soviet Russia*, 173.
[69] Reich, *The Sexual Revolution*, 223–5.

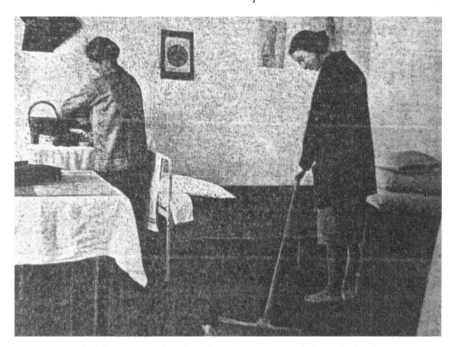

Fig. 3.4. The women of Mokrinskii Lane commune help with the cleaning
Source: 'Kommuna desiati', *Smena*, no. 12 (1928), 10–11.

However, the communards soon noted further problems. Irrespective of whether or not the relationship was deemed 'comradely', a lack of domestic space rendered sex and intimacy a rather awkward affair. With so few rooms at their disposal, where could couples slide off to? In addition, having seen something of a sexual liberation take root among youths after 1917, there was concern that things had gone too far by the mid-1920s. Tied up with reports about drunken behaviour, hooliganism, and NEP, cases of sexual exploitation and other unwanted side effects had started to circulate. 'Liberation', it was noted with unease in the press, was sometimes used as an excuse for the most heinous behaviour toward women. Certain unseemly men, fuelled with an excess of bravado, even decided that they had the right to judge a woman's revolutionary credentials based on how readily she dropped her underwear for them.[70] This was not what had been envisioned by the state or the communards. The alternative future of sexual relations was seemingly in danger. Reacting to these developments, the commune felt they had to make an amendment to the founding agreement. They added a stipulation: 'Sexual relationships among communards during the first few years of the commune are undesirable.' It was decided that it would be best if the commune took time to

[70] See Eric Naiman, *Sex in Public: The Incarnation of Early Soviet Ideology* (Princeton, NJ: Princeton University Press, 1997), esp. ch. 2; Frances L. Bernstein, *The Dictatorship of Sex: Lifestyle Advice for the Soviet Masses* (DeKalb: Northern Illinois University Press, 2011), esp. ch. 6.

Fig. 3.5. The men of Mokrinksii Lane commune do the ironing
Source: 'Kommuna desiati', *Smena*, no. 12 (1928), 10–11.

establish itself as a collective before it returned to the 'sexual' question'.[71] Ever rational, the communards voted for short-term caution.

The commune diary suggested that this internal abstinence held sway, more or less, for two years. During this time, the communards focused mainly on other aspects of the collective life, trying to find the money for more clothes, renovations, and modern provisions as they went. Occasionally, they gathered around the main table in 'the club' to discuss their standing on sex and relationships. As the commune stabilized and the communards matured, the possibility of serious relationships and even marriage was mooted. A series of hypothetical debates ensued. By 1927, one inhabitant was moved to say: 'It is quite in order for any communard to marry if he wishes to, and the commune may not stand in his way. On the contrary, the commune must make an effort to create the conditions necessary for family life.' But what would they do, they asked themselves, if one communard wanted to marry someone from outside the group? And what if that person was not a good match for the commune? Would they admit them anyway? Would they force them to live apart? Or would they have to face losing one of their number?

[71] Reich, *The Sexual Revolution*, 226.

They now seemed willing to accept marriage in principle, but they were unable to explain how it would work or what it would mean for the commune. Still undecided on the practicalities of the 'sexual question', the commune once again voted to put this issue on hold. It was not worth troubling themselves over such things until they happened. They would deal with these issues on a case-by-case basis, it was concluded.[72]

Of course, the fact that this debate had arisen at all suggests that marriage plans were already forming in some minds. It was not long before the commune had to make one of those case-by-case decisions. During the latter part of 1927, communard Vladimir had been spending more and more time with a young woman named Katia. He had fallen deeply in love with her. Plucking up his courage, he eventually told the commune of his intentions. 'Katia and I have decided on marriage', he announced. 'We're determined to live together, and, what is more, in the commune', he added, 'because we can't conceive of a life outside the commune.' Katia herself was present on this occasion. Standing before the group, there and then, she declared: 'I apply for admission to the commune.' One of the communards, Semion, immediately composed a trick question to test Katia's sincerity: 'How does Katia want to be admitted, as Vladimir's wife or simply as Katia?' 'I've been meaning to apply for admission for a long time; I know the commune and want to be a member of it', replied Katia. She wanted to be admitted on her own merits. A lengthy discussion ensued among the communards. Some were immediately in favour of admission; others raised fears that it could create a group within the commune and weaken their unity. But, eventually, the commune elected to accept Katia's application. They were impressed with her personal commitment to collective living.[73]

So, in a relatively short space of time, the commune had gone from rallying against all signs of traditional relationship norms, to accepting and supporting marriage as part of the revolutionary cause. Long before Stalin came to promote marriage in the supposed revolutionary retreat of the 1930s, activists such as these were rediscovering and re-embracing the virtues of this formal bond.[74] But this shift in policy was still seen as revolutionary by those involved. This was marriage envisioned not as the mainstay of bourgeois values but, as Trotsky had put it a few years earlier, the smallest version of a socialist cell.[75] It was a comradely unit built on socialist ideals. Instead of a marriage that isolated couples and dragged them away from the common good, this was to be a partnership based on revolutionary consciousness. In other words, this was marriage as something old, something new, something borrowed, and something *red*!

[72] Mehnert, *Youth in Soviet Russia*, 174.

[73] Mehnert, *Youth in Soviet Russia*, 175; Mehnert, *The Anatomy of Soviet Man*, 47–9.

[74] In 1936, for instance, divorce was made more difficult. A fee of fifty roubles was imposed on those registering for their first divorce, 150 roubles for those on their second, and 300 for the third. At the same time, the state increasingly incentivized marriage and the press promoted the virtues of a stable 'socialist family'.

[75] Naiman, *Sex in Public*, 88.

Other commune groups that found themselves in this position claimed that the most crucial component for an acceptable marriage, as with any successful cell, was class compatibility and class consciousness. As in so many other things, these activists vetted partners based on their class background.[76] Satisfied with Katia's class origins and her commitment to collectivism, the Mokrinskii commune welcomed a new member into the fold.

But revolutionary discussion did not stop there; nor did the hypotheticals. Now the commune was to contain a married couple, the question of children was raised. Would children be permitted in the commune? How would the commune care for them? For the present moment, it was decided, the commune should try to avoid children on account of a lack of space and limited finances. In keeping with wider discussions in the press, the notion of abstinence and contraception was broached. Some communards seemed to be desperately against abortion—shocked by stories of a rise in the number of terminations since the practice was legalized in 1920.[77] Some felt that abstinence went against the laws of nature, however, while others feared that contraception was coarse and prejudicial to health. Yet, it seems, one way or another, all communards sought to avoid pregnancy.[78]

As part of the ongoing debate about marriage and sex, it was subsequently agreed that if and when children did arrive they should not be allowed to compromise the commune's collectivist values. There would be no let-up in the principle of common ownership or in the drive for a 'new way of life'. Reaffirming their rejection of the old family, it was declared that children of the communards were to be regarded as the commune's children and brought up at the general cost.[79] In one of their more radical moments, following in the idealism of Aleksandr Bogdanov's *Red Star* (1908) and various other revolutionary writings, the communards were proposing to give up biological claim to their offspring. Where Bogdanov's popular Martian sci-fi envisioned a world of 'children's colonies', raising kids away from the individualism of the traditional family home, the communards vowed to renounce the last vestige of ownership from within themselves, embracing, theoretically at least, the idea of collective parenthood.[80]

---

[76] Timofeev, 'Staryi byt, novym bit', *Krasnoe studenchestvo*, no. 4 (1930), 26–7.

[77] See Bernstein, *The Dictatorship of Sex*, 147–58, 167–71. In Leningrad the abortion rate rose sixfold, from 5.5 abortions per 1,000 in 1924 to 31.5 per 1,000 in 1928, while in Moscow, 1928 marked the year that the number of abortions exceeded the number of live births. To put this in a wider perspective, in 1926 a total of 121,978 legal abortions were recorded in Russia; by 1935 this number rose to 15,000,000. See Wendy Z. Goldman, *Women, the State and Revolution: Soviet Family Policy and Social Life, 1917–1936* (Cambridge: Cambridge University Press, 1993), 288–9. Cf. Christina Kiaer, 'Delivered from Capitalism. Nostalgia, Alienation, and the Future of Reproduction in Tret'iakov's I want a Child!', in Christina Kiaer and Eric Naiman (eds), *Everyday Life in Early Soviet Russia: Taking the Revolution Inside* (Bloomington, IN: Indiana University Press, 2006), 183–216.

[78] Mehnert, *Youth in Soviet Russia*, 175–6.   [79] Mehnert, *Youth in Soviet Russia*, 176.

[80] A. Bogdanov, *Red Star. The First Bolshevik Utopia*, ed. and trans. Loren R. Graham and Richard Stites (Bloomington, IN: Indiana University Press, 1984), esp. 68–74. In this snapshot of the future, children grow up away from the potential pitfalls of wider society, receiving professional care and education, while parents learn to see their children as part of a wider cohort.

GENDER, *BYT*, REVOLUTION

Through all this back and forth, through all of these debates and discussions, the 'new way of life' and the 'new family' remained at the core of what the commune was about. Like so many other groups, the Mokrinskii communards found themselves engaged in the latest ideological concerns and revolutionary developments of their day, including the proliferating discourse on *byt*; the newly arising anxieties accompanying NEP; the apparent spike in the number of cases of sexual depravity, drunkenness, and reckless behaviour; and the unwanted side effects that came with the personal liberation granted in revolutionary policy. With each problem that arose, they sought to provide a revolutionary solution or a comradely example, sometimes adapting their own internal regulations to meet new challenges. They wanted to show what socialist life should look like and what the correct revolutionary response should be when issues did arise.

And yet, despite their desire to find the solution to all revolutionary problems, and despite their stated intention of overturning all those traditional attitudes that society had hitherto unthinkingly accepted, and perpetuated, there were times when the Mokrinskii Lane commune exposed their own contradictions. To judge by their own rhetoric on sexual equality, for instance, there were clearly certain assumptions that the commune failed to properly address. It was not just the darning of socks and chopping of wood that these communards willingly let slip through the equality filter. At the start of 1928, when Vladimir and Katia encountered relationship troubles, not long into their marriage, the men and the women responded differently—they became split along gendered lines. It turned out that Vladimir wanted to call the whole marriage off. On the whole, the men showed understanding toward Vladimir in this instance. 'When he married', they said, 'he loved Katia, but now he has nothing more than a purely comradely feeling.' But the women, who brought up the issue of increased divorce rates and careless male bravado, were furious: 'Vladimir is a swine ... He should have thought before he married; he simply can't first get married, and then run away after a bit. That's damned ... bourgeois romanticism: I love when I want to and I stop loving when I want to. To-day: I can't live without you, let's get married—a month later: I'm extremely sorry, I don't love you any more, we'll simply be comrades.'[81] The women felt that this was precisely the type of behaviour that was causing disorder in Soviet society—the same sort of attitudes exhibited by the hooligans that they had worked so hard to confront.

When, in the same year, Sergei decided to marry a woman named Olga (who was living outside the commune), then filed for divorce after just two and a half months, there was even more outrage. 'The decision to marry was taken too lightly', one of the women communards decried. 'Sergei', they punctuated, 'this is his fault.' As one of the architects of the commune, more was expected of him. 'This was the act of a man with common street ethics', it was added; the ethics of someone who would leave 'all grave consequences to fall on the woman'. Sergei's actions were said to

---

[81] Mehnert, *Youth in Soviet Russia*, 177.

'violate the new ethics' upon which the commune was built. In a moment of per-
ceptive self-analysis, someone even suggested that such occurrences were indicative
of the commune's inability to fully 'assess and tackle the issue of promiscuity' in
Soviet society.[82] It was felt that the men, like many of their revolutionary brothers,
still displayed an uncompromising male bravado in their attitudes towards sex and
relationships. They were seen to take too many liberties with women in general. In
other words, the men had failed to fully shake off the patriarchal attitudes that
taught them, as it had their fathers, that they could act with impunity when it came
to matters of sex and women. And, while Sergei got his comeuppance on this
occasion, it was still not clear whether the wider concerns of the women were
fully appreciated. Such concerns often seemed to get brushed to the side, never to
be addressed in full seriousness.

When the men dismissed these complaints, this told the women that they were
different, overly concerned, neurotic even. As Stephen A. Smith has noted regarding the behaviour of Komsomol cells in this period, women were often made to
feel excluded or out of place by men who consciously or unconsciously upheld
gender boundaries. This might take the form of men avoiding what they considered standard behaviour in these environments, such as the use of indecent language, in some sort of attempt to respect 'girlish bashfulness'.[83] Or, in the case of
the Mokrinskii Lane commune, the men might make the women feel that they
were displaying a propensity to be overly sensitive—that the women were some-
how failing to fully inhabit a male world, or, more specifically, a revolutionary
world that had been implicitly coded male.

Indeed, it must be said, in the urban communes the pursuit of sexual equality often
seemed to take place on male terms. As highlighted in the stories and publications
on these groups circulating in the mid-1920s, the communard fight against the old
'way of life' was often disproportionately directed toward women. As in activist
circles more broadly, the ideology of modern living was equated with the eradication of old family values. The old, illiterate, superstitious, and backward woman of
peasant society—the *baba,* in Russian—was seen as a stalwart of these old values.
She therefore became a symbol to rally against. In one portrayal of a commune, a
fictional story published in the literary section of *Molodaia gvardiia* (*Young Guard*)
in 1926, the cry rang out: 'a communist, in one phrase, is not a *baba!*'[84] Here was
a modern inflection of the traditional and disparaging Russian proverb, 'a *baba* is
not a person'.[85] Reflective of many contemporary communes, the communards of
this story challenged their own *baba* habits, alongside other 'noncommunist' and

---

[82] Pragera, 'Kommuna desiati', 11.
[83] Stephen A. Smith, 'The Social Meanings of Swearing: Workers and Bad Language in Late
Imperial and Early Soviet Russia', *Past and Present*, no. 160 (1998), 167–202, esp. 196–7.
[84] D. Kochetkov, 'Soloninnaia kommuna', *Molodaia gvardiia*, no. 4 (1926), 156–8.
[85] Cf. Richard Stites, *The Women's Liberation Movement in Russia: Feminism, Nihilism, and
Bolshevism, 1860–1930* (Princeton, NJ: Princeton University Press, 1978); Elizabeth A. Wood, *The
Baba and the Comrade. Gender and Politics in Revolutionary Russia* (Bloomington, IN: Indiana
University Press, 1997); Wendy Z. Goldman, *Women at the Gates: Gender and Industry in Stalin's
Russia* (Cambridge: Cambridge University Press, 2002); Barbara A. Engel, *Women in Russia, 1700–2000*
(Cambridge: Cambridge University Press, 2004).

'un-rational' tendencies. The pursuit of the 'new way of life', and the 'new people' (*novye liudi*) needed to populate this life, dictated that the communards purge themselves of all such traditional Russian characteristics.[86]

In groups such as the Mokrinskii Lane commune, the vices of the *baba* offered tangible challenges for activists to overcome. But the onus seemed to be on the women communards to emphasize the distance between themselves and the *baba*. In place of the *baba*, women looked to display a revolutionary 'steeliness' (*zakalennost*' or *zakal*) and a firm resolve. Common activist wisdom said that the process of *zakalivanie*, or 'tempering', was meant to induce the qualities of military discipline, endurance, and fortitude.[87] As Klaus Mehnert commented on his experience of Soviet youth in general, and of the Mokrinskii commune in particular: they spent a lot of time 'trying to turn women into men'.[88]

Other communes sometimes threatened members with expulsion for giving money to their parents. This showed an inability to cut ties with the old 'way of life', a failure of resolve. And it seems that women were more vulnerable to such accusations, too. They were less inclined to break with the family, it was thought. The desire to get married and leave the commune was also believed to be more of a risk with women communards.[89] Some of the early female walkouts did not help to alter these perceptions within the Mokrinskii commune. Women, in particular, had to guard against such shortfalls, maintain 'steeliness', and prove their unwavering commitment to revolutionary ideals. In many ways, then, this was a masculine environment, a masculine revolution. Again and again, the women—much more so than the men—were told they had to change in order to fit in.

Many urban communes and activists, at some level, evoked or found themselves complying with set, relatively unsophisticated ideas about masculinity and femininity. One of the few all-female communes, formed in the late 1920s, found itself besieged by men looking to mock their revolutionary ambition. Labelled, with derision, the 'womanly commune' (*bab'ia kommuna*), the activists involved felt that they had to be beyond reproach in all of their endeavours. Because they had to deal with these barbs on a daily basis, the women became particularly keen to prove that these scornful labels did not actually apply to them. Coming together in the traditionally male environment of a factory barracks, they were forced to accept a masculine vision of revolution. This was, after all, the only way they could earn respect and credibility in these circles. They tried to rid themselves of, or at least repress, anything that might be considered as *baba*-like behaviour. Being frivolous with one's clothing, it turned out, would certainly contravene the strong penchant for asceticism characteristic of many of their fellow male activists in and around the barracks.[90] Similarly, there was pressure to avoid 'pretty light shades' and 'decorations'

[86] Kochetkov, 'Soloninnaia kommuna', 156–8.
[87] Catriona Kelly, 'The Education of the Will: Advice Literature, Zakal, and Manliness in Early Twentieth-Century Russia', in Barbara E. Clements, Rebecca Friedman, and Dan Healey (eds), *Russian Masculinities in History and Culture* (Basingstoke: Palgrave, 2002), 131–51.
[88] Mehnert, *The Anatomy of Soviet Man*, 50.   [89] Kaishtat et al., *Kommuny molodezhi*, 25.
[90] B. Saparin, 'Bab'ia kommuna', *Molodaia gvardiia*, no. 24 (1930), 126–36.

in the bedroom. This was a sure-fire way to elicit criticism from male activists who thought that their plain rooms, full of books, though a little messier, were more revolutionary and more cultured.[91]

*

In all of these developments, and in all of these contradictions, however, the urban communes and communards remained marked by the evolving battle for *byt* and the prevailing concerns of the activist community. Soviet socialism in the mid-1920s was marked by uncertainty. The threat of NEP stiffened the resolve of some, while it led others to declare that the October Revolution had taught them nothing but 'how to drink'.[92] The Komsomol was quick to join in the panic when it was suggested that revolutionary excesses and the return of old habits were laying waste to the first generation of Soviets. The Komsomol leadership took seriously fears that the revolution was losing ground to hooligans, the ill-disciplined, and the regressive. In wild alarm, they discussed rumours and reports of Pioneer leaders establishing paedophile and paederasty groups, viewing such things as a sign of the times.[93] Amid all of this chaos, the certainty and stability of set gender assumptions seemed, on occasion, to help mark a clearer path to socialism. At times, with so many challenges to face, and so much change to embrace, it also seemed that a more sophisticated assessment of sexual equality was, for now, just beyond the reach of many communards.

In their own small way, therefore, the activists of these urban communes helped bring an added sense of urgency, masculinity, and *zakalennost'* to the forefront of revolutionary culture in the mid- to late 1920s. It is true that some of the more gender-conscious communes mimicked wider Soviet practices, implementing a 'women's division' (*zhenotdel*) or 'women's commission' (*zhenkomissiia*), which, like the official Women's Division of the Bolshevik Party, established in 1918, sought to provide a platform for female voices. But in the context of the urban communes—usually quite intermittent creations—the fact that women communards felt the need to make their own *zhenotdel* sometimes spoke to their continued sense of marginalization.[94] As with many other progressive movements taking place across the globe at this time, including the formation of rank-and-file trade union or cooperative groups in Britain and elsewhere, women and 'women's issues' were seen to overly complicate matters, resulting in them getting pushed to the sidelines.

The 'new way of life' and the 'new life' that the urban communards identified with was, in many ways, formed in opposition to a series of half-imagined, half-apparent

---

[91] L. Kassil', 'Kholostiatskaia kommuna', *Molodaia gvardiia*, no. 21 (1930), 76–9.
[92] RGASPI, f. M.1, op. 23, d. 584, l. 15.   [93] RGASPI, f. M.1, op. 23, d. 584, l. 17.
[94] For example, see *Otdel khraneniia dokumentov obshchestvenno-politicheskoi istorii Moskvy* (hereafter, OKhDOPIM; formerly, TsAOPIM), f. 459, op. 1, d. 28, ll. 87–87ob, 90–1 (Founding agreement of the M. N. Liadov commune, 4 October 1926); this document was first discovered and cited by David-Fox, *Revolution of the Mind*, 110.

obstacles to the revolution,[95] including the deep-seated habits of old Russia, the cultural surplus of NEP, the return of Oblomov and Onegin, the perversions of Soviet youth, and 'bourgeois femininity' and the *baba*. The '*byt* communes'—so labelled by a Soviet press that was itself embroiled in a moral panic over the derailment of revolution—offered a vehicle for activists to overcome all obstacles and press ahead, as fast as possible, with a socialist agenda. As they did so, these activists encouraged a distinctly plain, male asceticism and revolutionary dogmatism, a fervent passion for modern order, and an ever more vigilant approach to daily affairs and personal conduct.

This was where the interests of Stalin and those fed up with the compromise of NEP began to intersect.[96] The *byt* communards aided and abetted a vision of collectivism that would come to dominate the revolutionary experience of the latter part of the 1920s. The constant self-criticism and group-criticism of the communes marked a desire to seek out the personal aberrations possible in all revolutionaries; at the same time, their rallying against the dangers of NEPmen and kulaks revealed a hankering for heightened 'class war'. Likewise, their concern for the material conditions of revolution, alongside their impatience, would help galvanize the notion that it was possible to 'build socialism' and build it in 'one country'. The communards' key tenet of efficiency, which permeated everything the urban communes did, would not be lost on a Soviet Union poised to implement a programme of rapid industrialization and modernization. Indeed, as we will see in Chapter 4, work and new working practices—so precarious in the years of civil war, but now holding out the promise of permanence—would only become more important to these communards.[97] The spectre of industrialization provided a new opportunity for these enthusiasts to show how socialism should be lived.

In all of their actions, the *byt* communes and communards pushed relentlessly for full socialism. Thanks, in part, to the growth of human sciences in late Imperial Russia, as well as the materialist teachings of Marx, the first generation of Soviets were well aware that environment played a formative role in the development of individuals.[98] In their earliest form, this saw urban commune groups reject the traditional family and start to refashion domestic life along new, collectivist lines. With the coming of NEP, images of degeneracy and revolutionary stalemate, perceived as a by-product of this policy, led to a fixation on purity, overt displays of revolutionary commitment, and a more militant pursuit of the 'new way of life'. By 1926, even the upper echelons of the Komsomol were speaking of the '*byt* communes' as an example of how to overcome the imperfections of the present, with

---

[95] Here I extend and invert Michael David-Fox's description of the 'new way of life' (*novyi byt*) as a 'half-imagined, half-apparent' entity. See *Revolution of the Mind*, 83–4.

[96] Cf. Diane Koenker, *Republic of Labor: Russian Printers and Soviet Socialism, 1918–1930* (Ithaca, NY: Cornell University Press, 2005), esp. ch. 6.

[97] Cf. Koenker, *Republic of Labor*, 194.

[98] Daniel Beer, *Renovating Russia: The Human Sciences and the Fate of Liberal Modernity, 1880–1930* (Ithaca, NY: Cornell University Press, 2008), esp. ch. 5.

the urban communard experience seen as part of a mounting antithesis to those revolutionary perversions that were allowed to develop during the NEP years.[99] Along the way, it is clear, the communards displayed all the fragilities that one would expect of those eager to see revolutionary dreams enacted in the here and now. But when the communards themselves paused to survey Soviet life across the 1920s, they saw all the mistakes and shortcomings as yet further proof of the need for their continued struggle.

[99] RGASPI, f. M.1, op. 23, d. 584, ll. 26–7, 29.

4
Socialism in One Factory
Production Communes

'We do not need to impose the commune. We must wait, for when they come—and they will come—they will be voluntary.'

All-Union Congress of Shock Workers, Moscow, December 1929.

'Socialist competition has raised a conscientious attitude to work ... and it is not by chance that shock workers have become interested in the customs of the *kommunki*.'

Nadezhda Krupskaya.

Writing a letter to his former Red Army superior in the late 1920s, a young activist named Kochetov enthusiastically explained how he and some members of the old detachment had stayed together long after their military assignments, working alongside one another in a Moscow factory, eventually taking the form of a commune. In the factory setting—that mecca of socialism—these young men had continued to press for the revolutionary cause, joining in with local Communist Youth League (Komsomol) campaigns and attempting to promote worker solidarity, Kochetov explained. The idea of the commune was apparently first mooted by their own ever-determined Semen Pan'kov. 'You remember him', regales the letter: 'calm, tall, grey-eyed', with 'shaggy black hair'; always prepared to do 'what no other devil would'. 'Listen', he had said, 'we have all put a lot into advancing [the revolution], come on, now let's build a commune'.[1]

This was 1924, remembered Kochetov. By the end of July that year, with some assistance from a supportive individual at the local party *raikom* (district committee), Pan'kov had gone on to secure a modest home for the commune in a nearby workers' barracks. On moving day, Pan'kov and his collective recruits were taunted by some of their fellow workers. To these guys, it all seemed a bit too earnest. Worse still, Kochetov himself refused to follow the commune here at first. Over the preceding weeks, he had fallen in love with the daughter of one of the older workers at the factory. With his thoughts turning to marriage, he no longer relished the habits of life in the barracks, and could not seem to face the prospect of further collective endeavour. Nevertheless, the commune soon managed to pull in more like-minded activists. Before long, they totalled fifteen young men and eight young

---

[1] This letter was subsequently published as part of a wider collection of workers' accounts. M. Zagarnyi, 'Pis'mo kommunara', *Molodaia gvardiia*, no. 3 (1930), 79–81.

women. All agreed to hand over 50 per cent of their earnings to a common pot (*obshchii kotel*), and they quickly implemented a rota for washing the floors, ironing the clothes, and generally sharing all domestic duties. Luckily for Kochetov, when he found himself broken-hearted—his great love walking out on him for another man after just a few months—Pan'kov and the commune were there to offer him a home and, ultimately, a renewed sense of purpose.[2]

As a commune they set out to live the collective life and to press for socialism. At home, moving from their barracks to a larger residence near the site of an old monastery, they firmly rejected traditional social norms. In the factory, they established themselves in opposition to the closed-shop practices of the apprenticeship system still in operation under the New Economic Policy (NEP), as well as the doubt and scepticism they encountered from older workers. This enabled Kochetov to channel all his energies into the revolution. He felt part of something larger when he was with these activists. But that is not to say that life was without its challenges. He and the commune would have to overcome many hurdles in the coming months and years, Kochetov noted. In a style now familiar—a style common to those who had come to embrace the notion of social and collective reformation—Kochetov referred to commune life as a revolutionary journey. There would be disagreements and arguments over the cleaning, domestic arrangements, and the broader scope of their activities. At the tail end of 1925, a year and a half after Pan'kov had brought the commune together, a harsh winter, combined with a broken heating system, saw many would-be activists flee the group for an easier life. At this point they numbered fewer than ten. And for those left behind, at times, the original ideals of the commune seemed to fall by the wayside.

By 1926, the remaining communards had even started to splinter into factions, each with a different idea of how to proceed in light of recent troubles. One faction, labelled by Kochetov the 'conservatives', wanted to share costs and food but scale back on the collective arrangements. A second faction, the 'lodgers', were apparently 'only interested in their corner and their bed', effectively giving up on the ideals that had first brought them into the commune. In opposition to these, a third faction, the 'idealists', 'stubbornly fought for a full commune' and the fulfilment of Pan'kov's original plans. The group was at an impasse.

Then a fourth 'faction' emerged. Communard Zaichuk looked to recent developments in the activist community, taking particular note of the first sporadic 'shock-worker' (*udarniki*) initiatives in Leningrad, and proposed that the commune channel their collective efforts in a fashion similar to these activists. In time, following numerous discussions and much rumination, seven members of the original commune would come round to Zaichuk's thinking, including Pan'kov and Kochetov. They came to form what would be referred to as a 'shock commune' (*udarnaia kommuna*). They became very much taken with the shock-worker practice of 'storming' (*sturmovshchina*)—intensive efforts to fulfil productivity quotas and instil proletarian ethics across the shop floor of industry. This was not an unnatural shift for Kochetov and company, who, like many urban communes from this

---

[2] Zagarnyi, 'Pis'mo kommunara', 79–80.

period, had rallied hard against the ideological compromises of NEP. Reinvigorated by the latest push for socialism, these communards set about establishing themselves as the 'bearers' (*nositeli*) of proletarian values in the workplace, challenging and confronting those whom they considered obstructive to change. They looked to 'storm' the industrial setting.

Feeling better organized as a result of their reorganization, the remaining communards claimed they no longer had to forgo food, or as they put it, 'place their teeth on the shelf' (*zuby na polku*) at the end of every month, when the money ran out. The increased earnings and added job security that came with self-contracting (*samokreplenie*) as a collective unit certainly helped them in this regard. As Kochetov explained, with clear reference to Marx, 'socialist forms of organizing work called forth socialist forms of organizing life'. The prospect of a further revolutionary advance in Soviet industry motivated these communards and gave them something of a rose-tinted picture of how things were developing. Come 1927, as the Soviet press was gripped by fears of foreign invasion—'the war scare', as it became known—Kochetov and the commune only grew more determined. Indignantly, they vowed opposition to the imperial 'dogs of Great Britain' and all other aggressors, promising to build socialism to spite them.[3] In this way, they formed part of a cultural trend that invoked a more militant type of activism, reflected in rallying calls and press reports that, as contemporaries observed, read more like 'war communiqués', with absolutely everything becoming a 'campaign', a 'front', or a 'mission'.[4]

The commune now attempted to play a much larger role at work, summoning the memory of the *arteli* as they did so. They lived and worked as one collective unit, spending all their time together. They pushed for a disciplined working life to mirror the commune's domestic regulations, taking a collective vow to work hard and prove their proletarian credentials. Sensing that the local Komsomol and party *raikom* had grown more supportive of their actions, they also felt increasingly able to confront naysayers among the factory workforce and in the wider factory setting. Indeed, following the Shakhty Trial of 1928, when fifty-three mining engineers and technicians from the Donbass were publicly convicted of industrial sabotage, the language of 'wrecker' and 'saboteur' readily entered the commune's repertoire, along with a renewed, slightly modified, sense of 'class war'.[5] Along the way, there were accusations of 'careerism' from some of the more established adult workers, unhappy about being confronted or pushed aside by what they saw as a bunch of disruptive upstarts. But long-running tensions between youth and adult workers, coupled with the belief that NEP had put limits on youth training in Soviet industry, meant that such accusations only seemed to add fuel to the commune fire.

As they saw it, the communards pressed to extend 'new ways of doing things' across the barracks and factory. These 'new ways' were based on their understanding of

[3] Zagarnyi, 'Pis'mo kommunara', 79–80.
[4] Klaus Mehnert, *Youth in Soviet Russia*, trans. Michael Davidson (London, George Allen & Unwin, 1933), 67–8.
[5] Cf. Sheila Fitzpatrick, 'Cultural Revolution as Class War', in Sheila Fitzpatrick (ed.), *Cultural Revolution in Russia, 1928–1931* (Bloomington, IN: Indiana University Press, 1978), 8–40.

what it meant to be socialist and to work in a socialist manner. Out were hierarchical relations and established patterns of gerontocracy on the shop floor, all elite NEP specialists and technocrats, and anyone resisting change; in were new theories of collectivism, a focus on teamwork, calls for political consciousness, and activism in production. At the time of writing, it is clear that Kochetov was firmly in the grip of construction fever. As NEP gave way to calls for a concerted push towards industrialization, he and his fellow communards discovered a new zeal. Real change seemed to lie just ahead. Activist methods of work were taking root, and demands for an infrastructure upgrade in the barracks even seemed to have gained support from the local Komsomol cell. Worker settlements, public kitchens, dining rooms, laundries, clubs, and the general expansion of collective facilities appeared to be on the horizon now. With the bit between their teeth, the commune petitioned, with increasing boldness, for improvements across industry, envisioning a socialist world of proletarian consciousness in work and life, a productivity reflective of new scientific principles, and collective amenities bathed in electric light. They plastered the barracks and the factory in revolutionary banners calling forth this new world, and they tried to persuade other young enthusiasts to form collective labour teams and commune groups as they went.[6]

THE INDUSTRIAL FRONT

Those engaged in urban commune activism had always displayed an interest in Soviet industry and shared work. After all, a precedent had been set in Nikolai Chernyshevsky's *What Is to Be Done?*, with Vera Pavlovna's 'common apartment' also functioning as a sewing collective and production cooperative.[7] Student and *byt* communards debated collective labour and new methods of work alongside numerous other topics, as they contemplated the socialist future. And, as we have seen, youth activists, radical students, and enthusiastic workers could unite in the communes. Many were formed around Soviet factories or in working-class neighbourhoods, sometimes for practical reasons, sometimes as a sign of ideological affiliation. Some even seemed to predict Kochetov's 'shock commune', forming small comradely teams dedicated to living and working together as one. As early as 1921, while monitoring the development of the worker faculty schools (*rabfaki*) in her capacity as Deputy Commissar of Education, Nadezhda Krupskaya came across groups in the Basmannyi district of Moscow calling themselves 'labour-youth communes' (*kommuny trudovoi molodezhi*).[8] The 'founding agreement' (*ustav*) of one such commune, she discovered, pledged allegiance to the revolutionary labour force and advocated a new proletarian attitude towards manufacturing. As well as

---

[6] Zagarnyi, 'Pis'mo kommunara', 80–1.
[7] Nikolai Chernyshevsky, *What Is to Be Done?*, trans. Michael R. Katz (Ithaca, NY: Cornell University Press, 1989), ch. 3, esp. 188–202.
[8] *Gosudarstvennyi arkhiv Rossiiskoi Federatsii* (hereafter, GARF), f. A.2313, op. 1, d. 57, ll. 116–43 (Nadezhda Krupskaya's notes and materials from the People's Commissariat of Education, 1921).

living together and pooling their resources, this group tried to promote their own discussion circle (*kruzhok*) within the factory where they worked. They also petitioned the factory management to provide workers with a dedicated 'red corner' where all could read books, newspapers, and propaganda material. And, it turns out, like many activists around this time, they came to experiment with the ideas of Taylorism and the 'Scientific Organization of Labour' (*Nauchnaia Organizatsiia Truda*; acronym NOT), discussing a set 'rate of productivity' at work and a rational structure for life at home. Working practices and cultural revolution were thus entwined, as the commune looked for an 'overarching solution'. It was their ambition to revolutionize the whole factory setting.[9]

Clearly, the collectivist assault on the factory failed to materialize at this time. This is because a medley of local practices hampered any cohesive message from below in the immediate aftermath of October 1917. And, come 1921, with the party in control of the commanding heights of a temporarily mixed economy, the policy of NEP dictated the pursuit of stability over radical industrial reform. Nevertheless, Krupskaya, who would come back to the urban communes when writing about activism at the end of the decade, greatly admired the revolutionary energy of these groups. She noted their attempt to employ production targets, rationalized forms of organization, self-assessment, and mutually enforced labour discipline.[10] These were, Krupskaya believed, the seeds of proletarian mobilization. Later referring to such groups as 'public-worker activists' (*rabotnik-obshchestvennik* or *rabotnitsa-obshchest-vennitsa*), she declared that where once they were viewed as 'exceptions' or superfluous anomalies, the decline of NEP allowed the urban communes to form part of a wider 'common movement' (*obshchee dvizhenie*) pressing for change.[11]

Indeed, as Kochetov's experience shows, a continued sense of unease with NEP in the mid- to late 1920s, combined with a new economic urgency brought on by fears of foreign invasion, saw the urban communards drawn into a fresh populist offensive. Alongside other activists, and some local officials, communards started to call for a renewed revolutionary assault on industry. In this atmosphere, facing what was perceived by many contemporaries to be a moment of crisis, it has been argued that the party was ideologically predisposed to look for a combination of voluntarist and authoritarian solutions.[12] Hence they displayed a level of tolerance, and in some cases encouragement, towards the emergent shock-work movement with which Kochetov and other communards became embroiled. While the party

[9] GARF, f. A.2313, op. 1, d. 57, ll. 138–43.
[10] GARF, f. A.2313, op. 1, d. 57, ll. 8–9.
[11] N. Krupskaya, *O Bytovykh voprosakh* (Moscow, 1930), 9, 35.
[12] Diane P. Koenker, *Republic of Labor: Russian Printers and Soviet Socialism, 1918–1930* (Ithaca, NY: Cornell University Press, 2005), 216. Cf. Chris Ward, *Russia's Cotton Workers and the New Economic Policy: Shop Floor Culture and State Policy, 1921–1929* (Cambridge: Cambridge University Press, 1990); Lewis Siegelbaum, *Soviet State and Society between Revolutions, 1918–1929* (Cambridge: Cambridge University Press, 1992); David Shearer, *Industry, State, and Society in Stalin's Russia, 1926–1934* (Ithaca, NY: Cornell University Press, 1996); Sheila Fitzpatrick, *The Cultural Front: Power and Culture in Revolutionary Russia* (Ithaca, NY: Cornell University Press, 1992); Hiroaki Kuromiya, *Stalin's Industrial Revolution* (Cambridge: Cambridge University Press, 1988); Katrina Clark, *Petersburg: Crucible of Cultural Revolution* (Cambridge, MA: Harvard University Press, 1995).

moved to crack down in some areas of Soviet life, activists like Kochetov offered cause for optimism. Before long, with an example set, the number of urban communes would start to expand, as other activists and enthusiasts searched for a means of engaging in the latest revolutionary developments, and as the party sought to find more ways to mobilize the population for the latest projects and imperatives.

As Kenneth M. Straus has shown in relation to the shock-work movement, an activist assault on industry developed in three distinct phases towards the end of the 1920s. Firstly, between 1926 and 1928, young enthusiasts were allowed to form scattered and sporadic working experiments, including the formation of 'brigades' (*brigady*), which practised collective methods of labour, sometimes competing with one another and issuing comradely challenges to see who was the most productive. This was the party opening the gates to activist initiative, repeating Lenin's call for grassroots mobilization. Secondly, between 1929 and 1931, the party leadership moved to co-opt local initiatives and direct their energies toward official priorities. And thirdly, between 1931 and 1933, there was a move towards greater party control and regulation of worker initiative, ultimately resulting in a more individually focused 'shock-worker heroism', which also paved the way for the highly orchestrated Stakhanovite movement of the 1930s.[13] The activists that formed the urban communes—never averse to throwing themselves into ideological pursuits or engaging in the latest political developments—can be seen at every step as this industrial initiative unfolded, evolved, and became more entwined with state imperatives. The number of activists that chose to engage in the practices of the industrial-urban commune would always remain significantly lower than the number involved in the broader practice of shock work. But, in some cases, each can be seen to stimulate the other. Each was certainly born of similar revolutionary influences and desires, and the shock-work movement was likewise bringing together a great number of people looking to experiment with forms of collective association.

Here, then, is a picture that complicates our traditional understanding of this phase in Soviet history. The First Five-Year Plan, officially ratified at the Fifth Congress of Soviets, on 29 May 1929, has long stood as a historic marker. This is the point at which Iosif Stalin established his grip and his will on the revolution. Six months later, on the twelfth anniversary of the October Revolution, Stalin provided the term that has been used to define this period ever since: he declared that the move toward large-scale industrialization and collectivization was nothing short of a 'Great Break' (*Velikii perelom*) in Soviet policy.[14] But, as communard experience shows, and as historians have begun to argue, there was not necessarily much of a 'break' in the Great Break. At times, it can also be said, there did not appear to be all that much 'planning' in the First Five-Year Plan. In truth, the

[13] Kenneth M. Straus, *Factory and Community in Stalin's Russia: The Making of an Industrial Working Class* (Pittsburgh, PA: University of Pittsburgh Press, 1997), 138.
[14] I. V. Stalin, 'God velikogo pereloma: K XII godovshchinen Oktiabria', *Pravda*, 7 November 1929, 2.

vision of the First Five-Year Plan as a sudden switch from the structures of a mixed economy to the all-seeing ideals of a modern command economy—as well as the three-volume, two-thousand-page study upon which this policy was meant to be based—belies the true activism, indeterminacy, and improvisation at play on the ground during the latter half of the 1920s.[15] The party was hugely successful in promoting worker mobilization at the end of the 1920s, but this push did not represent a break with established revolutionary goals, nor did it free the leadership from the unexpected.

With NEP coming under increased scrutiny on ideological grounds, communard activists and other worker enthusiasts became part of what has been described as the 'spiraling cycle of local improvisation, central intervention, and All-Union bureaucratic warfare' that came to make up the First Five-Year Plan.[16] This was a policy that had its roots in the ideological and industrial tensions that fuelled people such as Kochetov. Even before the First Five-Year Plan was formally sanctioned, the push for worker mobilization and a reinvigorated class war had clearly started to take hold of Soviet industry. Communard Anikeev, for example, an activist based at the Moscow machine-tool plant Red Proletariat (*Krasnyi proletarii*), noted how the early years of NEP inspired much discussion about the 'new way of life' (*novyi byt*), working methods, and proletarian causes. The factory committee and party cell here even supported activist experimentation on these topics, he remembered.[17] In this way, the likes of Anikeev, his fellow activists, and the revolutionary leadership at the Red Proletariat factory acted as precursors to the industrial change that was to come at the end of the decade. Anikeev would engage in collective work, rally against the privileged role of NEP technocrats, and do many of the things that have become associated with industrial mobilization at the end of the 1920s. He was one of many who experimented with such ideas during the compromise of NEP.[18] He was, in other words, one of a number of activists who helped to instil the idea of a new revolutionary advance before the fact.

But his efforts did not stop there. By 1926–27, Anikeev, like Kochetov and company, found that local officials were becoming more receptive to shop-floor activism. Seemingly given permission from above, local officials encouraged workers to offer solutions to industrial problems, providing activists with a further outlet for their revolutionary energies.[19] A strong degree of lateral thinking seemed to be permitted in some places, as the gears of change slowly started to shift. By this point, the notion of the Five-Year Plan, and the move towards an idealized vision of Soviet industry, had been agreed in principle. The mobilization of activists was

---

[15] *Piatiletnii plan narodno-khoziaistvennogo stroitel'stva SSSR* (Moscow, 1929). For an in-depth study on the formation of the First Five-Year Plan and the Soviet command economy, see Eugene Zaleski, *Planning for Economic Growth: Soviet Union, 1918–1932*, trans. Marie-Christine MacAndrew and Gilbert Warren Nutter (Chapel Hill: University of North Carolina Press, 1971). Also, note Donald Filtzer, *Soviet Workers & Stalinist Industrialization* (London: Pluto Press, 1986).

[16] Kurt S. Schultz, 'Building the "Soviet Detroit": The Construction of the Nizhnii-Novgorod Automobile Factory, 1927–1932', *Slavic Review*, no. 2 (1990), 200–12.

[17] GARF, f. 7952, op. 3, d. 98, ll. 7–7ob. (Recollections of former Komsomol cell members at the Red Proletariat factory, 1920s).

[18] GARF, f. 7952, op. 3, d. 98, l. 7-ob.   [19] GARF, f. 7952, op. 3, d. 98, l. 7-ob.

arguably seen as a necessary prerequisite for such change to occur. Yet this was also a vision marred from the start by unreliable data and bitter struggles between the institutional bodies put in charge of making it a reality—namely the State Planning Commission (*Gosplan*) and the Supreme Council of the National Economy (VSNKh; *Vesenkha*). Even as the first semblance of the First Five-Year Plan came into being, then, so much time was spent debating and revising output targets that the actual methods of industrial fulfilment, alongside other practical issues, remained woefully underdeveloped. This lack of in-depth consideration meant that local authorities would continue to look to popular initiatives, such as the original shock-work movement and, occasionally, the urban communards, as a means of enacting revolutionary policy.

Party designs for centralized planning, which undoubtedly led to the establishment of an ever more restrictive state—limiting the sphere of revolutionary debate and placing immense power in the hands of Stalin—can be seen to be reliant on activists such as Anikeev, especially before 1931. From this angle, the 'Great Break', and to a great extent Stalinism, look less like the result of a triumphant, preordained plan, and more like a messy patchwork cobbled together, improvised, and finally brought under party control. The urban communes and communards became one small part of that patchwork. For Anikeev and a number of would-be or actual Komsomol and party members, the idea of the urban commune continued to offer an appealing means of enacting revolutionary visions on the ground. If the typical commune organizer was likely to be a Komsomol member, he or she was very often acting on his or her own initiative.[20]

*

As we will see, as they lent their voices to wider calls for structural and cultural change at the end of the 1920s, the urban communes and communards would enter their most popular and populist phase. Between 1927 and 1929, inspired by a renewed interest in collective ideals, and aided by the growing popularity of shock-work activism, the number of urban communes steadily began to rise. In some cases, it was said that the commune method of pooling money and working collectively offered a means of overcoming the inability of factory authorities to organize wages and labour effectively.[21] It was at this time that the idea of the urban commune started to spread across the Soviet Union. As revolutionary enthusiasts were encouraged to embrace the industrial drive and move to the new construction sites popping up across the Soviet Union, and as the press expanded their coverage of worker activism, new commune groups also began to spring up in urban settings as far afield as Novosibirsk, in Siberia, and Dnepropetrovsk (Dnipropetrovsk), in

---

[20] This can be gauged from a number of contemporary publications and studies concerning the urban communes. See A. Kaishtat, I. Ryvkin, and I. Sosnovik, *Kommuny molodezhi, po materialam obsledovaniia i pod redaktsiei instituta sanitarnoi kul'tury* (Moscow, 1931); S. Yarov, *Udarnye brigady v Gus'-Khrustal'noi* (Moscow, 1930); S. Zarkhii, *Kommuna v tsekhe* (Leningrad, 1930).

[21] V. I. Isaev, *Kommuna ili kommunalka? Izmeneniia byta rabochikh Sibiri v gody industrializatsii, 1920-kh–1930-e gg.* (Novosibirsk: Russian Academy of Sciences, 1996), 27.

Ukraine.[22] Some party representatives did express concern about this trend and its growing appeal among worker activists, but for now, most seemed to chalk it up to a propaganda coup for collectivism and collective working methods rather than a sign of potentially dangerous autonomy.[23]

Reflecting the industrial focus of the Soviet Union after 1928—and with some assistance from the Soviet press—groups, new and old, began to acquire titles such as 'worker communes' (*rabochie kommuny*), 'brigade communes' (*brigady kommuny*), 'production communes' (*proizvodstvennye kommuny*), and 'production-*byt* communes' (*proizvodstvenno-bytovye kommuny*).[24] These communes continued to concern themselves with revolutionary life, but it was becoming ever more apparent that the Soviet Union and its activist community had decided that this life and the industrial front were fundamentally connected.

As 1929 approached, with the Central Committee berating official organizations, including the trade unions, for not doing enough to enable worker activism, more and more Komsomol and party cells took an active role in promoting the virtues of commune association.[25] Before long, factory management and local leadership began to align commune activity with the now party-approved sponsorship of shock work. The urban communes even gained the endorsement of *Komsomol'skaia pravda* (*Komsomol Truth*), which claimed that such formations could become 'the main route towards' the reform of domestic and industrial life in the Soviet Union.[26] By the end of 1929, thanks to this sort of support—combined with an influx of urban migrants looking to settle into new homes and new working habits—it was thought that 30,000 people were attached to the urban communes in Moscow, Leningrad, and elsewhere in European Russia.[27] By March 1930, this time after a Lenin Enrolment campaign designed to further boost worker mobilization, the Central Committee of the Komsomol suggested the figure was more like 50,000.[28] And, as the urban communes became more embroiled in the industrial drive of the First Five-Year Plan, these numbers, and the number of copycat initiatives, would continue to grow; reports in subsequent years suggested that well in excess of 100,000 people were affiliated to such groups.[29]

It remains true that from this point on Soviet industry increasingly fell under the orchestration of the party leadership. But, clearly, there is more to this story. The urban communards might, in one sense, be seen to form part of a planned proletarian 'revival' (*ozhivlenie*)—the party hoping to rekindle the revolutionary energies of the workforce by invoking collectivist ideals and the proletarian heroism of 1917–21. This was certainly one way the party tried to galvanize the masses

[22] Isaev, *Kommuna ili kommunalka?*, 26–7.
[23] L. S. Rogachevskaia, *Sotsialisticheskoe sorevnovanie v SSSR: istoriia i ocherki, 1917–1970* (Moscow, 1977), 119.
[24] See Kaishtat et al., *Kommuny molodezhi*, 13–14.
[25] *KPSS v rezoliutsiiakh i resheniiakh s"ezdov, konferentsii i plenumov TsK* (Moscow, 1928), 143–4.
[26] 'Kommuny', *Komsomol'skaia pravda*, 18 January 1930, 4; first cited in Isaev, *Kommuna ili kommunalka?*, 25.
[27] 'Kommuny', 4.
[28] *Komsomol'skaia pravda*, 5 February 1930, 4; first cited in Isaev, *Kommuna ili kommunalka?*, 26.
[29] Iu. Larin, *Stroitel'stvo sotsializma i kollektivizatsia byt* (Moscow, 1930), 24.

around their latest plans. But this itself was in part a reaction to prevailing developments—the party looking to see which way the revolutionary wind was blowing. What is more, the party remained unable to dominate every facet of life at this time. Some reports suggest that new commune groups started to sprout up in certain locations specifically because there was a lack of guidance from party representatives.[30] Indeed, as we have seen throughout this book, Bolshevik ideas and ideology could be shaped and conditioned by the human reality on the ground. And, as the urban communes and communards show us here, on numerous occasions, before and during the establishment of an effective top-down system of control, the operational culture of the First Five-Year Plan would draw on revolutionary practices and demands nurtured in activist circles. Subject to less regulation and remaining more spontaneous in their actions than the shock-work brigades that appeared after 1928–29, some urban communes can be seen to exert a continued influence over revolutionary practices on the shop floor. While some factory settings proved more susceptible than others to actions emanating from unofficial or semi-official quarters, the urban commune and communards continually tried to implement new collective practices, Taylorist thinking, and efficiency drives. This was not, it should be said, a return to the workers' control of 1917— when bands of industrial workers were given the green light to seize control of their workplaces and help overturn the old order—but revolutionary policy was still subject to activist engagement, and it still mattered what activists lent their voices to. As Karl Marx said of the urban communards' Parisian forebears in 1871, the importance of such formations does not lie in what they sought or managed to achieve, but in their 'working existence'—the point being that they would inspire many thinkers and professional revolutionaries in the years to come. In their own small way, not wholly distinct from their forebears, the urban and production communes show that even in the Soviet Union of the late 1920s, actions could 'produce dreams and ideas', not just the reverse.[31]

THE DAWN CHORUS

The latter part of the 1920s, for all its uncertainty and upheaval, was an exciting time for the Soviet factory, opening up new ways of framing, reading, and taking part in the revolution. Sleeping until the first factory whistles went off, starting at six o'clock, worker activists woke to the prospect of advancing socialism a little further. The dawn call of industry beckoned them from their beds into a new day full of possibility. In establishments such as Moscow's electrical components factory, Elektrozavod, where the management proved very keen to promote local activism, young Komsomol members jumped at the opportunity to experiment with shock work, storming, and other collective practices. In this important factory—a

---

[30] D. Krymskii, 'Profsoiuzy na novom etape', *Partiinoe stroitel'stvo*, no. 2 (1929), 19.
[31] Kristin Ross, *Communal Luxury: The Political Imaginary of the Paris Commune* (London: Verso, 2015), 7, 24–5.

place charged with helping to enact Lenin's dream of electrifying all parts of the Soviet Union—it was not hard to equate daily work with the construction of socialism. Reports note that examples of 'young socialist enterprise' could be seen here as early as 1926.[32] At the same time, a group of trainee welders came together to form what was thought to have been the factory's first self-proclaimed 'worker commune'. Like many before them, they united around a 'common pot' in the local barracks, vowed to maintain a collectivist lifestyle at home, and looked to act as exemplary 'proletarian workers' in the factory.[33] As the dawn chorus called them from their beds, slowly rousing, they gathered together in the kitchen to eat breakfast and discuss their work for the day. Echoing a key tenet of Taylorism— and a theme much espoused in the Soviet discourse on NOT—every day they sought, above all else, to show the utility and necessity of disciplined labour. This push for discipline would manifest itself in their open denunciation of absentee-ism, shoddy workmanship, and drunkenness.[34] In a cultural sense, they looked to promote what they considered to be a socialist consciousness in the workforce. In a technical sense, they believed that this broader consciousness would open up avenues for new collective working habits, offering proof of the greater efficiency of socialism. Enacting the ideals of Soviet discourse, work and life became a uni-fied concern.

Under the shrewd guidance of Nikolai Aleksandrovich Bulganin, from 1927 Elektrozavod went on to utilize the actions of the communes and other activists at the factory. Early on, Bulganin, a youthful and confident industrial administrator, encouraged the factory Komsomol cell to harness the energy of those seeking to engage in shock work, subsequently managing to garner national headlines for himself and Elektrozavod as the workforce audaciously vied to meet their Five-Year Plan output targets in under three years. Come 1928, now calling themselves 'the Max Höltz commune'—after the German Communist bandit who had just made his way to the Soviet Union—the welder activists were working with the Komsomol cell to promote productivity targets, as well as rallying against forces of resistance and older workers.[35] Some officials were fearful of the precedent the activists set for equal salary distribution, but the local Komsomol continued to call on the com-mune to help press through their agenda. Plus, the communards seemed to have struck up a good working relationship with some cell representatives. Both were desperate to leave behind what they saw as the revolutionary stasis of NEP indus-try. In this context, the commune became particularly interested in the notion of 'brigade work' which was taking root in the factory at the time, choosing to lend its full support to the formation of more collective teams of activists, or 'brigades'

---

[32] A. Kliushin, 'Proizvodstvennye kommuny kak opyt kollektivnogo truda', *Partiinoe stroitel'stvo*, no. 11 (1931), 23.

[33] Kliushin, 'Proizvodstvennye kommuny kak opyt kollektivnogo truda', 24.

[34] Kliushin, 'Proizvodstvennye kommuny kak opyt kollektivnogo truda', 24.

[35] Kliushin, 'Proizvodstvennye kommuny kak opyt kollektivnogo truda', 24–5. For more on the development and revolutionary promotion of Elektrozavod, see S. V. Zhuravlev, *'Malenkie liudi' i 'bol'shaia istoriia': inostrantsy moskovskogo Elektrozavoda v sovetskom obshchestve v 1920–30 gg.* (Moscow: ROSSPEN, 2000).

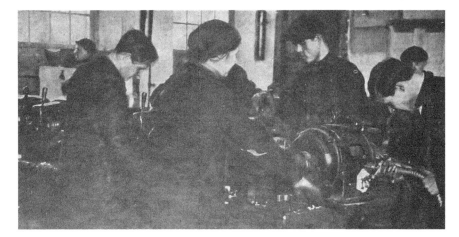

Fig. 4.1. A production commune engaging in shock work at the Lepse engineering works, Leningrad, c.1930
Source: 'Zavod kommuny', Smena, no. 8–9 (1930), 10.

(brigady), on the shop floor. Some of these cooperative formations went on to take the label 'commune-brigades'; certain groups even followed the lifestyle of the welder activists. Still showcasing what they believed to be the ideal socialist approach to work and life, the commune remained ardently involved in the revolutionary push that was taking place inside Elektrozavod.[36]

Much as they had elsewhere, these factory-based commune groupings also offered the most enthusiastic would-be radicals the chance to close the gap between promise and reality (see Fig. 4.1). As the industrial shift took hold of the Soviet Union, dispatches from factories outside of Moscow and Leningrad, such as the Bolshevik Plant in Kiev (Kyiv), stated that some activists were complaining about the slow pace of change. A few looked for ways to rectify this problem. Replicating some of the commune ideals they had read about in the Soviet press, for instance, six young men and one woman, the eldest of whom was twenty-one years old, set upon promoting the collectivist lifestyle from a one-room attic apartment near the Bolshevik Plant.[37] In their view, things did not look as good here as they did at Elektrozavod. Having arrived at the factory, they very quickly became aggravated about the state of the residences available for workers, as well as the lack of leadership regarding the local shock-work effort. The Komsomol did 'almost nothing' to inspire the youth of the factory, while older workers remained inflexible when it came to new approaches, they complained. Frustrated by what they saw as a lack of action, these activists formed their commune, pledging to make up for the local revolutionary shortfall and confront all the 'conceited blockheads' who were resisting

[36] Kliushin, 'Proizvodstvennye kommuny kak opyt kollektivnogo truda', 25.
[37] Iu. Ber, Kommuna segodnia. Opyt proizvodstvennykh i bytovykh kommun molodezhi (Moscow, 1930), 34–5.

change.[38] Again, the commune gave activists a chance to press through change and engage in the latest revolutionary causes.[39]

Similarly, forming a commune in May 1928, five young Komsomol members from Kiev–Avrashkov, Zurakhov, Manziuk, Spielberg, and Hain—declared that they were 'at war with the administration', older workers, and 'even the local cell' at the Red Banner Factory. They believed the factory was lagging behind those in Leningrad and Moscow at the time, and they thought it necessary to make an effort to show what could be done.[40] Among other things, they embarked on a campaign to help change the 'psychology' of the factory floor, promoting collective labour and friendly competition between workers. In turn, starting from the barracks, they waged a struggle against vodka, insisting that a healthy and cultured workforce was a productive and happy workforce. They tried to fill the boots of the idealized socialist worker that they read about in the youth press, while inviting fellow youths and Komsomol members to join them in their evening discussions at home and their daily efforts at work.[41]

In Kharkov (Kharkiv), Ukraine, a young man named Brover, determined to see the promise of revolution enacted then and there, formed a fifteen-person commune at the State Electro-technical Factory (*Gosudarstvennyi elektrotekhnicheskii zavod*; acronym GEZ). The 'Il'ich commune', as they called themselves, honouring the great leader of October, resolutely set about pooling resources, advancing collectivism, and behaving as 'exemplary workers'. Appropriating the language and ideas they encountered in their reading materials, they pressed to eradicate 'absenteeism, tardiness, ... and waste', showing the utility and necessity of discipline in all their actions. Extending the efficiency of Taylorism and NOT one step further, the Il'ich commune went on to advocate ergonomic innovations. On one occasion, much to the annoyance of some workers, they even changed the arrangement of tools at various workbenches across the factory. By rationalizing the layout of workspaces, Brover posited, the factory could improve productivity and ensure greater care of its equipment.[42] There was always a better way to work, a better way to live, and a better way to be. Brover and company most definitely wanted to be part of that better way.

In these instances, new 'scientific approaches', alongside the collective structure of the commune alliance, seemed to offer young activists the chance to feel as though they were at the forefront of revolution. Activists, and in some cases local Komsomol cell representatives, turned to the urban commune as a means of challenging what they considered to be forces of resistance and limitation. At the same time, participating in productivity campaigns offered them the chance to catch up with the revolutionary undertakings of Leningrad and Moscow. Within the context of a rapidly developing shock-work movement, mounting calls for an industrial

---

[38] Ber, *Kommuna segodnia*, 36.
[39] Also note correspondence from the Bolshevik factory: *Rossiiskii gosudarstvennyi arkhiv sotsial'no-politicheskii istorii* (hereafter, RGASPI), f. M.1, op. 23, d. 922, l. 81 (Postal correspondence, *Komsomol'skaia pravda*, April 1929).
[40] Ber, *Kommuna segodnia*, 46–7.   [41] Ber, *Kommuna segodnia*, 50–2.
[42] Ber, *Kommuna segodnia*, 37–40.

overhaul, and growing political confidence emanating from Moscow, the urban commune was becoming an ever more appealing construct of youth activism.

SEARCHING FOR THE SOVIET HAMMER

Moving from the Caucasus to Moscow, in 1928, an enthusiastic young worker named Marusa Arushanova found herself joining in this activist trend. She arrived in Moscow—just as Stepan Balezin and Ali Ianbulat had arrived in Petrograd/ Leningrad a few years earlier—full of hope and optimism, eager to participate in socialist revolution. She was offered a room, sharing with some local Komsomol members in a barracks that served as home to the young workers of the Hammer and Sickle steel plant, the Automobile Society of Moscow (AMO) plant, and the Dinamo Electro-machine construction plant.[43] The politically active Arushanova had certainly landed in the right spot. Evening discussions and debates abounded in this barracks. Those that lived here were already familiar with the shock-work movement and collective practices. Inspired to do more, Arushanova brought up the prospect of forming a 'production commune' with her Komsomol roommates. Her fresh-faced positivity met with enthusiasm, and they agreed to turn their existing cohabitative arrangement into the basis of a commune-collective. They started by introducing a system of shared wages and mutual responsibility, presenting their actions as an example of the 'new way of life' (*novyi byt*) within the barracks. Then they arranged to work together as a collective shock-work unit in the wire manufacturing shop at the Hammer and Sickle plant. Their life, they agreed, was now to be an exercise in collectivism.[44]

Urging their peers at work and at home to join them, they expanded to a peak of eighteen members. Eating, sleeping, and working together did present its fair share of problems, and, over the course of the year, some members would come and go. One card-carrying Komsomol member was actually kicked out for working too slowly and not displaying enough commitment to the group. But Arushanova successfully managed to establish what was reported to have been one of the first production communes at the Hammer and Sickle plant.[45] A year later, the commune was still eagerly nailing its colours to the wall: advocating the virtue of collectivism and discipline in all activities. They continued to invite fellow Komsomol activists over to their residence in an attempt to persuade them to establish their own communes.[46] And they seemed to have an impact. Figures from the Metalworkers' Union show that by June 1930, the Hammer and Sickle plant, Arushanova's primary place of work, was home to four established production communes and forty-eight registered 'communard workers'. In addition, the union listed thirty-three known 'collectives', with 248 workers, which had adopted

---

[43] GARF, f. 7952, op. 3, d. 341, ll. 32–4 (State Publishing files for 'History of Factories and Plants'—Maxim Gorky's archive—1931–38). I was led to this file thanks to Straus, *Factory and Community in Stalin's Russia*, 147–8.
[44] GARF, f. 7952, op. 3, d. 341, l. 34.   [45] GARF, f. 7952, op. 3, d. 341, ll. 34–5.
[46] GARF, f. 7952, op. 3, d. 341, ll. 35–6.

many of the daily working practices and cooperative principles of the commune, but did not necessarily all live together under one roof.[47]

Arushanova's work in this area got her noticed. By 1930, moving on from her commune responsibilities, she was chosen by the local party cell to organize and lead a Women's Section (*Zhenotdel*) at the Hammer and Sickle plant. So began her rise into the machinery of local revolutionary politics in the south-eastern Rogozhsko-Simonovskii region of Moscow—a place that was soon to acquire the title of 'Proletarian District'.[48]

Similarly, another industrial hopeful and urban migrant from the North Caucasus, a young man by the name of Sorokin, became part of this proliferating trend. Starting out his working life in a small steam mill in the mid- to late 1920s, Sorokin looked to the revolutionary horizon. Reading the Soviet press, he became inspired by stories about the building of Avtostroi—a new automobile factory complex on the outskirts of Nizhnii Novgorod—as well as by reports on the shock workers that were helping to build it. He positively consumed newspaper articles on the topic, feeding his growing interest in both worker activism and that great vehicle of the future, the motorcar.[49] The desire to take part in the construction of this modern vision led Sorokin to start planning a move to this part of central European Russia, 400 kilometres east of Moscow. He enrolled on a technical course in the nearest town to improve his qualifications, and, with some fellow students, organized his own shock-brigade-cum-study-group. At the end of the course, Sorokin persuaded the shock brigade and the forty-two students who had completed the class to apply to Avtostroi for work. Eventually, in May 1930, after much planning, and with a certain amount of trepidation, twenty-two of them made their way to this Soviet Detroit, where Sorokin then led them in the formation of another socialist vision: a 'working-commune'.[50]

He secured the group residence in a makeshift tent-barracks, erected just outside the construction site. They slept, ate, and shared everything within the lining of these improvised quarters. All under the age of twenty-two, the communards quickly became part of the youth-activist struggle at Avtostroi. Eighteen of these communards became members of the Komsomol, one attained a party card, and they all poured their energy into fulfilling the local plan. Their indefatigable insistence on replicating collective shock-work patterns did come to grate on some workers, resulting in one local manager trying to split the commune up by allocating each communard to a different job across the site. But, with the tacit support of the Komsomol, Sorokin and the others hounded this manager until he relented and agreed to move on. They also reported to the Komsomol cell to request the challenge of particularly arduous tasks, viewing 'hard graft' as a proletarian virtue. And, sometimes working knee-deep in mud and water, readying swampland for construction,

[47] GARF, f. 5469, op. 14, d. 193, l. 132 (All-Union Meeting of Metalworkers, 11 June 1930). Also first uncovered in Straus, *Factory and Community in Stalin's Russia*, 147–8.
[48] GARF, f. 7952, op. 3, d. 341, ll. 35–7.
[49] Mehnert, *Youth in Soviet Russia*, 179. For more on Avtostroi, see Lewis H. Siegelbaum, *Cars for Comrades: The Life of the Soviet Automobile* (Ithaca, NY: Cornell University Press, 2008), esp. ch. 2.
[50] Mehnert, *Youth in Soviet Russia*, 179–80.

they clearly relished the opportunity to exhibit their revolutionary commitment to their peers and local party operatives.[51]

After nigh on six months of this sort of effort, the commune lost four members: one expelled because he failed to match the working example set by the group, the rest simply deciding that such a lifestyle was not sustainable, especially with winter drawing near. But, with growing and visible support for all forms of shock-work activism within Avtostroi, the commune pressed other young enthusiasts to follow their lead. When Sorokin and company first arrived on site, there were sixty-eight registered shock brigades made up of 1,691 shock workers. By the autumn of 1930, the number was 253 registered brigades, with seven communes among them. And by the spring of 1931, this would rise to 339 brigades composed of 7,023 shock workers, with thirteen communes among them. Again, the number of full-blown communes remained very much in the minority, but they clearly fed off the expanding shock-work movement. Indeed, for his role in promoting shock work, Sorokin was later nominated and went on to receive the Order of the Red Banner for Labour.[52] He, like the commune, was operating between authority and autonomy—showing the operational realities of the nascent Soviet state.

PROLETARIAN *PERESTROIKA*

A dramatically expanding urban population—in excess of ten million people moving from rural and unindustrialized areas to the cities between 1928 and 1932—meant that the aspirational communes formed by Sorokin and Arushanova were far from unique.[53] And so, as this torrent of new workers flowed into the cities, the cultural mission that fuelled many urban communes, particularly the more established groups, was only going to become an issue worthy of greater consideration.

Among the urban communards that attached themselves to the Automobile Society of Moscow (AMO) factory, for instance, A. Bychkov tells the story of continued cultural revolution through the mid- to late 1920s. Upon joining the AMO workforce, Bychkov became part of a vibrant youth activist and Komsomol community.[54] Some 10 per cent of the factory was thought to be under twenty-five years old in 1924.[55] As elsewhere at this time, a certain amount of generational tension between new and old workers helped to fan the flames of revolutionary desire. There was a feeling that a number of 'dead souls' were acting as a block to change.[56] Komsomol workers threw themselves into organizing evening clubs, reading groups, and discussion circles (*kruzhki*). A clear sense of cultural mission was attached to everything

---

[51] Mehnert, *Youth in Soviet Russia*, 180.   [52] Mehnert, *Youth in Soviet Russia*, 181.

[53] Sheila Fitzpatrick, 'The Great Departure: Rural–Urban Migration in the Soviet Union, 1929–1933', in William G. Rosenberg and Lewis H. Siegelbaum (eds), *Social Dimensions of Soviet Industrialization* (Bloomington, IN: Indiana University Press, 1993), 21–2.

[54] *Tsentral'nyi arkhiv goroda Moskvy* (hereafter, TsGA Moskvy; formerly TsAGM), f. 415, op. 16, d. 76, ll. 1–50 (ZiL factory, reflections of A. Bychkov on 'brigades, communes etc.', 1927–30).

[55] TsGA Moskvy, f. 415, op. 16, d. 656, l. 4 (AMO factory, reflections of Komsomol members, 1923–26).

[56] TsGA Moskvy, f. 415, op. 16, d. 76, l. 1.

they did. The logic seemed to be that cultural advance would beget all other advances and promote a socialist consciousness.[57]

Bychkov explained that many of them felt emboldened to attempt to take the lead on factory life. With some AMO youths already experimenting with urban commune living, Bychkov amassed a few friends to organize a barracks 'cell'. Nearly all carrying Komsomol cards, members of the 'cell' concerned themselves with the domestic arrangements of their fellow workers and sought to promote domestic collectivism. From 1927, they pushed to make revolutionary inroads in this area, petitioning for more to be done in relation to the 'housing question'. But, with the advent of shock work at the factory and, like others, inspired by the legacy of the Russian *arteli*, Bychkov and company looked to turn themselves into a 'production-*byt* commune'. From 1928, they extended on their practice of promoting shared living in the barracks, functioning as a unitary 'brigade' at work. This was collective teamwork by day, everyday-domestic revolution by night.[58] The bonds of their collective association became part of a broader revolutionary strategy for these activists. They continued to concern themselves with the 'housing question' and exemplary living. But in this form they would join in various Komsomol campaigns across AMO, including the organization of factory inspection committees, monitoring the labour methods and revolutionary credentials of the workforce. The ground war of the commune revolution had moved to encompass factory life in its entirety. Sometimes, admitted Bychkov, they went too far, much to the detriment of more experienced workers, whom they treated quite badly, rallying to replace them with Komsomol members whenever possible.[59]

The move to curtail NEP, and the shift this brought about in the ideological landscape of revolution, gave fresh inspiration to Bychkov and his fellow communards. In their efforts to instil socialism at home and at work, they tried to affect the social composition of the factory—forming part of a renewed vision of 'class war'. In the same vein, they became active in forming revolutionary 'seminars', teaching new workers about not only shock-work practices, but the correct codes of behaviour for socialists at work. This was a revised and reinvigorated vision of the 'class education' (*klassovoe vospitanie*) that formed part of the cultural mission undertaken by the Red Army and Komsomol in the years immediately following the October Revolution.[60] Come 1929, they even requested and obtained permission from the party cell to partake in 'cultural campaigns' (*kul'tpokhody*) in the countryside, where some young activists were being sent to help organize collective farm models and advocate the virtues of collectivization. Visiting Novo-Annenskii, situated to the south-east of the Moscow oblast, they talked about offering 'sponsorship' or 'guardianship' (*shefstvo*) based on their experience of collective association and new working methods in the factory.[61] Embracing the language of the day, they also

---

[57] TsGA Moskvy, f. 415, op. 16, d. 656, ll. 2–6.
[58] TsGA Moskvy, f. 415, op. 16, d. 76, ll. 8–14.
[59] TsGA Moskvy, f. 415, op. 16, d. 76, l. 7.   [60] TsGA Moskvy, f. 415, op. 16, d. 76, l. 37.
[61] TsGA Moskvy, f. 415, op. 16, d. 76, l. 34. Similar instances can be seen in Michael David-Fox, *Revolution of the Mind: Higher Learning among the Bolsheviks, 1918–1929* (Ithaca, NY: Cornell University Press, 1997), 110.

discussed tackling 'alien elements'—those things they had come to see as distinctly un-proletarian or non-socialist in character—including drunkenness, poor hygiene habits, and weak revolutionary consciousness. In this regard, they were not beyond exhibiting a sense of superiority over the peasants they encountered on these campaigns, mocking the 'rough manners' and 'petty conventions' of rural commu-nities.[62] Such missions were to serve as a precursor to the 'Twenty-five thousanders' (*Dvadtsatipiatitysiachniki*) movement of 1930—a state-backed initiative that saw a wave of 25,000 front-line industrial workers sent out into the countryside to help improve the performance of Soviet state farming and instil proletarian values among the peasantry.[63]

Still, then, the urban commune offered a mode of revolutionary engagement—a method of association informed by cultural and revolutionary trends specific to the Soviet experience—that helped give meaning to the lives of young activists such as Bychkov. Functioning outside or in-between the apparatus of state, the commune gave these activists the space to appropriate components of the revolutionary mes-sage. Amid the push for volunteer shock work, socialist competition, a revival of collectivism, a return to socialist economics, and industrial modernization, the commune, even as it took on certain new characteristics, continued throughout to provide these activists with a way to understand and interact with the changes taking place around them.

MOBILIZING THE ACTIVISTS

Ultimately, by encouraging worker mobilization and opening the floodgates of activist initiative, the party and local representatives, whether they meant to or not, would begin the process of co-opting and codifying some of the revivalist actions of the urban communards, and, in the short term, help to facilitate more commune experimentation. There formed here a virtuous circle of party ambition and activist inventiveness. In the coming years, this mode of revolutionary engagement and popular association reached new heights and developed new dimensions, as parts of the ideological establishment took a more considered interest in their commune. After all, with activists such as Bychkov, Arushanov, and Sorokin gaining the attention of local leadership, the urban commune, in its various forms, was becoming a small but established component of Soviet industrialization. And as scattered examples came to the fore, some found themselves readily—even enthusiastically—included in official mobilization strategies.

Indeed, by the end of 1929 the urban commune trend was deemed significant enough for the Central Committee of the Komsomol to contribute funds toward a gathering of urban commune activists in Moscow. Alexander Kosarev, appointed Secretary of the Komsomol in March 1929, initially rejected the idea of supporting

---

[62] TsGA Moskvy, f. 415, op. 16, d. 76, l. 35.
[63] See Lynne Viola, *The Best Sons of the Fatherland: Workers in the Vanguard of Soviet Collectivization* (New York: Oxford University Press, 1987).

such an event. Believing that such initiatives did not yet concern the Central Committee, he suggested *Komsomol'skaia pravda* should take the lead.[64] But he soon changed his mind. A few months later, he offered to fund a 'conference' of urban commune activists on the condition that it led to the production of a report on 'the socialist reconstruction of everyday life and [...] communes' in the workplace.[65] The party leadership had recently reiterated its call for all ideological bodies to embrace worker initiatives as part of the wider mobilization drive. And, thereafter, an increasing number of Komsomol cells were urged to report on the activities of the urban communards, some noting the 'serious attention' these groups were starting to pay to 'the cultural and political development of workers'.[66]

Kosarev, who had some first-hand experience of commune alliance, seemed to come round to the idea that these groups could be advantageous to the Komsomol leadership, especially in pursuit of their policy of 'self-criticism' (*samokritika*)—the idea of involving workers in the governing of the Five-Year Plan by getting them to offer correctives to revolutionary aberrations in trade union practice, practical work, bureaucratic excesses, and general abnormalities in industrial life.[67] After all, these groups did bring a panoptic quality to their endeavours. Soon the urban communes were being cited as a means of organizing daily life in the factories,[68] persuading the Central Committee of the Komsomol to refer to them as 'agitators for new forms of life', before they formally asked local representatives to support all such formations where possible. 'It is necessary to lend full support and guidance [to the initiatives] of those young people in the organization of production communes', announced the Central Committee.[69]

Crucially, as a result of Kosarev's change of heart, a quasi-official 'All-Union Congress of Communes and Collectives' would meet in Moscow in January 1930, just one month after the first, party-backed All-Union Congress of Shock Workers. In the depths of a dry and icy winter, a reported 200 'communard delegates', collectivism enthusiasts, and Komsomol representatives gathered to discuss the role of the urban communes, and similar collective variants, in the development of Soviet industry.[70] Here, delegates and supporters excitedly declared: 'the commune is no longer a dream. With the grand plan of socialist construction our concerted efforts can become a joyful reality.'[71] Three months earlier, they noted, *Pravda* had

---

[64] RGASPI, f. M.1, op. 4, d. 41, ll. 143–52 (Meeting of the Central Committee of the Komsomol, 18 December 1929).
[65] RGASPI, f. M.1, op. 4, d. 42, ll.147–55 (Meeting of the Central Committee of the Komsomol, 23 February 1930).
[66] RGASPI, f. M.1, op. 4, d. 42, ll. 23–32 (Meeting of the Central Committee of the Komsomol, 23 January 1930).
[67] See A. Kosarev, *Proizvoditel'no rabotat' kul'turno zhit'. Doklad na 7-I vsesoiuznoi konferentsii VLKSM* (Moscow, 1932), 43–9. For more on the policy of 'self-criticism', see Koenker, *Republic of Labor*, 247–59.
[68] RGASPI, f. M.1, op. 3, d. 65, ll. 61–9 (Komsomol Provision on the workplace, no date, 1930).
[69] RGASPI, f. M.1, op. 4, d. 45, ll. 36–7 (Protocol: 'Restructuring the way of life', 15 July 1930).
[70] The proceedings of this 'All-Union meeting' were recorded by L. Bernshtein, 'Kommuna—ne mechta', *Iunyi kommunist*, no. 1 (1930), 30–9.
[71] Bernshtein, 'Kommuna—ne mechta', 39.

reported that 'in the very near future ... [the] communes will constitute a mass of one hundred thousand people'.[72] This marked the organizational pinnacle of the urban commune phenomenon, bringing it as close as it had ever been to what might be considered a fully coherent ideological or political movement. With the support of the Komsomol leadership—whose greatest fear was common disaffection with the industrial programme—the 'delegates' present discussed the parameters of commune activism in relation to the latest revolutionary developments.

Perhaps reflecting the Komsomol's input to proceedings, some 'delegates' spent less time discussing their various domestic arrangements, and more time discussing the virtues of introducing a new working culture on the shop floor. With all that had happened in the past few years, they were keen to spell out the difference between the first *byt* communes—apparently too inward-looking for some—and the latest production-based groups, active in spreading 'self-criticism', 'socialist competition', and a renewed 'class consciousness' among the workforce. Others were at pains to stress that their *byt* communes represented the society of the future, and that the idea of 'from each according to his abilities'—the fundamental principle upon which these groups were based—created new opportunities for all workers. The urban communes had never belonged to the so-called 'visionaries', they insisted. Simply put, they did not consider their communes to be utopian islets cut adrift from the revolutionary struggle.[73]

Representing the activists of AMO, one communard said that with 'socialist competition', their collective alliance had become stronger and more determined. In this context, it was argued, they could better function as what some at the meeting were inclined to call 'associations of class struggle', helping new workers find a role and a purpose in the factory, while eroding the old structures of elite industrial management.[74] This might just have been the same communard who, later that year, wrote to *Iunyi kommunist* (*Young Communist*) declaring: the 'commune that asks purely domestic ... questions has no right to existence'. He argued that the march of the Five-Year Plan required all communards to extend their experience of labour activism, social engagement, and comradeliness.[75] Others, however, including a communard from the *Skorokhod* shoe factory in Leningrad, insisted that groups that concerned themselves with the 'way of life' had set up the social dimensions of the proletarian assault on industry.[76] Such activists appeared less willing to accept or highlight the distinction between the earliest *byt* communes and those that were now adopting the title of 'production commune'.

Yet most accepted that the assault on industry had become a part of the urban commune existence. Alongside the revolution in domestic and social life, for instance, the communes at *Skorokhod* apparently welcomed the prospect of overturning the existing structure of the factory, embracing the slogan: 'less red tape,

---

[72] Bernshtein, 'Kommuna—ne mechta', 39.   [73] Bernshtein, 'Kommuna—ne mechta', 30–1.
[74] Bernshtein, 'Kommuna—ne mechta', 31.
[75] 'Pis'mo AMO kommuny', *Komsomol'skaia pravda*, 24 November 1930, 4; cited in Kaishtat et al., *Kommuny molodezhi*, 70.
[76] Bernshtein, 'Kommuna—ne mechta', 33–4.

more comradely sensibility!'[77] This was the 'red tape' of the old elite and the specialists who had run the factories through much of the 1920s, as well as the compromised structures of NEP that allowed them to remain—that is, the same 'red tape' that the emerging Stalinist leadership had vowed to eradicate when referencing what it considered to be the forces of opposition to Soviet industrialization. Some viewed the revolutionary 'discipline' exhibited by the communards as a means of helping the party-driven crackdown on absenteeism and poor working habits. This was something that those most interested in the 'scientific organization of life' were particularly keen to promote, believing 'rational behaviour' and 'discipline' to be key to the revolutionary values for which they were striving.[78]

With a helping hand from the Komsomol leadership, the discursive notion of the urban commune was clearly expanding to include more of the revolutionary politics that were driving the First Five-Year Plan. This was also reflected in the names that some of the latest communes adopted. Be it the 'Five in Four' commune at the Hammer and Sickle factory, or the 'Our Frenzy and Labour Front' commune at the Zlatoust machine works, such titles showed how heavily involved these groups had become in official campaigns to over-fulfil the production targets.[79] In some cases, reacting to central demands, Komsomol cells moved to make their presence better known: orchestrating their own official collective groups, or forcing existing communes to take on new members. In one Volga-based factory, the local Komsomol cell felt obliged to initiate its own 'production commune', which it viewed as a means of helping the state get more of the urban poor and unemployed to adopt good working habits.[80] Some party representatives even argued that communes might be used to ease the mounting burden of youth homelessness in the Soviet Union.[81]

This is not to say that the communards' embrace of the Five-Year Plan was necessarily superficial or coerced. At the Moscow gathering, some communards, including a group from the Baumanskii district in Moscow, appeared to be genuinely in step with the Stalinist centre's distrust of trade unionism, complaining that the unions had always stood 'completely aloof' from the urban communes and their attempts to revolutionize factory life. It was also noted that when they approached union representatives to ask for funds towards their 'All-Union Congress', absolutely nothing was forthcoming.[82] Furthermore, it was thought by some among the Komsomol leadership that interest in the commune initiative was piqued because these groups were challenging everyone 'to keep up' with 'rapid responses in manufacturing'.[83] From this perspective, if the onset of the First

---

[77] Bernshtein, 'Kommuna—ne mechta', 34.   [78] Bernshtein, 'Kommuna—ne mechta', 31.
[79] Lewis H. Sieglebaum, 'Production Collectives and Communes and the "Imperatives" of Soviet Industrialization, 1929–1931', *Slavic Review*, no. 1 (1986), 68.
[80] RGASPI, f. M.1, op. 3, d. 68, ll. 155–62 (Memorandum: Volga Regional Committee of Komsomol, no date, 1928/29).
[81] Zagarnyi, 'Pis'mo kommunara', 80. Also see GARF, f. 5515, op. 15, d. 225, ll. 3–5 (People's Commissariat of Labour on 'help for the homeless', no date, 1930).
[82] Bernshtein, 'Kommuna—ne mechta', 36.
[83] RGASPI, f. M1, op. 3, d. 68, l. 26 (Survey for Central Committee and Regional Committees of the Komsomol, no date, 1928).

Five-Year Plan was based on the rejection of gradualism and the shackles of NEP, the urban communes and communards were showing more resolve than the leadership. They were showing everybody up. With the most engaged groups still organizing meetings, workshops, and discussions, the popular stamp of the urban commune, it was reported, galvanized activists around new approaches.[84]

Establishing themselves in opposition to 'traditional' or 'non-revolutionary' practice, as well as to 'bureaucratic inertia', the urban communes were very much seen to be involved in promoting the proletarian contours of the industrial assault.[85] As they confronted the 'backward strata' of new workers—those exhibiting 'petty bourgeois and kulak moods' on the shop floor—they furthered their reputation as class warriors.[86] By engaging in the battle for the culture of the factory, and by pursuing socialist consciousness at work and at home, they helped turn the language of a renewed class struggle into an active proletarian mood at the base.[87] In some cases, the communes clearly took it too far. At the Elektrozavod factory, for instance, one card-carrying adult worker, a certain comrade Plotnikov, was harassed and tormented by a group of communards until he agreed to join with them. Plotnikov was more qualified than the rest of the commune, but it was they who dictated the working and cultural dynamics of this particular factory section. And as these communards saw it, with the likes of Plotnikov on their side, the group could seek to exert more pressure on their peers.[88] This was not what the factory management intended or desired when it came to supporting rank-and-file activism, but it did promote a sense of common cause and a professed 'proletarianism'. Where they were able to establish themselves, then, the production communes were frequently on the verge of attacking those who failed to embrace the latest revolutionary habits. A renewed sense of 'proletarian morality', and, to some extent, a reinvigorated iconoclastic attitude, informed the communards' day-to-day actions and demands.

---

[84] RGASPI, f. M.1, op. 4, d. 43, ll. 106-ob. (Report: 'The state of mass labour among youth workers in the textile industry', no date, 1930).

[85] Kliushin, 'Proizvodstvennye kommuny kak opyt kollektivnogo truda', 23–5.

[86] S. Samuelii, 'Rabotu proizvodstvennykh kommun i kollektivov—na novye rel'sy', *Partiinoe stroitel'stvo*, no. 15–16 (1931), 12–18.

[87] This assessment has been influenced by recent publications on what has been called the 'affective turn' or the 'emotional turn', in other words, studies that view reason and emotion as complexly intertwined, forming a crucial component of historic development—the interconnection of cognition and emotion. These publications reject the notion of universal emotion or emotion as a psychological state. Instead they argue that emotion and affective dispositions are formed through discourses with environment and society. Emotion is, in other words, specific. As Sara Ahmed suggests, emotion is constantly 'moving', 'relational', and active in its formation. She calls this 'the sociality of emotion'. See Sara Ahmed, *The Cultural Politics of Emotions* (Edinburgh: Edinburgh University Press, 2004), 8–12. For an assessment of emotion relating to Russia and Eastern Europe, see Mark D. Steinberg and Valeria Sobol (eds), *Interpreting Emotions in Russia and Eastern Europe* (Dekalb: Northern Illinois University Press, 2011). Also see Patricia T. Clough, ed., with Jean Halley, *The Affective Turn, Theorizing the Social* (Durham, NC: Duke University Press, 2007); Richard A. Shweder and Robert A. LeVine, *Culture Theory. Essays on Mind, Self, and Emotion* (Cambridge: Cambridge University Press, 1997); Jan Plamper, *The History of Emotions: An Introduction*, trans. Keith Tribe (Oxford: Oxford University Press, 2015).

[88] Samuelii, 'Rabotu proizvodstvennykh kommun i kollektivov—na novye rel'sy', 13.

TOWARDS INDUSTRIAL *PERESTROIKA*

The co-opting and codifying of the urban communes reveals both the strengths and the limitations of the leadership's command economy visions at this time. Both the Komsomol and the party moved to absorb these activists, alongside the shock-work movement, within an increasingly professionalized state apparatus. As they did so, they tried to influence the form, purpose, and language of these associations. This facilitated more press coverage, and helped to publicize the idea of the urban commune even further. By 1929, local representatives started to meddle far more actively in the daily affairs of these groups. From this point on, the production-based urban communes and communards had to operate in an environment where the boundaries of acceptable revolutionary debate were visibly shrinking. And, as we will see in Chapter 5, with the party developing a more effective system of top-down management after 1929–30, there would be rapid growth in the number of orchestrated communes and lesser 'collectives', which were more directly focused on officially endorsed working imperatives. But, on the way to this greater statist efficiency, the ideological and practical trajectories of the First Five-Year Plan were not charted as meticulously as some would have us believe. In some cases, the evolving structures of the production commune served as a constituency for revolutionary and collective populism where cell activity alone had failed. And, with the end of NEP, at a time of rising urban immigration, rapid industrial growth, and considerable tumult, the urban commune found new meaning.

On a localized basis, some production communes managed to affect working habits and influence Komsomol representatives. These representatives, after all, could not ignore the predominance of youth within these groups.[89] Sometimes communards helped to galvanize other activist workers around new practices and messages in the factory setting. This was why the leadership came to take such an interest in these formations. Like the Russian workers organizing and making political demands in 1905, many production communards saw themselves, in an idealized view of the world, making the case for ideological advance now. Indeed, some contemporaries noted that the communards they encountered were early advocates of 'the daily exchange of production experience'—the idea that sharing knowledge of best practice and competing on a level playing field offered the Soviets an economic advantage over capitalism.[90] This became a theoretical staple of Soviet economic reasoning. But, as the communes were absorbed into an increasingly interventionist and professionalized apparatus, and as more people flooded into industrial settings, we can see that while they were not straightforwardly leading events, their biggest impact came in the attitude they helped bring to the shop floor.

---

[89] See RGASPI, f. M.1, op. 4, d. 45, ll. 36–7 (Protocol: 'Komsomol objectives on restructuring the way of life', 15 July 1930).
[90] Samuelii, 'Rabotu proizvodstvennykh kommun i kollektivov—na novye rel'sy', 17.

Emerging from the youth activist rejection of NEP, the production communes were a kernel of revolutionary ambition and desire, a culturally specific model by which the promises of Soviet socialism could be anticipated, contemplated, and, importantly, shared. Labour studies have shown that, by 1930, the production communes were most numerically strong in the Moscow metallurgical industry. Indeed, with greater support and input from local Komsomol forces, and with well-established shock-work activities in place, it was these workplaces that gave rise to a proliferation in commune experimentation after 1929–30.[91] But, equally, a range of contemporary reports point to a broader sociocultural trend within activist and rank-and-file circles, spreading across a range of workplaces.[92] With the prospect of industrial modernization just around the corner, those engaged or looking to engage in urban commune activities became increasingly obsessed with extending the ascetic focus and rational reorientation of collective living to working life. Indeed, in Leningrad, a small group of bakery workers were inspired to band together to form their own production commune. Far from the oil and steel of heavy industry, they nevertheless embraced the same ideas, concepts, and structures. They pledged, with the same earnest intensity, to live and work together as an exemplary association of comradely orientation. To prove their revolutionary credentials, and the superiority of socialist organization, they also vowed to 'lower waste to 0.05 per cent and analyse the best means of producing French buns'—very much adopting the language of the day.[93] Discussing waste, absenteeism, and partaking in broader cultural campaigns, the bakery communards showed themselves to be well versed in the latest revolutionary readings. They even attempted to assimilate the idea of 'continuous production' (*nepreryvka*), proposing that the bakery ovens stay on between batch preparation and shift handovers.[94]

In reality, when it came to seeking out greater efficiencies, the bakery communards, and others like them, spent much of their time castigating co-workers and each other for things such as excessive chatting or unscheduled breaks at work. Some resorted to posting the names of certain 'offenders' on bulletin boards in an attempt to shame co-workers into conforming to what they had come to consider the correct socialist practice.[95] On their own, these were not developments that would change Soviet industry. But in the context of the First Five-Year Plan, and with the prospect of revolutionary change tantalizingly close, these uneven actions spoke to a world of socialist possibilities. As the full force of ideology was thrust upon industry, formations such as the production communes helped give meaning to socialism on the shop floor. What they did, thought, and said here—the

---

[91] Siegelbaum, 'Production Collectives and Communes', 69.
[92] Z. L. Mindlin and S. A. Kheinman (eds), *Trud v SSSR: statisticheskii spravochnik* (Moscow, 1932); P. Dubner and M. Kozyrev, *Kollektivy i kommuny v bor'be za kommunisticheskuyu formu truda* (Moscow, 1930); S. Zarkhii, *Kommuna v tsekhe* (Moscow, 1930); V. Ol'khov, *Za zhivoe rukovodstvo sotssorevnovaniem, opyt vsesoiuznoi proverki sotssorevnovaniia brigadami VTsSPS* (Moscow, 1930).
[93] Dubner and Kozyrev, *Kollektivy i kommuny*, 16–17.
[94] Dubner and Kozyrev, *Kollektivy i kommuny*, 17–18.
[95] Dubner and Kozyrev, *Kollektivy i kommuny*, 17–18; Also see L. Tandit, 'Proizvodstvennye kommuny i zadachi partorganizatsii', *Partiinoe stroitel'stvo*, no. 6 (1930), 45.

ideas they embraced and the things they rejected—helped to effect a culture of change in which the First Five-Year Plan would take root. But, what would become of the production communes and the discursive notion of commune alliance as a more effective system of top-down management came into being? That is the topic of Chapter 5.

5

Early Stalinism and the Urban Communes

Between 1929 and 1931, more young activists and enthusiastic workers experimented with urban commune association than ever before. The communes were now wrapped up in a dramatic urban and industrial expansion. Reflecting the greater level of party input and attention, this collective phenomenon also acquired a new trope around this time: supporters of the production communes began referring to these formations as 'the highest form of collective labour' or 'the highest form of socialist competition'.[1] Some local leaders and factory managers started to view these formations as part of a broader drive to provide collective working solutions to Soviet industrial problems. And a more systematic effort to promote the communes emerged in early 1930, following a spike in the number of reports and press articles on these groups.[2] In places such as the Zlatoust Machine Works in the Urals and Elektrozavod in Leningrad, for instance, the factory management ensured a proliferation in commune formations.[3] It is hard to say precisely how many people were involved in genuine commune activities at this time because no comprehensive study was produced, and a greater range of managerial input meant that the term was also being employed more indiscriminately. But the studies that were produced all suggest a figure in excess of 100,000 by 1931; some even hint at a likely inflated and conflated figure of around 300,000.[4]

Yet, despite a growth in numbers and a favourable outlook from some quarters, the period 1929–31 also witnessed the swansong of the urban commune idea. Sucked into the local machinery of state, with mass mobilization the commune idea was itself made vulnerable to shifting industrial imperatives and management priorities. Rising concerns about the number of unskilled, peasant workers flocking

[1] For example, see L. Tandit, 'Proizvodstvennye kommuny i zadachi partorganizacii', *Partiinoe stroitel'stvo*, no. 6 (1930), 44; L. Bernshtein, 'Kommuna—ne mechta', *Iunyi kommunist*, no. 1 (1930), 39; D. Reznikov, *Udarnye brigady sotsializma* (Moscow, 1930), 32.

[2] For example, see P. Dubner and M. Kozyrev, *Kollektivy i kommuny v bor'be za kommunisticheskuyu formu truda* (Moscow, 1930); S. Zarkhii, *Kommuna v tsekhe* (Moscow, 1930); V. Ol'khov, *Za zhivoe rukovodstvo sotssorevnovaniem, opyt vsesoiuznoi proverki sotssorevnovaniia brigadami VTsSPS* (Moscow, 1930).

[3] V. N. Kuikov and V. V. Vadim, *Istoriia industrializatsii Urala, 1926–1932 gg.* (Sverdlovsk, 1967), 454; and A. Kliushin, 'Proizvodstvennye kommuny kak opyt kollektivnogo truda', *Partiinoe stroitel'stvo*, no. 11 (1931), 23–5.

[4] Z. L. Mindlin and S. A. Kheinman (eds), *Trud v SSSR: statisticheskii spravochnik* (Moscow, 1932), 123; S. Samuelii, 'Rabotu proizvodstvennykh kommun i kollektivov—na novye rel'sy', *Partiinoe stroitel'stvo*, no. 15–16 (1931), 12; Dubner and Kozyrev, *Kollektivy i kommuny*; Zarkhii, *Kommuna v tsekhe*; Ol'khov, *Za zhivoe rukovodstvo sotssorevnovaniem*; I. Zaromskii, 'Proizvodstvennye kollektivy—novaia forma organizatsii truda', *Voprosy truda*, no. 4 (1930), 19–20.

into industry also made commune collectivism start to look increasingly incongruous by 1931. Was it fair that these new workers entered the factory on an equal footing when they possessed so little knowledge of industry? Certainly, after this point, a consensus started to build around the need for professionalized command structures that could better manage the macro picture. But, in truth, there was still a great deal of confusion and indeterminacy among the local and national leadership when it came to the urban commune initiative. This was exacerbated by Stalin's warnings against forcibly enacted collective farming in the countryside—a shift in policy caused by peasant resistance and declining agricultural yields. As a result, in some cases, doubts were raised about collective labour organization in the cities, too. Ultimately, the fall of the urban communes and communards was a story of uncertainty and tumult brought on by the sheer pace of change during the First Five-Year Plan, as well by as the party leadership's resultant desire to stabilize Soviet industry after 1931.

Never fully endorsed by the party, the rapid expansion of commune experimentation at the end of the 1920s would weaken this trend and introduce a number of internal and external tensions. As we saw with the 'All-Union' meeting of urban communards in early 1930, the desire to stress one's allegiance to the productivity drive led some communes to criticize those not as engaged in industry as themselves. Not all communes felt the same way or followed the exact same path, but a new insecurity was introduced, as groups began to fear the accusation and the label 'utopian'. From this perspective, to neglect industrial duties and imperatives was to follow an irrational path. More managerial input also meant that the original simplicity of the urban commune idea was coming under strain. And with simplicity had come group cohesion. In addition, with their penchant for wage levelling and shaking up labour methods, commune growth inevitably led to worker resentment, complaints, confrontations, and, to some minds, the threat of industrial instability.[5] In this environment, a constant back and forth between pro- and anti-commune commentators developed. In others words, a new uncertainty had appeared which, when combined with a lack of guidance from the top, meant there was no next step available to the urban communes. There was no clear breakthrough moment when the urban commune became part of mainstream, party-approved schemes. So, after a spike in numbers, and far more press attention than ever before, the urban communes were suddenly left in a tentative position. With local leadership support starting to disappear, some of the newest groups began to crumble, and confidence in the urban commune started to decline.

Following two years of rapid growth in urban commune numbers, the phenomenon found itself effectively proscribed within industry when the Supreme Soviet of the National Economy (VSNKh; *Vesenkha*) and the All-Union Central Council of Trade Unions (VTsSPS) issued a joint resolution, on 11 September 1931, calling on all 'administrative-technical personnel and trade union organizations' to prepare

---

[5] See V. Turov, 'V tsekhakh giganta', *Iunyi kommunist*, no. 8 (1930), 66.

for the conversion of brigades to cost-accounting units (*khozraschety*).[6] The implementation of cost-accounting contracts was meant to help factory management direct brigade teams and collective-worker groups, establishing a professionalized and routinized form of shock work.[7] This was buttressed at the Seventeenth Party Conference, in January 1932, which passed a resolution ratifying the managerial approach to industry and, despite some opposition, limiting wage-levelling practices.[8] In the end, as the ideological tide turned, the urban commune was cast aside. Many of the revolutionary causes championed by the communes lived on, but industrial conditions elevated professionalized structures above activist initiative. This chapter shows the activists of the urban commune coming to terms with this revolutionary change.

It is worth noting that, unlike so many others under Stalin's rule, there was no violent end for the urban communes or the activists who aspired to live and work in these groups. The full force of terror had yet to manifest. Besides, few leading figures would have wanted to alienate enthusiasts and aspiring Bolsheviks such as these, especially during the height of industrialization. Indeed, many contemporaries remained uncertain as to whether all the new resolutions actually applied to the urban communes. Some commune groups continued, almost as before, in the guise of 'cost-accounting brigades' (*khozraschetnye brigady*), even after 1931.[9] They did not become agents of resistance or victims of coercion; their reaction to events, and the local leadership's reaction to them, was too un-dramatic, random, and even ill organized to suggest this. In many cases, the Communist Youth League (Komsomol) and party activists that formed these groups were the same people that went on to populate and operate the institutions of state in the years to come. Had the urban communes developed into a more dominant movement or offered an alternative source of power, they most certainly would have been tackled more directly. But this was not the straightforward 'war on dreamers' that some have envisioned when considering revolutionary experimentation across the opening decade of the Soviet Union.[10] Some party members maintained relatively positive views of the communes; others became sceptical of these formations. The urban communes and communards did not meet their end through the swift, calculated movements of a totalitarian state. They were not decreed out of existence. As much as anything, the urban commune as an idea and a trend dissipated amid the ongoing pressures and shifting ideological imperatives of Soviet industrialization. This is not to suggest that power resided anywhere other than the upper echelons of the party—where policy shifts were ultimately decided—but it does help to reveal the lived experience and evolving realities of revolution as a new era was being defined.

[6] Lewis H. Sieglebaum, 'Production Collectives and Communes and the "Imperatives" of Soviet Industrialization, 1929–1931', *Slavic Review*, no. 1 (1986), 81–2.

[7] See Kenneth M. Straus, *Factory and Community in Stalin's Russia: The Making of an Industrial Working Class* (Pittsburgh, PA: University of Pittsburgh Press, 1997), ch. 6.

[8] *XVII Konferentsiia VKP(b): stenograficheskii otchet* (Moscow, 1932).

[9] Samuelii, 'Rabotu proizvodstvennykh kommun i kollektivov—na novye rel'sy', 12–18.

[10] Richard Stites, *Revolutionary Dreams: Utopian Vision and Experimental Life in the Russian Revolution* (New York: Oxford University Press, 1989), ch. 11.

Indeed, at points along the way, it did look as though some sections of the activist community and the party were gearing up to further embrace commune association. As early as December 1929, at the Shock Workers' Congress in Moscow, the urban and production communes were being cited as a source of great potential for industry. With one-sixth of delegates already on some form of collective pay, this is not that surprising.[11] Around this time, Nadezhda Krupskaya was also singing the praises of the *kommunki*.[12] In turn, the State Planning Commission (*Gosplan*), VTsSPS, and *Vesenkha* were instructed to carry out investigations and collect data on the communes for the Sixteenth Party Congress in June 1930. Yet, very little of this data was published or available in time for the event. One scholar has speculated that, had the materials been delivered on time, then this Congress might have served as a launching pad for a more centralized and vigorous programme of commune development, much as it did for the shock-brigade initiative.[13] This seems unlikely. There were still many aspects of the urban communes that would never have suited the centralizing ambitions of Stalin and the party leadership in the years to come. And, from the party's perspective, other issues were starting to take precedence. But, as ever, History is full of chance.

COMMUN-IS, COMMUN-ISN'T

When looking at the sequence of events that led to the collapse of the urban commune phenomenon, it is worth remembering that these groups could be volatile. The observant reader will have noticed that the urban communes were always suscepti-ble to bust-ups and walkouts. As one *Komsomol'skaia pravda* (*Komsomol Truth*) article warned in 1925, these groups could 'fall apart as quickly as they are created'. The issue of fund contribution, it was noted, was the most likely reason for 'bicker-ing in the commune'.[14] This did not change after 1929. If anything, the greater publicity they now enjoyed meant that this aspect of commune life became more acute and attracted more attention. Stories of bad communes were circulating with greater frequency, too. Some stories mocked collective groups for descending into 'little more than warm company', devoid of any sense of political mission. At the 'All-Union' meeting of communards, in early 1930, one young woman warned those attending that bad internal arrangements caused her fellow communards to

---

[11] *Politicheskii i trudovoi pod"em rabochego klassa SSSR, 1928–1929 gg: Sbornik dokumentov* (Moscow, 1956), 360.

[12] N. Krupskaya, *O Bytovykh voprosakh* (Moscow, 1930), esp. 33–6.

[13] John Russell, 'The Role of Socialist Competition in Establishing Labour Discipline in the Soviet Working Class, 1928–1934' (unpublished PhD dissertation, University of Birmingham, 1987), 251–2. Also note John Russell, 'The Demise of the Shock-Worker Brigades in Soviet Industry, 1931–1936', in Stephen White (ed.), *New Directions in Soviet History* (Cambridge: Cambridge University Press, 1990), 141–59.

[14] K. Shilov and A. Stratonitskii, 'Zhizn' molodezhi. O komsomol'skikh kommunakh', *Komsomol'skaia pravda*, 9 September 1925, 6.

lose all sense of comradeliness. 'I was left alone crying in bed, with nobody to care for me', she explained.[15] This was hardly in the spirit of collectivism.

One commune group, founded in May 1930, came to register similar concerns. Engaged in intensive working practices at the Elektrozavod factory for most of the day, this eight-person alliance was reduced to a state of 'chronic half-sleep', which did nothing for their comradely sensibilities.[16] In close proximity all day, every day, at home and at work, arguments and resentment started to abound. At points, the communards noted in their diary, they went through the day without saying 'good morning' or 'hello' to one another. The animosity felt towards certain individuals was reflected in their mutual character descriptions. One Shura Kogodova, for instance, was described as 'sharp-nosed, thin, with a Socratic forehead'. Tania Molchanova, likewise, was disparagingly referred to as a 'chubby, curly-toed ... lazy' girl, with 'plump white hands and short fingers' that apparently did little to aid the infuriatingly slow pace at which she worked.[17] The commune, its members agreed, did not always bring out the best in them. Subsequently, in early 1931, they decided to disband. They continued to work in brigade teams in the same factory, but they sought to avoid what was seen as the intensity of the commune.[18] Such occurrences were now being discussed among both communards and those less enamoured with these young activists and their collective approach to life.

In some cases, the urban communes were also seen as intrinsically antagonistic. They unsettled things. In 1929, naturally sceptical of youthful activists, the head of the Red Banner plant's 'Norm-Setting Bureau' (*Tarifno-normirovochnoe biuro*; acronym TNB) was particularly frustrated by the fact that the new production communes were playing havoc with his labour recordings. These internal factory departments were put in charge of monitoring performance and accounts. Like a true bureaucrat, the head of this particular bureau even accused these groups of being 'selfish' for failing to follow proper accounting standards. However, by 1930, perhaps under pressure from the Komsomol cell, his stance mellowed somewhat. He even professed admiration for the enthusiasm of these groups, while presumably still doing his level best to get them to adhere to proper accounting procedures.[19]

In the same vein, one commune noted that the sight of women in the factory proved too much for some of their fellow workers. 'They will hold us back', 'the whole factory will stop', were the common refrains.[20] Women did not always feature as prominently in the new wave of production communes as they had in some earlier *byt* communes. Heavy industry, notably the metallurgical sector, was com-

[15] Bernshtein, 'Kommuna—ne mechta', 34.
[16] E. Mikulina, 'Budni kommuny (iz zapisnoi knizhki brigadira)', *Molodaia gvardia*, no. 15–16 (1931), 76.
[17] Mikulina, 'Budni kommuny (iz zapisnoi knizhki brigadira)', 77–8.
[18] Mikulina, 'Budni kommuny (iz zapisnoi knizhki brigadira)', 83–4.
[19] Iu. Ber, *Kommuna segodnia. Opyt proizvodstvennykh i bytovykh kommun molodezhi* (Moscow, 1930), 49–50.
[20] V. Saparin, '"Bab'ia" kommuna', *Molodaia gvardiia*, no. 24 (1930), 126.

posed of predominantly male workers and gave rise to a number of predominantly male communes at this time. But, even here, the commune remained one of the more likely spaces for women workers to be seen. For some, this only served to confirm the rabble-rousing reputation of these groups.

As they made their presence known in the factory, urging older workers to follow new practices and challenging what they saw as traditional habits, the urban communes and communards sometimes encountered shouts of 'We do not need your commune!' and 'To hell with your commune!'.[21] When things went wrong, sceptical workers were all too ready to jump on the communes. Some decried double standards when they saw self-proclaimed communards and advocates of the 'new way of life' (*novyi byt*) revelling amidst 'booze', 'debauchery', and 'girls'.[22] Holding these groups in contempt, others were quick to highlight cases of over-zealous behaviour, complaining to line-managers when the communards tried to dictate on matters that did not concern them or on factory jobs where they had little or no experience.[23] One of the main complaints, however, related to pay and job security. As the First Five-Year Plan progressed, some workers were worried that they would be crowded out. As incremental pay increased, and as the communes sought to organize their own collective contracts, there was also a perception that these activists were better off and that they were self-seeking. One group of unhappy workers expressed their disgruntlement through creative word play and derogatory workplace rhyming slang:

Кому-на, кому-не, кому дуля—кому две . . .
Komu-na, komu-ne, komu dulia—komu dve . . .[24]

Splitting the Russian word '*kommuna*' (commune) into '*komu*' (meaning 'to whom', 'to someone') and '*na*' (meaning, 'here, take this'), and then replacing '*na*' with '*ne*' (nothing), this phrase translates as something like: 'To some—it's here you go, to others—nothing at all, to some a big up yours, while others get two [of everything] . . .'. More accurately, '*dulia*' refers to the derogatory Slavic '*fig*' gesture: a clenched fist with the thumb sticking through the index and middle fingers. This obscenity was being used, in this case, to drive home the extreme displeasure of these workers when faced with the communes at work. They were rejecting the notion that the communards were working for the 'common good'. If this was the 'common good', they were saying, it was not a version that they recognized, nor did it seem to include all workers. Similarly, some expressed disgruntlement at what they saw as the broader inequalities and pitfalls of the Soviet system with another *kommuna*-based pun: '*komu-na, komu-net*', which might be read as 'for some it's commun-is, for others it's commun-isn't' or 'the commun-haves, the commun-haven'ts'.[25]

---

[21] E. Mikulina, 'Kommuna sliudianits', *Molodaia gvardiia*, no. 8 (1931), 68.

[22] Ber, *Kommuna segodnia*, 70.

[23] A. Iuzhnyi, 'Proizvodstvennye kommuny, kak opyt sotssorevnovaniia', *Partiinoe stroitel'stvo*, no. 8 (1931), 11.

[24] Ber, *Kommuna segodnia*, 70.

[25] *Tsentral'nyi derzhavnyi arkhiv hromads'kykh ob'iednan' Ukrainy* (hereafter, TsDAHOU), f. 1, op. 20, d. 3198, l. 8 (Report bulletin on anonymous letters, as collected by the State Political Directorate, GPU,

The critics of the urban communes would raise all of these existing and developing concerns and animosities. Increasingly, from 1929 onwards, publications such as *Partiinoe stroitel'stvo* (*Party Construction*), which closely followed the story of Soviet industrial modernization, started to run a mix of pro- and anti-commune opinion pieces on the production communes.[26] Other publications, too, started to pick up on cases of experienced workers denouncing communard 'bullies' in factory newspapers and on the factory bulletin boards.[27] Some observers argued that the Komsomol needed to 'temper' these activists.[28] But, despite entrenched opposition in some quarters, a clear consensus had yet to develop.

COMMUN-HAVES, COMMUN-HAVEN'TS

As commune numbers started to rise, *Komsomol'skaia pravda* saw fit to share the reservations of some of its readers. A letter written to the editors by a certain N. Klavdiia, and subsequently published in the autumn of 1929, expressed grave concern and doubt over the feasibility of the urban commune trend that was taking root in Soviet industry. Entitled 'Harmful Dreams', Klavdiia's letter noted that she had recently been part of a protracted, three-day Komsomol cell discussion about the production communes and the organization's stance on these formations. She was aware that they were not alone in this endeavour. In the universities, as in the factories, she had heard, 'they are doing the same thing, discussing [the communes] in their bureaus and cells' (see Fig. 5.1). 'But', warned Klavdiia, with more than a hint of bitterness and annoyance, 'I believe they aren't worth this, these guys are a waste of time.' 'There is no way that they will advance equality', she continued, 'the stronger characters get more … and lead things.' Klavdiia seemed to draw on the presumption that many communards were better off or self-seeking. She claimed that it was just too soon for such formations. '[W]e are not ready for the commune either culturally or economically', she insisted. At the present moment, she explained, the communards were only serving to antagonize other workers and confuse factory accounts. Instead, she believed, all the energy of the Komsomol and its membership should be channelled into facilitating the infrastructure needed to fulfil the statist visions of the party. Klavdiia could see the point of collective canteens (*stolovye*) and orphanages (*detdoma*) run on collective principles, but not these personal and provocative associations.[29]

Aggrieved at Klavdiia's position, supporters of the commune noted defensively that while it was possible to find the odd 'shining egoist' (*iarkii egoist*) among these groups, they were, on the whole, made up of committed, self-sacrificing individuals.

between January and March 1930). I would like to thank Jonathan Waterlow for drawing my attention to this source.
    [26] For example, see Iuzhnyi, 'Proizvodstvennye kommuny, kak opyt sotssorevnovaniia', 9–11; Samuelii, 'Rabotu proizvodstvennykh kommun i kollektivov—na novye rel'sy', 12–18.
    [27] Turov, 'V tsekhakh giganta', 66.   [28] Turov, 'V tsekhakh giganta', 66.
    [29] N. Klavdiia, 'Vrednye mechty', *Komsomol'skaia pravda*, 12 October 1929, 4. Also reproduced with additional commentary in Ber, *Kommuna segodnia*, 64–6.

Fig. 5.1. A cartoon mocking the chaos caused by the daily exercise regime of the student commune, ZhBK

Source: 'V univerbarake', *Kranoe studenchestvo*, no. 2–3 (1930), 25.

If there was a problem with the communes Klavdiia encountered, it was suggested, then she and the paper really should have printed advice for them to follow.[30] As it was, to those inclined to advocate for commune association, the logic of her letter was flawed. '[T]he main thought of the letter', it was surmised with a strong sense of irony, 'is ... fulfil the Five-Year Plan, but please don't interfere with my cosy, little room or with my muslin curtains, as it is warm here and you can easily dream of anything, even socialism'—the insinuation being that, for all their faults, at least the communards were 'doers', living and building socialism here and now.[31]

All the same, the urban communes and communards continued to face calls for them to answer their critics and prove their value. Writing in early 1930, one observer, L. Tandit, commented that the urban communes offered a way to 'lift the working class' and push forward industrial growth. In many cases, Tandit said, these groups acted like the 'new shoots' that Lenin had predicted. They already functioned as the 'highest form of collective labour and socialist competition', while their voluntary charters (*ustavy*), he proclaimed, were a testament to the

---

[30] Ber, *Kommuna segodnia*, 65.   [31] Ber, *Kommuna segodnia*, 66.

revolutionary 'creativity and ... commitment' of these groups.[32] But, he cautioned, they also encouraged haste and some unwelcome developments. In some cases, it seemed, the promotion of the production commune led to a certain amount of confusion and disorder. Where a number of commune groups were formed in quick succession, Tandit noted, work often suffered from a 'lack of direction'. In certain factories, this was made worse, he continued, when management sponsored or joined the communes. This led to what Tandit referred to as the danger of 'false paths' (*lozhnye puti*) and 'pseudo-communes' (*lzhekommuny*). To avoid these pitfalls, Tandit recommended two things. Firstly, he said, it was incumbent upon all commune activists to keep the party mission in mind and work towards state imperatives. Secondly, he insisted that local party leaders, unions, and even the press, all needed to offer care and support to the communes, rather than trying to incorporate them in management structures or encouraging activists to force them on new workers.[33]

Tandit's comments were, in part, inspired, or at least informed, by Stalin's 'Dizzy with Success' article from 2 March 1930, which blamed local officials for running too far ahead and antagonizing peasants by implementing collective farming too forcefully in the countryside.[34] Picking up on the idea that some local officials had 'lost all sense of proportion', Tandit stressed the need to allow the urban communes to grow voluntarily. He thought new workers, in particular, should not be pushed or bullied into joining these groups.[35] Similar murmurings came out of those factories where entire sectors were being declared 'communes' without any real thought as to the practicalities.[36] Although aimed at proceedings in the countryside, the idea of revolutionary excess still resonated with observers of Soviet industrial activism. In the coming months, the Komsomol leadership, still interested in the potential of the urban communes and communards, warned that in some places local management were in danger of pushing this phenomenon too far or expecting too much from it.[37]

Such concerns and criticism did not go unnoticed among those that had formed the urban communes. Many were at pains to emphasize the difference between themselves and problematic examples of labour activism. Many were also keen to highlight just how well versed they were in recent revolutionary developments, as well as the needs of party and state. In some cases, predictably, local management also started to swing things in the other direction, now putting more pressure on activists and urban communards to conform to set factory procedures. The result was that by the time bodies such as *Gosplan* had completed their commissioned studies into the urban communes, a number of new developments and a change of behaviour were discernible among these groups. Communards had become far

---

[32] Tandit, 'Proizvodstvennye kommuny', 44–5.
[33] Tandit, 'Proizvodstvennye kommuny', 47–8.
[34] I. V. Stalin, *Sochineniia,* vol. 12 (Moscow, 1949), 191–9.
[35] Tandit, 'Proizvodstvennye kommuny', 47.
[36] *Industrializatsiia SSSR, 1929–1932gg.: dokumenty i materialy* (Moscow, 1970), 517.
[37] *Rossiiskii gosudarstvennyi arkhiv sotsial'no-politicheskii istorii* (hereafter, RGASPI), f. M.1, op. 4, d. 45, ll. 36–7 (Protocol: 'Restructuring the way of life', 15 July 1930).

more concerned with things such as worker qualifications and the effect of their wage-levelling practices on factory management.[38] Indeed, responding to the issues raised in Klavdiia's letter directly, as well as broader concerns flagged up in the press, some of the communards in attendance at the 'All-Union' meeting in early 1930 had already started to equate accusations of 'utopianism' with ignorance of wider factory practices.[39] They were keen to disprove those who had said that 'life in a commune was life in a bubble', and they vowed to show that they could function as part of a productive whole.[40]

So, by the start of 1931, *Gosplan* investigations into collective working patterns in European Russia would already distinguish between four main organizational approaches among the out-and-out production communes: firstly, a collective of workers with the same qualification level, sharing wages equally; secondly, a collective of workers of a similar qualification level, sharing wages equally; thirdly, a collective of workers with different qualifications, sharing or distributing their wages through a tariff system; and fourthly, a collective of workers with different qualifications, sharing part of their earnings among the group. Of the thousands surveyed, a majority of communes, 78.8 per cent, were of the first two types, with most participants sharing the same or similar qualification levels. A mere 13.8 per cent and 6.3 per cent of participants fell within categories three and four respectively.[41] In part, these figures reflect the fact that many communards worked and trained together, helping one another to advance their worker qualifications (*razriady*). But they also show that many of these groups had moved to prove their critics wrong on the issue of wage levelling and the potential adverse effects that such practices might have on factory management. Many were keen to challenge what was referred to as this 'mistaken public perception' of commune organization. By taking account of worker qualifications, they hoped to show that their actions were not having an adverse effect on factory accounting and that they were not attempting to arbitrarily enforce collectivism on all workers without consideration of wider forces. This in itself was portrayed by some communards and commune advocates as a sign of their commitment to the 'rational' development of industry.[42]

In the midst of a rapid expansion in their number, and experiencing a greater level of interest from a range of sources, the urban communes clearly felt pressure to fit in with the latest industrial demands. The urban commune trend was, as ever, evolving. Young communards, working out of Elektrozavod and many other sites, were now more concerned than ever to show that they had the well-being of ordinary workers, factory structures, and the broader interests of Soviet industry in mind as they sought to pursue their collective visions.[43] In addition, with an increase in the number of rural migrants, and questions being raised over the

---

[38] Samuelii, 'Rabotu proizvodstvennykh kommun i kollektivov—na novye rel'sy', 17.
[39] Bernshtein, 'Kommuna—ne mechta', 30–1, 35.
[40] Bernshtein, 'Kommuna—ne mechta', 36.
[41] Samuelii, 'Rabotu proizvodstvennykh kommun i kollektivov—na novye rel'sy', 17.
[42] Samuelii, 'Rabotu proizvodstvennykh kommun i kollektivov—na novye rel'sy', 17.
[43] See A. Kliushin, 'Proizvodstvennye kommuny kak opyt kollektivnogo truda', *Partiinoe stroitel'stvo*, no. 11 (1931), 23–5.

importance of skill levels, many commune activists readily accepted that the state needed to maintain order. Indeed, in some quarters, over the course of 1930–31, it was not seen as contradictory to advocate collectivism and shared resources among communards, while also supporting the notion of piece-rate payment. This, it was argued, offered a fair means of incentivizing skill acquisition and preventing new workers from hopping from one job to another. The fear was that an influx of unskilled labour might see the unqualified pursuit of equalization turn into nothing more than a mass descent towards the lowest common denominator, rather than a positive, collective advance towards the next stage of History—the higher stage of socialism.[44]

COMMUNARD MOLODTSOV

These pressures were present in the minds of most communards by 1930–31. But the urban commune remained appealing to many young activists—those joining the Komsomol and the aspiring party-membership types—because it continued to offer them a readily accessible way of contributing to, and feeling part of, the revolution. In 1930, as the diary of Vladimir Molodtsov reveals, the urban communards retained their reputation as leaders in the struggle for the 'decor of life', and the commune continued to be spoken about in terms of the 'highest form' of labour organization.[45] Molodtsov, a young, aspiring activist, would himself seek to join their ranks. At just eighteen years old, Molodtsov decided to up sticks, planning to move to the now-famous construction site at Magnitogorsk. But upon reading an article in *Komsomol'skaia pravda* appealing for workers to help excavate the Mosbassa coal mines in the Tulga region, to the south of Moscow, Molodtsov immediately changed his plans and went where he thought his revolutionary energies were most needed. Finding himself in the mining town of Bobrik-Donskoi in the fall of 1930, Molodtsov noted the wet, black earth of the region and how it made everything seem dirty. He also recorded how hard he had found his first few shifts in the mine. After just four trips underground, he was exhausted and ached all over. But he was determined not to lose heart. He knew things would get better. This was his right of passage into the world of proletarian work.[46]

Here he was, in unfamiliar surroundings, apprehensive and tired, but fuelled by a sense of revolutionary mission. After a couple of weeks, as things started to settle a little, Molodtsov wrote in his diary that everyday life was 'so-so'—not great, but manageable. Sometimes the mud got dragged into the living quarters, he complained. And the electricity supply was intermittent, meaning that they never knew if there would be light when they got home in the evening. At the same time, he turned his mind to improving life and dreamed of advancing the revolutionary

---

[44] Kliushin, 'Proizvodstvennye kommuny kak opyt kollektivnogo truda', 23–5.
[45] V. A. Molodtsov, 'On byl shakhter, prostoi rabochii . . .', in M. Kataeva (ed.), *Dnevniki i pis'ma Komsomoltsev* (Moscow: Molodaia gvardiia, 1983), 49–68, quotations at 58, 62.
[46] Molodtsov, 'On byl shakhter, prostoi rabochii . . .', 49–51.

cause in Bobrik-Donskoi. He arranged to attend his first Komsomol-cell meeting, previously lacking the energy after a day in the pit. He also spoke to his friend Misha about pooling their money together and, thus, began to contemplate commune life.[47]

Indeed, upon attending his first cell meeting at the end of October, Molodtsov learned that there was already a 'production-*byt* commune' (*proizvodstvenno-bytovaia kommuna*) in existence in Bobrik-Donskoi. It was composed of Komsomol members, and membership was overseen by the Komsomol cell bureau that was attached to mine number seven. He and Misha immediately applied for entry. Taking stock of recent developments, it seemed that the policy of the Komsomol bureau was to pay close attention to the way the commune operated, but to avoid forcing commune life on the 'wrong' people. They tried to prevent oversubscription to the commune; and to ensure all members were similarly qualified. As a result, Molodtsov and Misha were in for a wait. In the meantime, they continued to turn up to cell meetings, and they tried to make a good impression wherever possible.[48]

A matter of some distraction arose on 5 November, when Molodtsov, expecting a pay packet of thirty roubles, received just nine. He had put in six shifts over the last few days and had been hoping to spend the money on a number of posters and pictures of the party leaders. This was not to be. And Molodtsov was not the only one to lose out. But little did he know that the issue was to become a bone of contention within Komsomol circles, especially in the cell at mine number seven.[49] So, when Molodtsov decided to lead the charge for remuneration, while still volunteering for extra shifts in honour of the anniversary of the 'Great Revolution' (7 November by the new calendar), he clearly impressed sections of the local Komsomol hierarchy. Indeed, by 17 November the cell bureau at mine number seven had dissolved and reformed. Recent events had persuaded the cell that their old head was unfit to lead. Then, amid the shake-up, on 23 November Molodtsov was given full Komsomol membership and elected to the bureau. Misha was allocated candidate status. And, crucially, both were given the seal of approval and admitted into the commune. The new cell leader gave them glowing reports, and they entered the commune with a reputation—the latest bright young things in Bobrik-Donskoi.[50]

Once inside the commune, as Molodtsov noted on 24 November, he and Misha immediately found themselves embroiled in a somewhat lively discussion on the issue of swearing and foul language. Existing members Zaitstev and Barkov, who opposed a collective ban on swearing, were in the minority, but insisted on teasing the rest of the group by putting forth examples of the language that was to be banned. Over the next few days, discipline, absenteeism, working habits, and class all came up for discussion.[51] Language and labour would sometimes be discussed

[47] Molodtsov, 'On byl shakhter, prostoi rabochii . . .', 51–2.
[48] Molodtsov, 'On byl shakhter, prostoi rabochii . . .', 52.
[49] Molodtsov, 'On byl shakhter, prostoi rabochii . . .', 54–5.
[50] Molodtsov, 'On byl shakhter, prostoi rabochii . . .', 56.
[51] Molodtsov, 'On byl shakhter, prostoi rabochii . . .', 57.

in the same breath. The communards were judging new workers on these issues, passing comment while on their breaks at work, or during evening meals back in the barracks. Molodtsov quickly learned that the commune was as concerned with internal, domestic best practice as it was with being seen as a bastion of good labour. Clearly, even now, in late 1930, with Stalin's First Five-Year Plan in full swing, the cultural revolution (*kul'turnaia revoliutsiia*) remained a key component of commune life. The only difference was that, since 1928, a more prominent anti-specialist, class-driven, productivity-obsessed workers' assault was added to the rubric of cultural revolution. The behaviour of an individual at work was, therefore, discussed alongside their hygiene, political consciousness, and commitment to cultural enlightenment—all of which was understood to make up their general cultural standing. Personal habits and working habits were now seen as part of the same, intertwined cultural goal: the making of a revolutionary environment and the making of revolutionary identity.[52]

Molodtsov enjoyed the camaraderie of the commune, discussing the day while reclining in bed each night, sharing in each other's success and failure, and walking into the mine canteen together 'like a happy family'. He also enjoyed the group competition, as they each vied to see who could dig the most coal.[53] As it had for many others, then, the commune offered Molodtsov a lifestyle. This did not mean that life was without its hardships. In the weeks and months to come, Molodtsov wrote frequently about missing family and friends back in Moscow. This feeling was especially acute upon receiving a parcel from his mother in mid-December; she had sent him some homemade mittens for the harsh winter that was setting in. But Molodtsov seemed to view such moments as a test of his revolutionary character. This was another adversary to contemplate and overcome. He wrote about his 'ideology' and 'psychology' pulling in different directions on the issue of home. With great determination, he challenged himself to look past homesickness, doubt, and the inevitable bad day. He began instead to ask about advancing his qualifications; his aim was to prove and improve himself as a revolutionary.[54]

Be it his internal self-development, his labour productivity, or the physical realities around him, Molodtsov sought constant progression in all areas. Together with his fellow communards, he took pride in fixing up their barrack accommodation, improving the 'decor of life' bit by bit, implementing a modern sanitary routine, and even looking ahead to establishing their own collective canteen. When several women applied to join the commune at the start of 1931, Molodtsov read it as yet another sign of the group's gradual advance. He relished the fact that these women brought with them the 'new way of life' (*novyi byt*), including organized trips to the cinema.[55] They were improving the cultural infrastructure of the commune. In the same vein, he liked to think that he was improving as a miner, measuring himself against others not just in terms of productivity, but in 'productive

---

[52] Cf. Michael David-Fox, *Crossing Borders: Modernity, Ideology, and Culture in Russia and the Soviet Union* (Pittsburgh, PA: University of Pittsburgh Press, 2015), ch. 4, esp. 125–8.
[53] Molodtsov, 'On byl shakhter, prostoi rabochii . . .', 58–9.
[54] Molodtsov, 'On byl shakhter, prostoi rabochii . . .', 60.
[55] Molodtsov, 'On byl shakhter, prostoi rabochii . . .', 64–5.

enthusiasm'. When elected to treasurer of the commune around this time, he also liked to think he was improving as a communard—as an exemplar. Just to make sure, he even looked to sign up to cultural enlightenment missions in the village and to confront the kulaks they had all read so much about. To Molodtsov's mind, you could not be classified as either a 'shock worker' (*udarnik*) or a 'communard' (*kommunar*) through hard work alone; you had to show that you had 'grown ideologically'.[56]

Like many communards, Molodtsov described his work, time, life, and self in terms of linear development, ever advancing and progressing. He subscribed to a teleological understanding of the world in which the enlightening processes of cultural revolution and collective association were seen, like the rockets of Soviet science fiction, as the vehicles to launch humanity to new heights—to escape the past in search of the future.[57] Such an outlook certainly made the hard days more bearable for young activists like Molodtsov. It helped the self-proclaimed communards of Bobrik-Donskoi to see past the mud, the dirt, and the cold, as well as the occasional falling out or poor working day. And it clearly offered hope and purpose, too. For these young enthusiasts, the commune offered a means of participation and a sense of fulfilment. It gave them the room to develop their revolutionary understanding.

In this sense, the urban commune was not out of keeping with contemporary developments, and the communards certainly were not inherently un-Stalinist in their outlook. Indeed, for one thing, their understanding of cultural revolution was not, as some might assume, wholly divorced from the drive for 'culturedness' (*kul'turnost'*) that would come to form an important aspect of Stalinism—albeit with a more conservative edge and with Soviet consumerism added into the equation.[58] These communards, as many activists would continue to do, maintained that socialism was attainable via a journey of revolutionary enlightenment, ideological commitment, and self-reflection. 'This was how to live well', exclaimed Molodtsov, 'fighting and struggling to live!'[59] More to the point, Molodtsov's experience shows that the idea of the urban commune, despite the added attention of recent years, could still serve to offer some young activists the space they needed to form their revolutionary characters. While there were growing reports of compromised, lost, or 'forced' communes, Molodtsov tells us that his collective alliance maintained a degree of autonomy within the pit's revolutionary community, putting most practical issues to the collective vote and helping each other on a day-to-day basis. They remained respectful of management hierarchies—perhaps reflecting recent concerns—but enjoyed the chance to undertake daily initiatives. Here, if not to all observers elsewhere, the commune and the objectives of the Great Break were considered largely coterminous. As Molodtsov continued to develop his revolutionary ambition, becoming a party candidate in April 1931, his ultimate

---

[56] Molodtsov, 'On byl shakhter, prostoi rabochii . . .', 61–3.
[57] For more on revolutionary perceptions of time and progress in the early Soviet state, see Michael G. Smith, *Rockets and Revolution: A Cultural History of Early Spaceflight* (Lincoln, NE: University of Nebraska Press, 2014), intro, esp. 6–7.
[58] Cf. David-Fox, *Crossing Borders*, 125–8.
[59] Molodtsov, 'On byl shakhter, prostoi rabochii . . .', 58.

decision to leave the commune was not to be based on ideological grounds. Instead, he would go in pursuit of new opportunities and the prospect of 'growing ideologically' elsewhere in the Mosbassa system.[60] In Molodtsov's case at least, the prospects of advancement within party-state structures rendered the urban commune a joyous but temporary construct.

AN UNCERTAIN END

At the start of 1931, then, it was not obvious that the urban communes were going to become something of the past. They were still adapting to revolutionary circumstances. Pointing to these formations, Iurii Larin had recently declared that collectivization in the countryside was proving less successful than collectivization in the city. An influential party man and leading figure within *Gosplan*, Larin praised those who had taken to the urban communes voluntarily. They were the first to engage in 'the collectivization of *byt*' and had shown the rest of the Soviet Union that their material base was 'sufficient to strive towards these goals', he insisted. The 'collectivization of *byt*', Larin reiterated, was not beyond Soviet means.[61] Others were praising the urban communes and communards for reducing the gap between daily working life and cultural revolution. Comparing everyday realities and socialist culture to the expanding blades of the 'scissors crisis'—the term given to the widening gap between industrial and agricultural prices at the start of the 1920s—one commentator portrayed 'the collectivization of *byt*' as a vital component of the present revolutionary moment. In this scenario, the urban communes and communards were major players in the battle to bring daily matters and cultural enlightenment closer together. When it came to health, 'prevention is better than cure' was the communard motto, it was heavy-handedly explained. The communards, it was asserted, had embraced a vision of socialism that was modern, fair, rational, and efficient. They were seen to be setting a good example to all workers and had apparently shown great 'cultural hunger' (*kul'turnyi golod*).[62]

Similarly, in a report on urban reconstruction delivered to the Central Committee in June 1931, Party Secretary Lazar' Kaganovich, one of Stalin's closest associates, declared that the state still had a duty to 'give every possible encouragement to urban communes where they arise voluntarily'—again echoing Lenin's call to support 'new shoots'. Kaganovich even insisted that an excessively 'bureaucratic attitude toward them must not be tolerated' and local officials had no right to 'hinder their formation'. Recounting the example of one commune group in Moscow, Kaganovich explained how these activists frequently became constructive members of the Komsomol and the party, while, he added, also distinguishing

---

[60] Molodtsov, 'On byl shakhter, prostoi rabochii . . .', 67–8.
[61] Iu. Larin, 'Kollektivizatsiia byta v sushchestvuiushchikh gorodakh', *Revoliutsiia i kul'tura*, no. 7 (1930), 54–62, quotation at 54. Larin also made a point about the lack of force used in these urban communes and urged his peers to learn from the mistakes they had made in the countryside.
[62] I. Oleinikov, 'Kul'tura i byt kommuny "Plamia Revoliutsii"', *Revoliutsiia i kul'tura*, no. 4, (1930), 64–5.

themselves among the shock workers of Soviet industry.[63] The Party Secretary freely criticized what he considered the 'leftist' excesses of Leonid Sabsovich, the architect who proposed the construction of numerous state-built phalanxes across all Soviet cities, each supposedly designed to house two to three thousand persons in perfect harmony. He also ridiculed the author of *Sotsgorod* (1930), Nikolai Miliutin, who had advocated for a number of similarly grand communal city projects. Themselves products of the growing craze for collectivism at this time, figures such as Sabsovich and Miliutin were shown to have gone too far. They sought to extend from constructivist architectural theory the idea of the 'social condenser'— the notion that all Soviet buildings could act to influence social behaviour and forge new communities through the design of new, socially equitable spaces.[64] Kaganovich accused these architectural visionaries of revelling in 'absurd and impossible propositions'. He said they were 'pseudo-theoreticians, ... distorting Marx, Engels and Lenin'.[65] But, having encountered a number of urban communes, including groups based out of the Hammer and Sickle steel plant, the Automobile Society of Moscow (AMO) plant, and the Dinamo Electro-machine construction plant, Kaganovich did not view these formations as a distraction or as a source of alternative priorities.[66] He saw these urban communes as they wanted to be seen, as a possible appendage of the Komsomol and the party.

Kaganovich, in other words, was capable of supporting the collectivism of the urban communards, while dismissing the collective visions of Soviet planners and architects. He, like other observers, warned against the 'artificial implementation of the [urban] commune'. He did not want to see the development of 'pseudo-communes' enforced under the guise of party remit. Yet, he remained hopeful that the urban communes would help to implement socialism on the ground. His criticism of recent collective discourses was instead levelled at city planners and architectural visionaries that concerned themselves only with 'the wholesale abolition of the individual kitchen'. He deliberately invoked an image of banal triteness when referring to such figures. The socialization of life and society, he argued, was better achieved by those activists that spent their common funds refurbishing their own apartments and improving existing facilities. Maybe he was concerned with keeping activists onside at a time of great upheaval. But he convincingly advocated socialism 'not by phrases' and fantasy, 'but by living acts and deeds'.[67]

Yet this would not prove to be enough. Over the course of 1931, the urban communes and communards came under increased scrutiny and pressure, swept

---

[63] This report was subsequently published as L. M. Kaganovich, *Socialist Reconstruction of Moscow and other Cities in the USSR* (Moscow, 1931). For quotations, see 85–6.

[64] This approach was closely associated with the Organization of Contemporary Architects (OSA), and it was very much the driving force behind Moisei Ginzburg's famous Narkomfin building (constructed between 1928 and 1932).

[65] Kaganovich, *Socialist Reconstruction of Moscow and other Cities*, 86–8, 97.

[66] Kaganovich, *Socialist Reconstruction of Moscow and other Cities*, 86. Lazar' Kaganovich's encounters with the urban communes are confirmed in *Tsentral'nyi arkhiv goroda Moskvy* (hereafter, TsGA Moskvy; formerly TsAGM), f. 415, op. 16, d. 76, ll. 36–7 (ZiL factory, reflections of A. Bychkov on 'brigades, communes etc.', 1927–30).

[67] Kaganovich, *Socialist Reconstruction of Moscow and other Cities*, 26–7, 86–7.

up in a frenzy of management-focused policies designed to tackle the problem of organizing a new, seemingly unwieldy, mass workforce. The managerial turn—that is, the notion that Soviet industry needed to improve top-down management structures, standardize procedures, and limit labour fluidity—had been gaining traction within the political discourse for several months when Stalin delivered his famous 'New Conditions' speech on 23 June 1931. Labour turnover and absenteeism remained a problem, and impossibly high output targets, set at the end of 1930, had served to make matters worse by putting a tremendous strain on workers and factory systems. Stalin chose this moment, therefore, to call for 'new methods of management', specifically citing the need for a more organized system of labour recruitment, better control of wage structures, and a more orderly mechanism of response for dealing with poor workmanship or, put another way, cases where individual workers had shown a lack of 'personal responsibility' (*obezlichka*). This was a call for industrial accounting to be undertaken in a distinctly modern fashion. The stated goal was greater stability and efficiency.[68] However, the true context for all of this was a broader realization that the frenzied push for collectivization and mobilization had come at a cost. Agricultural production had plummeted and Soviet industry remained quite sporadic and unreliable. The party leadership needed to advocate a more modest and measured—certainly a more controlled—pathway to economic fulfilment.

While Stalin was not concerned with urban communes specifically, and while Kaganovich had, just days earlier, delivered a report praising certain aspects of the communard approach, the further move toward managerial solutions initiated by the 'New Conditions' speech would come to have a detrimental effect on this collectivist trend. Critics of the urban communes and communards certainly acquired a new stridency in 1931. They latched onto the issue of wage levelling. Indeed, in his speech, Stalin expressed concern that some 'leftist' managers had implemented wage scales that failed to reflect the difference between skilled and unskilled labour—a particular danger when Soviet industry was dealing with a rapid influx of peasant labour.[69] And this at a time of growing anti-kulak sentiment, resulting from reported cases of peasant protest and non-cooperation in the countryside. Critics were also cognizant that Stalin had also previously expressed concern about party-sponsored agricultural communes being promoted as the primary means of collective organization in some parts of the countryside. Agriculture should be run along utilitarian lines, and ruled with an iron fist, seemed to be the message; there was no time to promote collectivist/levelling practices or primitive socialism here. That represented a violation of 'the principle of voluntarism and accounting for local circumstances'.[70]

In many cases, established urban communards showed awareness of these issues. As we have seen, some commune groups were keen to show that they could fit in with factory structures. Communards at Elektrozavod insisted that the selective nature of their alliances meant that wage levelling was not a problem for the

---

[68] I. V. Stalin, *Sochineniia*, vol. 13 (Moscow, 1951), 53–82, esp. 78–82.
[69] Stalin, *Sochineniia*, vol. 13, 55–8.   [70] Stalin, *Sochineniia*, vol. 12, 191–9.

factory.[71] The Soviet press had also received letters from urban communards expressing concern about waves of new peasant workers and seasonal workers; those sending these letters were showing how attuned they were to the latest developments of Soviet industry.[72] But their detractors saw it differently. As contemporaries noted, critics of the urban communes could be absolute in their condemnation of wage-levelling tendencies and anyone associated with wage levelling, to the point that they were unwilling to consider the example that such groups set in regard to labour discipline, working habits, and class consciousness.[73] Reports of overzealous management trying to implement collective organization across the shop floor served only to persuade some to adopt a wholly negative view of the communes, collectives, and brigades. And, reinforcing these views, when approached, disgruntled co-workers were only too pleased to share their frustrations with the critics.[74] The idea of the urban commune was coming under attack; it was being weakened in the public eye.

Compounding negative perceptions, at the same time as the 'New Conditions' speech was being circulated in the press, *Pravda* published calls for a campaign against 'forced' or 'involuntary' urban communes and collectives. While such demands focused mainly on overzealous management and offending officials, the commune story was, nevertheless, starting to look a little more complicated than it had in previous years.[75] It was no longer such an easy sell, with activists starting to feel the need to justify their actions. Indeed, reports were coming to light that some managers and officials had threatened to lower pay, dole out less desirable jobs, sack people, and even remove Komsomol and party cards in an attempt to enforce their own collective formations.[76] Even as those responsible for these acts of over-zealousness were removed, and as involuntary communes were disbanded, suspicion remained. *Komsomol'skaia pravda* found itself going to print with articles by observers that wanted to criticize the newspaper for what was seen as its broadly positive take on the urban communes. In response to an article claiming that Komsomol members would benefit from time spent in an urban commune, for instance, one critic retorted that it was 'deeply wrong' for people to view these groups as if they were part of the 'class struggle in the form of ... anti-property mood'.[77] Before long, commune support started to come with a caveat: the urban communes and communards had 'produced many good workers and had encouraged many women into industry', but it was time for them to 'submit to factory management and official accounting', it was reiterated within the pages of *Partiinoe stroitel'stvo*.[78]

[71] Kliushin, 'Proizvodstvennye kommuny kak opyt kollektivnogo truda', 26.
[72] 'Staryi byt, novyi byt', *Krasnoe studenchestvo*, no. 4 (1930), 26–7; 'Podelites' opytom kollektivnoi zhizni', *Smena*, no. 19 (1930), 14.
[73] *Na novom etape: sotsialisticheskogo stroitel'stva: sbornik statei*, vol. 1 (Moscow, 1930), 182.
[74] Iuzhnii, 'Proizvodstvennye kommuny kak opyt sotsialisticheskogo', 11.
[75] *Pravda*, 21 July 1931, 1; referenced in Samuelii, 'Rabotu proizvodstvennykh kommun i kollektivov—na novye rel'sy', 14.
[76] Samuelii, 'Rabotu proizvodstvennykh kommun i kollektivov—na novye rel'sy', 13.
[77] V. Izmailov, 'Ostavit' individual'nii otbor lozung "sto protsentov kommunarskoi molodezhi v komsomol"—ne veren', *Komsomol'skaia pravda*, 4 January 1931, 3.
[78] 'O partiinoi i massovoi rabote v tsekhe i brigade', *Partiinoe stroitel'stvo*, no. 7 (1931), 64–6.

Among a cohort that traditionally liked to display their loyalty to the revolution and the party, this was an unsettling development. More than before, the urban commune now seemed open to accusations of deviation. Even one of the central staples of commune life, the 'common pot' (*obshchii kotel*), was developing negative connotations in the wake of Stalin's 'Dizzy with Success' article.[79] While the debate around wage levelling was often targeted at management and local functionaries of the party-state, confidence in the idea of urban commune itself was reduced. New communes were still being formed, but local cells and factory managers were sometimes uncertain how to manage them, or perhaps were simply too wary to try.[80] The energy and idealism that sustained the urban commune initiative, as well as its backers, had been well and truly checked.

NEW PRIORITIES

Simultaneously, and perhaps inevitably, the urban communes and communards found themselves being folded into the latest drive for one-man management and command-economy efficiencies. They got caught up in the grander visions of the party leadership, which was moving to unify working methods and professionalize industrial controls. There was no official call to incorporate the urban communes in these visions, but their weakened image certainly made it easier for local party representatives to enact blanket changes. In particular, the cost-accounting contract was introduced to formalize relations between shock workers and management. In effect, this led to brigade teams and other socialist competition workers being adopted into the lowest link of the managerial hierarchy.[81] As Kenneth M. Straus has shown, where shock work and socialist competition—and, in turn, the work of production communes—was based on a contract that required management to supply raw materials and workers to fulfil or exceed output targets, cost-accounting contracts were supposed to incorporate counter-planning and make the brigade team responsible for all the important economic indicators at shop-floor level. In many ways, this formalized the rationalization, labour-efficiency, anti-waste, and anti-absenteeism drive of the shock workers, as well as the work of urban communes and communards active in Soviet industry.[82] In this form, these leading workers and working groups were to be made accountable to shop-floor supervisors, and they were promised remuneration for their 'administrative responsibilities'.[83]

The first trial cost-accounting units (*khozraschety*) arose, with official approval, in January 1931. Working with management, they formally undertook to minimize

[79] See N. I. Pershin, *Kommunisticheskaia partiia—organizator osvoeniia tekhniki proizvodstva v traktornoi promyshlennosti v period stroitel'stva sotsializma* (Volgograd, 1974), 119.
[80] See G. L'vov, 'Partorganizatsiia Elektrozavoda v bor'be za khozraschet', *Partiinoe stroitel'stvo*, no. 14 (1931), 37.
[81] Lewis H. Siegelbaum, 'Production Collectives and Communes and the "Imperatives" of Soviet Industrialization, 1929–1931', *Slavic Review*, no. 1 (1986), 82.
[82] Straus, *Factory and Community in Stalin's Russia*, esp. 148–51.
[83] Siegelbaum, 'Production Collectives and Communes', 82.

the cost of production. Inspectors were duly selected and appraisals requested. An economist, L'vov, was, for example, put in place to monitor their implementation at the Hammer and Sickle (*Serp i molot*) plant in Moscow.[84] Early feedback gradually seemed to foster greater confidence and commitment. Thus, by the spring of 1931, there were reports of the first urban communes turning into *khozraschety*.[85] In some cases, communes seemed to convert willingly; in others, local management cajoled them or they just got caught up in the wider push to professionalize socialist competition. After Stalin's 'New Conditions' speech, there were certainly calls—usually directed at the shock workers more broadly, but some specifically targeting the urban communes—for groups to convert. Many of these came from local functionaries keen to promote the latest working imperatives. But they also came from those that wanted desperately to see the urban communards and their ilk submit to factory structures.[86]

By July, the Moscow Trade Union Council was also urging its district committees to encourage and aid the conversion of all brigades into cost-accounting contracts.[87] The unions, which had never known how to deal with the communes, displayed little sympathy for these formations now, either.[88] And as the year progressed, so it appeared that fewer and fewer cells wanted to promote or support the likes of the urban communards. Ideological imperatives were shifting, and belief in the commune had started to dissipate quickly. More and more urban communes converted or undertook cost-accounting roles. It appears that those commune groups that had come together at the behest of local representatives or management were among the first to convert. They, presumably, had less allegiance to the idea of the commune in the first place. The overall effect was to further emasculate the very idea of commune alliance. Then, on 11 September 1931, *Vesenkha* and the VTsSPS issued their joint resolution, demanding of 'administrative-technical personnel and trade union organizations maximal attention to, and careful preparation of, the conversion of brigades to cost accounting'.[89] With hindsight, this can be seen as the death knell of the urban commune. It was soon followed by a more officious drive to implement cost accounting and a more standardized wage scale. Reports of forced conversions undertaken by local management started to proliferate, even though this practice was nominally prohibited in the joint resolution.[90] The momentum of industrial change, and the new managerial approach then in favour with the

[84] Straus, *Factory and Community in Stalin's Russia*, 149.
[85] *Bor'ba klassov*, no. 3–4 (1931), 83; cited in Russell, 'The Role of Socialist Competition in Establishing Labour Discipline', 283. Also see *Rabotnitsa na sotsialisticheskoi stroiki* (Moscow, 1932), 67–75; A. L. Orishchenko, *Istoriografiia sotsialisticheskogo sorevnovaniia rabochego klassa SSSR* (Khar'kov, 1975), 60.
[86] See Samuelii, 'Rabotu proizvodstvennykh kommun i kollektivov—na novye rel'sy', 18; M. Eskin, *Osnovnye puti razvitiia sotsialisticheskikh form truda* (Leningrad, 1936), 79.
[87] *Trud*, 9 July 1931, 3; cited in Siegelbaum, 'Production Collectives and Communes', 81.
[88] See communard discussion in Bernshtein, 'Kommuna—ne mechta', 35–6. Some commune activists accused trade union representatives of acting 'completely aloof' towards them.
[89] 'Postanovlenie VSNKh SSSR i VTsSPS. O khozraschetnykh brigadakh', *Pravda*, 12 September 1931, 2.
[90] G. Shadek, 'O khozraschetnykh brigadakh', *Ratsionalizatsiia proizvodstva*, no. 8 (1933), 4–5; Siegelbaum, 'Production Collectives and Communes', 82.

leadership, had, in many ways, already overwhelmed the urban commune by the end of 1931. In some quarters, there was still a degree of confusion and indeterminacy when it came to adopting new management strategies. It was not always clear how the latest industrial imperatives should be applied to the urban communes and other established collective teams. There were examples of local management providing brigades and communes with the funds to purchase tools and undertake cost-accounting duties, while, at the same time, allowing them to elect their own leaders and retain much of their collective autonomy. As a result, some even began to wonder 'whether cost-accounting brigades will signify a return to *arteli* or ... a new form of labour organization'.[91] There were also reports of Komsomol members defending the record of the urban communes and warning against the blanket rejection of collectivist forms of pay, especially among consciously formed groups. And so, one survey of the Leningrad oblast, conducted at the beginning of 1932, suggested that there were still 14,400 workers engaged in some form of production commune or collective brigade.[92] Clearly, even in Stalin's Soviet Union, change was not instant.

The continued existence of these and other groups notwithstanding, the writing was on the wall for the urban communes. Moving away from the revivalist ideas and mass mobilization that had helped launch the First Five-Year Plan, the message from the party leadership now was unity, order, and standardization.[93] Individually determined and progressively structured piece rates, it was argued, would improve the quality of production and worker responsibility as a whole. The artisanal were to be replaced with the command structures of modern industry. In this environment, with the critics of the commune highlighting their every weakness, production communards, now the dominant face of the commune phenomenon, had to work harder to justify their existence to the local authorities and even to themselves. It was just a matter of time. Over the course of 1931–32, most commune activists would gradually come to embrace the new approach to industry or move on to other things within the ever more professionalized infrastructure of the Soviet party-state. Those that did not risked becoming redundant to the Komsomol, the party, and the revolution.

It is one of the ironies of the urban commune phenomenon that having got caught up in the 'spiraling cycle of local improvisation, central intervention, and All-Union bureaucratic warfare' of industrial mobilization at the end of the 1920s,[94] and having seen numbers rise dramatically thanks to the support of various local functionaries, come 1931–32, the commune had been laid open to the innovation of cost accounting. The rapid growth in numbers, a new embrace of Soviet industry and the discourse of 'socialist construction', greater interference

[91] *Trud*, 18 June 1931, 2; cited in Siegelbaum, 'Production Collectives and Communes', 83.
[92] *Trud i profdvizhenie v leningradskoi oblasti 1932g* (Leningrad, 1932), 63.
[93] Cf. David Priestland, *Stalinism and the Politics of Mobilization: Ideas, Power, and Terror in Inter-war Russia* (Oxford: Oxford University Press, 2007), ch. 4.
[94] Kurt S. Schultz, 'Building the "Soviet Detroit": The Construction of the Nizhnii-Novgorod Automobile Factory, 1927–1932', *Slavic Review*, no. 2 (1990), 200–12.

from official sources, as well as the inevitable criticisms that came with this, had all served to bring the urban commune to this end point. As well as a change in the working parameters set from the top, what we can see across 1931–32 is the curtailment of a trend—in this case, something originally informed, but not wholly controlled, by Soviet discourse and by youth's natural tendency to play around with the ideas of their age. And so it was that cost accounting finally secured the fate of the urban commune. Urban commune activists would move to pursue their revolutionary ambitions within newly professionalized structures. As one means of chasing socialism came to an end, another was just beginning—albeit in a form greatly routinized and compromised.

A RETURN VISIT

As Klaus Mehnert discovered when he went back to the Soviet Union at the end of 1932, things had changed irrevocably among the urban communards he knew. It had been over a year since he last communicated with one of his favoured groups, the young activists based at 6 Mokrinskii Lane, in Kitai-Gorod, Moscow. At the time, he had known them as a *byt* commune, partially formed from the remnants of student commune experimentation. And he had also witnessed their first forays into Soviet industry, as, like so many others, they sought to participate in 'socialist construction'. Tracing his way through the narrow streets of Kitai-Gorod upon his return, he was pleased to find the red-bricked tenement block that had housed these activists. As he entered the building's unlit hall, he bumped into one of the other residents. Mehnert inquired about the commune, only to be told that the group had 'disbanded', although, apparently, some of the participants still remained. Confused, Mehnert struggled by match-light up the staircase to the second floor. The apartment door ajar, he could hear familiar voices. They were still there! The smell of cabbage soup and the paraffin of a primus stove met him as he headed towards the apartment. Stepping through the door, he immediately noticed his old friend, Valodia (referred to, slightly more formally, as Vladimir before this trip), who was busily pinning information on the commune's noticeboard. Valodia's eyes turned to Mehnert, and there was a sudden cry of 'Kolia Germanski, so you haven't forgotten us!'[95]

With a bookcase full of Soviet journals, Lenin's works bound in brown, as well as prints of Lenin, Stalin, and the People's Commissar for Military and Navy Affairs Kliment Voroshilov mounted firmly to the wall, Mehnert's initial thoughts were that nothing had changed at all. The resident downstairs must have been a fool! Valodia and company certainly appeared no less dedicated to revolutionary life than before. In fact, Valodia was keen to press on his German friend that while some people had left, and new faces had taken their place, things were actually much 'improved'. 'You won't recognize the old ruins', he said. 'We've got the next-door flat too', continued Valodia. They were still looking to advance their surroundings

[95] Klaus Mehnert, *Youth in Soviet Russia*, trans. Michael Davidson (London: George Allen & Unwin, 1933), 249–51.

and strive for socialism, then. As he was summoned to tea, however, Mehnert soon learned that things were not quite as they once were.[96]

Those gathered told Mehnert that six months previously the commune had voted to abandon the rules and regulations of their charter (*ustav*). Not all members had agreed at the time. Alexei, a communard and a party member, had apparently 'voted against disbanding to the last'. But a majority eventually passed the motion. They elected to become an 'ordinary collective' for 'bed and board', each paying a flat rate of thirty-five roubles towards the rent. The uncompromising collectivism of the commune had been rejected. Mehnert was shocked and baffled by the news: 'How ever did you light upon that idea? You were such a topping commune! One of the best I know! [*sic*]'[97]

'D'you know, that was all wrong', interjected Valodia. 'Tell me—isn't it really a contradiction', he started to explain, 'when we in the Soviet Union are trying by every means, even with piece rates and premiums, to increase production, and at the same time are living in communes, where everyone has to chuck what he's earned by the hardest personal work into the common pot? [*sic*]' 'Of course, there was a mighty row at first', Mehnert was told, but circumstances had forced a rethink. Mehnert queried the mention of piecework and what this meant for the activists.[98] Vassia, who had been smoking a cigarette until this point, explained that piecework rates had been introduced in the factory a year earlier. What is more, Vassia continued, the 'Party maximum'—a 300-rouble limit on pay for party members, after which everything went back to the state—had been 'completely abolished' for workers. The resultant increase in take-home pay for communard Alexei, armed with his party card, caused unease among the others at first. At one point, he was bringing back 480 roubles a month for the general kitty—a lot more than everyone else. Broadly speaking, those present seemed to accept that the implementation of piecework rates was entirely necessary. 'Who d'you suppose was against piece-work rates and for levelling [*sic*]?', Vassia suddenly added with a hint of malice, '[t]he unqualified "black" [vis-à-vis benighted] workers, who had come from their village to the town a few weeks or a month before, thinking that here one could live wonderfully and in joy without work and without qualification'. '[They had] no notion of the machines and how to operate them', he scoffed.[99]

And there it was, one of the prime reasons for the demise of Mehnert's favoured commune: Vassia and the others had evidently grown wary of the influx of peasant workers in recent years. Perhaps they were too easily led down a path of Stalinist scapegoating. But, whatever the reason, resentment had certainly developed, and Vassia seemed to blame these newcomers for necessitating change. Apparently, they were unskilled and entered the factory 'with a crash', making collective life impossible.[100] Order needed to be restored. Vassia insisted that while the commune was a 'great and beautiful idea', to continue in that vein, at this time, was

[96] Mehnert, *Youth in Soviet Russia*, 250.
[97] Mehnert, *Youth in Soviet Russia*, 251.
[98] Mehnert, *Youth in Soviet Russia*, 251.
[99] Mehnert, *Youth in Soviet Russia*, 252–3.
[100] Mehnert, *Youth in Soviet Russia*, 254.

nothing short of 'a Utopia'.[101] That basic staple of commune life, the aspiration for total equality, had been eroded by what Vassia saw as the unconscious and dangerous masses. That age-old fear of the backwardness of the Russian peasants had reared its head once again. Piece rates were seen to offer a solution, but they also pushed aspects of commune life into the future.

Aggrieved, Vassia explained that 'you can't ask people to pump the last ounce out of themselves day and night, and bear the heaviest responsibilities' while all this was going on—at least not without some reward or means of distinguishing their activism and sacrifice. In one rather heated moment, Vassia even exclaimed that this would be 'the sum total of petit bourgeois, left-deviation, Trotsky-ist levelling mania'. Vassia had attended evening classes at a 'worker faculty' (*rabfak*); he had been a card-carrying member of the Komsomol since 1923, entering the ranks of the party in 1928; he had fought to increase production in the factories; in his own words, he had 'done nothing but grind'. He felt he had earned more. So now he welcomed some aspect of material incentive and allotted provision.[102] He and the others had certainly become more sensitive about grade scales. This new attitude also seemed to have developed, in part, due to the anti-kulak sentiment and suspicion that was being stoked through reports of peasant resistance.

Meeting up with his old friends at various points over the next few days—at work and at public events—Mehnert tried to learn more about their reaction to recent developments. Walking back from a parade with Valodia on his final evening, Mehnert spoke candidly, returning to the subject of piece rates. 'In all branches of daily life to-day, in all newspapers and pamphlets', he noted, 'I meet ... those words of Lenin's which call the differentiated distribution of goods the sharpest tool for increasing output.' 'I think it is very wise of you to throw what you describe as the levelling tendencies of recent years overboard', Mehnert said, invoking Vassia's previous argument. 'I know, too', he went on, 'that Marx himself regarded a period of pay according to output as necessary, before the last phase of Communism is reached with remuneration according to needs.' But, he added with some reservation, 'I ask myself, are you not, from your point of view, afraid of the differentiation'. He also hinted that there was an element of inconsistency in promoting voluntary activist work alongside new grade scales.[103] Valodia interrupted:

> It doesn't matter how much Marx and Lenin you read in Germany, you still don't get rid of the point of view which we can only describe as vulgar Marxism. After all we're not a welfare association, not the Salvation Army! Yes, we acknowledge the principle of output, we demand that he who produces more and consequently serves the entire community more, shall also share more in the total produce.... Our equality consists in this, that we have destroyed class and that each is judged according to his personal output, not according to inherited rank or banking account. That is at the moment the sole equality we want. What remains decisive is that fact that, for all the differentiation, even the man with the highest salary, even the man who wins ... in a lottery, can do

---

[101] Mehnert, *Youth in Soviet Russia*, 253.   [102] Mehnert, *Youth in Soviet Russia*, 252–3.
[103] Mehnert, *Youth in Soviet Russia*, 261–3.

nothing with this money ... The means of production are firmly in the hands of the State; no private person can acquire them; his money does not give him power over others.[104]

Sensing he had pressed his friend too far, Mehnert expressed sympathy and understanding with much that Valodia had said. But, still, he could not see why 'this state of differentiation' was needed or why the commune had to end. He questioned how it would lead to communism. 'Man, Kolya, but you're slow in the uptake!', blurted an exasperated Valodia. 'Don't you understand', he persisted, 'that by unfolding all productive energies we are coming, by way of principle of output, to such an immense increase in production that one day this state of shortage in everything, in which we are present, will be overcome, and in its place abundance will appear?' Valodia—ever the activist, still attuned to the Soviet press, an ideologue—had come to accept that the urban commune had run its course. In helping to abolish the latent apprenticeship system and the old specialists (*spetsy*) that lingered throughout NEP, Valodia even seemed to claim that the commune had been a success. For him, the commune was never an end in itself, never an islet or an idyll, but a means of fighting for a revolutionary cause. He was willing to believe that Soviet socialism was entering the next phase of its development, and he was adapting his life accordingly.

Upon reaching the outside of the apartment building, Mehnert and Valodia resumed pleasantries. They had argued as principled socialists. Mehnert was not entirely convinced by what he had heard, but he was still full of respect, love, and admiration for his young friend. He and Valodia said a fond goodbye. Valodia wished his German comrade a safe journey back to Berlin. But, before parting, Valodia added: 'Next year, if you come again, Kolya, we'll be a long way further forward. Then you'll understand all the better!'[105]

So, even the people that Mehnert associated most with commune activism had, it seemed, come to embrace the latest approach to socialist construction. There was a sense that these aspiring revolutionaries had outgrown the commune. Their youth and enthusiasm had coincided with the moment when activist initiative was most possible. But now the professionalized organs of the Komsomol and party offered the best means of revolutionary advancement. Mehnert's subsequent reflections on his trip and the state of the October Revolution offer an epitaph as good as any for the likes of Valodia's old commune: 'To-day the road to victory seems less simple than it did in the years of the Civil War, or during the first ardour of the Five-Year Plan, when the assault went forward unchecked. But the goal is the same, even if the procedure varies...'[106]

COMMUNE ENDINGS

Not all communards converted with as much certainty and conviction as Vassia and Valodia, but among the varied responses that there must have been, there was

---

[104] Mehnert, *Youth in Soviet Russia*, 263–4.   [105] Mehnert, *Youth in Soviet Russia*, 265.
[106] Mehnert, *Youth in Soviet Russia*, 269–70.

also acceptance, and, in some cases, a sense that the urban commune had run its course. Along the way, then, as well as a curtailment of commune promotion from above, from below there was willingness to embrace new directives. These aspiring revolutionaries were increasingly making their way into the structures of the party-state. Among their number was the making of a new proletarian elite. This presents us with an uncomfortable picture if we wish simply to celebrate the initiative of the collective activist against our full knowledge of Soviet socialism under Stalin. But, one thing is clear, in this environment the full autonomy and idealism of the urban commune alliance was no longer deemed possible. Alongside the shock brigades and other advocates of collective labour, the urban commune was being cast out-side the parameters of current ideological thinking, as 'the logic of storming' was gradually surpassed by 'the logic of rationalization'.[107]

Between the mobilization drive of 1929–31 and the Stakhanovite campaigns of 1935–37, Soviet socialism moved towards the command visions of a centralized party-state. In terms of the economy, the 'mastering' of construction would be promoted over the clamour and innovation of the First Five-Year Plan.[108] Stalin had justified the move back towards monetary incentives by arguing that money would only disappear under full communism.[109] In turn, the revolutionary ambitions of activists would be fully absorbed into the Komsomol and party apparatus. The massive growth in commune numbers from the end of the 1920s, and the support that these groups managed to acquire at this time, was reflective of both the optimism and the mass proliferation in activist initiative that accompanied the First Five-Year Plan. The urban commune was pulled into what turned out to be a chaotic mobilization effort, before, in the end, suffering the consequences of the rapidly changing policy objectives and instability that came to define this attempted leap forward—this Great Break.

As attention turned to the command economy and larger state mechanisms, the idea of the commune gradually became anathema to contemporary conditions, a development that—given time for the commotion of the First Five-Year Plan to pass, and with future leaders keen to prevent the appearance of alternative pathways—the Soviet Union would eventually convince itself had always been considered impractical.[110]

---

[107] Straus, *Factory and Community in Stalin's Russia*, 153. Also see Robert W. Davies and Oleg V. Khelvniuk, 'Gosplan', in Edward A. Rees (ed.), *Decision Making in the Stalinist Command Economy* (Basingstoke: Macmillan, 1997), esp. 41–3.

[108] Straus, *Factory and Community in Stalin's Russia*, 156.

[109] Stalin, *Sochineniia*, vol. 13, 342–3.

[110] See B. Vviedenskii (ed.), *The Great Soviet Encyclopedia* (Moscow: Foreign Languages Publishing House, 1953), vol. 22.

Conclusion
The Commune is Dead, *Vive le Communard!*

'I have created communism on the second floor'—these assured words are proudly declared by Artamon, a figure of collective agitation and a leading character in Nikolai Pogodin's 1930 play *Daring (Derzost'*), which centres on a group of twelve young revolutionary enthusiasts boldly engaged in the construction of an urban commune inside the confines of a factory barracks.[1] Artamon is presented as a determined activist, impatient for change. By redesigning the living space made available to him and his friends on floor two, Artamon claims to have facilitated collective dining, learning, and leisure. In this scene, Pogodin seeks to capture the directness and immediacy of the revolutionary activism driving his cast of determined communards (*kommunary*).

As a playwright, Pogodin liked to draw on his previous journalistic experience, choosing to dramatize factual reports on current events, especially in his early theatrical works.[2] Reading various newspaper articles about the self-proclaimed urban communards at the end of the 1920s, Pogodin saw a story that encapsulated the energy, promise, and tension of the age. These enterprising youths epitomized the swell of voluntarism and initiative accompanying the push for Soviet industrialization. In their desire to collectivize space, time, clothing, materials, money, work, social duty, cultural activities, and political campaigning, Pogodin also saw scope for drama. These were aspiring socialists, intent on advancing both the October Revolution and their own understanding of 1917. They were an avant-garde at the forefront of a clash between socialist modernity and tradition.

Perhaps seeking to create something of a Chekhov play for the Soviet period, Pogodin opens *Daring* by turning the unremarkable into an object of intense inquiry. We join our band of would-be activists as they debate the possibilities of the urban commune. Here, juxtaposed with their surroundings, in a neighbourhood renowned for prostitution and depravity, they agree to embark upon a 'new way of life' (*novyi byt*) designed around rational and scientific ideals. Artamon and company turn that which is hidden in plain sight—routine, habits, and lifestyle—into the centrepiece of their revolution. This was to be a revolution enacted on both the self and society's norms. Together they establish a 'common pot' (*obshchii*

---

[1] N. F. Pogodin, 'Derzost'', *Sobranie dramaticheskikh proizvedenii*, vol. 1 (Moscow, 1960), 103–98, quotation at 172.
[2] Marc Slonim, *Russian Theatre: From the Empire to the Soviets* (New York: Collier, 1962), 337.

kotel), press for a more equal existence, and begin to feel the first quivers of a 'dialectical process' taking place in their minds.[3]

Again, mirroring contemporary reports, Pogodin has the communards seek out work as a collective team, which adds suspense to the play. For, inside the factory, party representatives are nervous about the 'unplanned' nature of this new alliance. Other workers mock their idealism. One character offers a disparaging assessment, suggesting that, for all the good it would do, he might as well change his first, middle, and last name to Communard; he would be, he taunted, 'Kommunar Kommunarovich Kommunarov'. The play's principal antagonist, Master Blagodetelev, an old foreman who vociferously opposes this commune alliance, enters the fray, accusing one of the five women communards, Ada, of 'kissing under bridges'—code for prostitution. He can barely comprehend the sight of women at the factory. This was a space for men! For that, and the communards' championing of collective labour, he labels these activists 'daring' and 'audacious' agents of disruption and change.[4]

And so, the scene is set for a battle between the forces of progress and the forces of resistance. Pogodin picks up on the conflict between new and old workers, as well as the inherent tension between activist initiative and industrial management during the opening years of the First Five-Year Plan. The second act follows the communards as they struggle against the naysayers, the numerous obstacles put in their path, and instances of self-doubt. Amid a panorama of hostility, the communards are forced to deny claims that they function as a 'sect' of self-interest and isolation. And, of course, they continue to face ridicule for introducing women to the workforce.[5] The stress of it all puts a strain on commune relations, testing the group's comradeliness to the limit. They strike out against Master Blagodetelev, denouncing him in the factory wall-newspaper (*sten-gazeta*), which seems to represent a turning point in his character's development. He will soon undergo a process of 'dialectical reassessment'—he will begin to question his actions and doubt old certainties. But by now the commune is on the edge of a precipice: the communards have lost sight of each other's concerns; they even fail to notice that one of their own, Dimka, has fallen ill.

Shocked at their own failings, the final act opens with the communards deciding to redouble their efforts. They introduce a system that requires all members to write 'personal reports' (*lichnye otchety*) so that they can better monitor each other's physical and mental health. Communard Katia hopes that this will make them a more 'like-minded' (*edinomyshlenniki*) group. This is also when Artamon redesigns their accommodation, seeking to enhance their collective development. When a central party representative turns up to investigate the complaints and accusations made against the commune, we do not know what he will uncover. He starts to interview the communards. Soon, however, he comes to a resolute conclusion: he declares that the commune was not the problem; the problem lay in the culture of the factory and the persistent small-mindedness of

[3] Pogodin, *Sobranie dramaticheskikh proizvedenii*, vol. 1, 108–17.
[4] Pogodin, *Sobranie dramaticheskikh proizvedenii*, vol. 1, 116–17, 127–9.
[5] Pogodin, *Sobranie dramaticheskikh proizvedenii*, vol. 1, 142, 146–7.

certain established workers! Master Blagodetelev, who, as the audience knows, has been experiencing an existential crisis, is finally forced to publicly repent for his actions. And with the communards regaining a stable footing in the factory, the prospect of revolutionary advance seems to be back on the agenda.[6] Attempting to rally the spirits once more—the communards having suffered through their trials and tribulations—Stepa rehearses Vladimir Mayakovsky's inspiring revolutionary poem, *Left March*: 'the Commune will not be conquered | Left! | Left! | Left!' The direction of travel begins to present itself. The communards begin to replenish their revolutionary stocks. The quest for socialism will continue. As the play draws to a close, Dimka interrupts to ask his fellow communards, 'who will walk right?' In unison, all reply with the main refrain of Mayakovsky's poem, 'Left! Left! Left!'[7]

*

Pogodin strikes a sympathetic, but at times cautionary, tone. '[H]istory will progress on to communism and take something good from us', he has communard Stepa proclaim at one point. He accurately observes the urban communards' belief that they offered something more than a 'sect'. His model communards position themselves as 'pioneers of the communist future', assisting the leftward march of History.[8] They, like the communards he read about in the press, were activists and Communist Youth League (Komsomol) members keen, if not impatient, to enact the latest revolutionary slogans. Pogodin celebrates their vitality and gusto in the context of a broader drive towards revolution in industry. These were the people to shake up established working structures, uproot the old specialists (*spetsy*), reject the compromises of the New Economic Policy (NEP), and, at last, instil socialism within the factories. But Pogodin also observes the tensions at play within the urban commune phenomenon at this time. Despite their protestations, his communards are forever open to the accusation of utopianism. The primary concern relates to their domestic arrangements. The danger was obvious: they might end up isolating themselves from the imperatives of the outside world. That would be 'pure Trotsky', we are told.[9] The communards' insistent claim to wider significance suddenly appears to contain a note of defensiveness. At the same time, while his consummate activists come to symbolize the positive work of volunteerism, the limitations and pitfalls of this agitation formula are made abundantly clear. These activists and communards had the power to unsettle not just a few older workers, but whole swathes of people within the factory and barracks. Plus, their unplanned, uncoordinated, and largely instinctive approach left some wondering where the party stood on such formations. In this form, mobilization and the lustration of Soviet industry had to be a finite affair.

---

[6] Pogodin, *Sobranie dramaticheskikh proizvedenii*, vol. 1, 184–7, 191–3.
[7] Pogodin, *Sobranie dramaticheskikh proizvedenii*, vol. 1, 198.
[8] Pogodin, *Sobranie dramaticheskikh proizvedenii*, vol. 1, 142, 169.
[9] Pogodin, *Sobranie dramaticheskikh proizvedenii*, vol. 1, 113.

SOCIALIST ASPIRATION

Like Pogodin's *Daring*, this book has placed the urban commune and communard centre stage. It has shown how the idea of the *kommuna* alliance emerged out of the antecedents of the Russian revolutionary movement and Soviet understandings of the Paris Commune, and how in the hands of urban activists, would-be radicals, and those aspiring towards Komsomol or party membership, this collective vision turned into a trend that offered participants the chance to enact socialism within their own dormitories, apartments, or barracks. We have seen how this gave enthusiasts a chance to feel part of the change going on around them, and how their diverse attempts to live the socialist lifestyle intertwined with developing ideological discourses, local Komsomol and party support, local revolutionary campaigns, and, towards the end of the 1920s, workplace mobilization initiatives. For the first time, we have seen the urban commune phenomenon up close and in detail.

For ignoring the potential of Pogodin's urban communards, Master Blagodetelev is presented as a man in danger of being cast aside from History by the forces of revolution. When it comes to writing the history of that revolution, however, it is the urban communes and communards that have been cast aside. Irina Gordeeva recently argued that while the heavily promoted 'agricultural commune' (*sel'skokhoziaistvennaia kommuna*)—the label attached to collectively organized forms of Soviet farming—has attracted more attention over the years, perhaps because it received official backing from the Commissariat of Agriculture, the cultural significance of the '*byt* commune … is not fully appreciated'.[10] Historians of Soviet agricultural experimentation, such as Dominique Durand and Robert Wesson, acknowledged the existence of the urban communes, but underestimated their number and contemporary standing.[11] Largely arising in response to the state-enforced Chinese commune movement, initiated in 1958, early studies of Soviet agricultural experimentation focused on the countryside and communist rural policy. These works looked for precedents to Mao Zedong's 'people's communes' (*rénmín gōngshè*)—municipal organizations comprised of many thousands of households and smaller farms. Back in the Soviet Union, Nikita Khrushchev stifled any such response by banning the press from reporting on the Chinese communes for fear they would present an alternative view of communism, or draw attention to a path that had by that point been relegated to the status of an anomaly unworthy of Soviet hagiography.[12]

By definition, then, 'commune' has come to mean a form of agricultural collective organized 'to share the activities of production'.[13] This is true for the Soviet Union

---

[10] I. Gordeeva, 'Predislovie', in *Kommunizm svoimi rukami: Obraz agrarnykh kommun v Sovietskoi Rossii* (St Petersburg: European University at St Petersburg Press, 2010), 59. This is from the introduction subsequently provided for the Russian translation of Dominique Durand, *En communisme des 1918: sociographie dès communes agraires en URSS* (1978).

[11] See Durand, *Kommunizm svoimi rukami*, 77; Robert G. Wesson, *Soviet Communes* (New Brunswick, NJ: Rutgers University Press, 1963), 226, 228–9.

[12] See Richard Hughes, *The Chinese Communes* (London: The Bodley Head, 1960), esp. ch. 6; Anna L. Strong, *The Rise of the Chinese Communes* (Peking: New World Press, 1959).

[13] Moshe Lewin, *La paysannerie et le pouvoir soviétique 1928–1930* (Paris: Mounton, 1966), 468.

and twentieth-century communism more broadly. The urban, activist commune, missing from the legislative records of the Soviet Commissariat of Agriculture, has been dismissed as an unimportant offshoot, or overlooked entirely. Inside the Soviet Union it was eventually erased from official public memory. The leadership's desire to avoid the appearance of alternative routes to communism meant that *kommuna* came to be associated with impractical developments in early agricultural experimentation.[14] Save for a few accounts produced in more recent years, the full dynamism and discursive appeal of the commune alliance had been all but lost from the pages of Soviet history.[15]

Now we see that the notion of the commune alliance had particular cachet across the opening decade of the revolution, and, in the hands of the urban activists and would-be radicals at the heart of this book, such alliances came to form a vibrant part of the revolutionary experience. Banding together and embracing the idea of the commune, urban revolutionary enthusiasts discovered a means of bringing the promise of socialism to life. This was a particularly pertinent development during the opening years of the revolution because of the obvious inadequacies of the urban housing stock. The basic principle of cohabitative cooperation, very much at the heart of the commune idea, seemed to offer revolutionary solutions to immediate problems. In the urban commune one could overcome the shortfalls of the present while chasing a vision of the future.

With some of the first urban communes arising inside the student dormitories of the new revolutionary state, a good deal of youthful idealism was present from the start. Surveying the objective conditions of their surroundings, while also picking up on aspects of a nascent 'cultural revolution' (*kul'turnaia revoliutsiia*) already under way within the Soviet Union's institutes of higher education, some students took it upon themselves to help press the local revolutionary agenda. They forged assertively collective living arrangements, inside often cramped dormitory rooms, and declared their intention to both enact and prove the virtues of comradely union. They undertook agreements to share clothes, money, books, and living space, as well as a responsibility toward each other and the revolutionary development of their institutes—all under the banner of the 'commune'. As much as anything, these early associations sought to convince themselves, their peers, and their teachers that they had found a way to progress socialism.

---

[14] B. Vviedenskii (ed.), *The Great Soviet Encyclopedia*, vol. 22 (Moscow: Foreign Languages Publishing House, 1953).

[15] Most notable here is Richard Stites, *Revolutionary Dreams: Utopian Vision and Experimental Life in the Russian Revolution* (New York: Oxford University Press, 1989), esp. 213–19. Further to this, a number of Russian studies have recently included passages that seek to contextualize the actions of the urban communards. See V. S. Izmozik and N. B. Lebina, *Peterburg sovetskii, 'novyi chelovek' v starom prostranstve, 1920–1930-e gody* (St Petersburg: Kriga, 2010), 142–52; N. B. Lebina, *Povsednevnaia zhizn' sovetskogo goroda: normy i anomalii, 1920/1930 gody* (St Petersburg: Letnii Sad, 1999), ch. 2; A. E. Bezzubtsev-Kondakov, 'Kommuny Leningrada,' *Klio*, no. 3 (2004), 158–63. Outside Russia, Anne E. Gorsuch also made strides in this direction, noting how urban communes engaged with the press, while also representing a product of generational conflict. See Anne E. Gorsuch, *Youth in Revolutionary Russia: Enthusiasts, Bohemians, Delinquents* (Bloomington, IN: Indiana University Press, 2000), 51–7.

Students such as Ali Ianbulat, Stepan Balezin, and Ol'ga Komova, entering higher education in the early 1920s, wanted to extend upon the mission statements of the local Komsomol cells; they wanted to enact what others were merely debating. As they formed their own communes, they publicly renounced the 'bourgeois family', believing, as Komova put it, that they could remake the very notion of the 'family' into something much 'richer and wealthier'.[16] But, beyond their personal bonds, they also engaged their fellow students in various political and cultural campaigns, they pressed their institutes to promote collective activities and build more collective facilities, and, on occasion, they even harangued non-socialist teaching staff or individuals that they considered to be acting in a manner detrimental to the wider revolutionary cause. The Leningrad flood of 1924 proved to be a turning point, at least as far as Balezin was concerned; his efforts to form a salvage-relief team to help with the clear-up operation developed into the nucleus of a new, more determined student commune alliance. This commune started to actively recruit new members, took over multiple dormitory rooms as it started to grow, and aspired to turn the whole building into one large commune, complete with a collective library, group recreation areas, and debate rooms.[17]

In the hands of activists such as these, the student commune became a place to digest, absorb, and experiment with the ideas of the age. Inspired by Soviet visions of a 'new way of life' (*novyi byt*), the notion of scientific organization, and the promise of socialist modernity, Balezin and company discussed and practised new approaches to their daily routine, personal relations, and political development.[18] Socialist aspiration and the politics of disappointment combined, as they challenged both themselves and the ideological standing of the student and pedagogical body as a whole. That is, they positioned themselves to function as an avant-garde unit of revolutionary progression, eager for the day that socialism would reign supreme inside their institutes of higher education.

Likewise, with the policy of 'revolutionary housing repartition' (*revoliutsionnyi zhilishchnyi peredel*) legalizing the seizure of residential property between 1917 and 1921, collective activists started to organize commune alliances in requisitioned apartments, hostels, and barracks. Housing repartition helped to stimulate what the anthropologist Aleksandra Piir has called 'the principle of compulsory self-enforcement' (*printsip prinuditel'nogo samoupravleniia*)—when the residents of reclaimed properties took it upon themselves to monitor the ideological practice of their neighbours, assessing their revolutionary worthiness.[19] This was the ideal environment for those who wanted to set themselves up as exemplary practitioners of socialism.

From 1918–19, there were reports of youths and returning Red Army volunteers establishing their own commune formations inside the requisitioned properties of

---

[16] *Muzei istorii Rossiiskii gosudarstvennyi pedagogicheskii universitet im. A. I. Gertsena* (hereafter, MRGPU im. Herzen), d. K-38, ll. 25–18 (Personal file of Ol'ga Sergeevna Komova).
[17] MRGPU im. Herzen, d. B-5, ll. 10–9 (Personal file on Stepan Afanas'evich Balezin, 1904–82).
[18] MRGPU im. Herzen, d. B-5, ll. 16–15.
[19] A. Piir, '(Samo)upravlenie v petrogradskikh/leningradskikh zhily domakh', *Antropolocheskii forum*, no. 17 online (2012), 175–218.

Petrograd and Moscow.[20] These groups united around a 'common pot' and a sense of revolutionary opportunity. In a fit of anti-private egalitarianism, some vowed to overturn the old order; others swore to confront social and sexual inequality. They viewed the requisitioning of homes and the establishment of collective arrangements as a moral act. This was the declaration of a new social order. As the party leadership tried to address the country's post-war financial plight, curtailing the practice of housing repartition and reintroducing a limited market economy with the implementation of NEP in 1921, commune activists only seemed to gain in conviction. With NEP came NEPmen-profiteers and the threat of 'NEPification' (*oneprivanie*)—the political degeneracy and visible challenge to socialist ambition associated with the return of things such as fine dining, cabaret, and private interests. It is one of the paradoxes of the revolution that while NEP was implemented to alleviate social and economic tensions, activist circles, including large sections of the Komsomol, rallied against the negative ideological developments of this policy.[21] Those forming the urban communes became galvanized in opposition to the undesired cultural surplus of NEP.

In turn, these self-proclaimed communards, and the activists joining their ranks at this time, latched on to the growing discursive interest in the 'new way of life', the 'new life', and 'cultural revolution'. Avid readers of the revolutionary press, they could hardly miss the fact that everyday life was being billed as a crucial site in the battle for socialism. The growing number of articles on the topic helped to define what the communards were fighting for. Again, socialist aspiration and the politics of disappointment combined to drive the urban communards in their struggle against the compromises of the present. Some groups vocally renounced the slovenly, unproductive 'old way of life', as symbolized by Ivan Goncharov's archetypal Oblomov, determined to live more like the 'Good, strong, honest, capable people' of Nikolai Chernyshevsky's *What Is to Be Done?*[22] Before long, with the Soviet press running stories on the communes and their approach to the 'new way of life', the title of '*byt(ovaia)* commune' started to gain traction. The urban commune alliance was becoming ever more associated with the socialist struggle for *byt*.

To some extent, in the hands of these idealistic types, the urban commune adhered to a variation of the Marxist-Leninist conception of the dialectic. Here activists tried to establish the physical and the psychological means for revolutionary advance. The commune was a bastion of collectivism that served to enable them to stand as exemplary revolutionaries and agitate for a 'new way of life'. As they evolved from spontaneous formation to disciplined organization, the communes were, by their own reckoning, taking one step closer to realizing their collectivist

---

[20] See Aktivnyi rabotnik, 'Kommuny molodezhi', *Iunyi kommunist*, no. 3–4 (1919), 10–11; and V. I. Dunaevskii, 'Oktiabr' i trud rabochei molodezhi', *Iunyi kommunist*, no. 15 (1919), 2–5.

[21] See Michael David-Fox, *Revolution of the Mind. Higher Learning among the Bolsheviks, 1918–1929* (Ithaca, NY: Cornell University Press, 1997), 104; and Peter Gooderham, 'The Komsomol and the Worker Youth: The Inculcation of "Communist Values" in Leningrad during NEP', *Soviet Studies*, no. 4 (1982), 506–28.

[22] See M. Afanas'ev, 'Novomu bytu—byt', *Krasnoe studenchestvo*, no. 13 (1928), 20–1; and L. Bernshtein, 'Kommuna—ne mechta', *Iunyi kommunist*, no. 1 (1930), 31.

dreams. In Leninist terms, if 'full collectivism' and a 'collectivist society' belonged to the communist stage of humanity's development, then the urban commune came just before that; it was part of the socialist phase, attempting to lay the foundations of the future civilization. As the utopian thinker Aleksandr Bogdanov may have seen it, just as the 'idea of justice' becomes nullified when crime disappears, and new theories replace the old, the idea of the commune alliance would become obsolete when mankind was no longer restricted by bourgeois individualism.[23] But these self-identified communards, born at a time of revolutionary action, were not preoccupied by the abstract or theoretical nature of their undertakings. They tied their revolutionary outlook to the practical, political, and cultural development of the world around them.

Hence, attuned to the prevailing mood, these same aspiring socialists came to embrace a shift in revolutionary attitudes towards the end of the 1920s. A more militant ideological discourse, coming off the back of the 1927 war scare—when revolutionary calls and press slogans started to read more like 'war communiqués'— was far from anathema to the urban communes, many of which were composed of activists who had served time in the Red Army, had set themselves in opposition to old class enemies, and were in the habit of eagerly trying to enforce their understanding of revolution on others.[24] What is more, alongside calls for a return to the militant idealism of 1917–21, many existing urban communes and communards were inspired by the resurgence of volunteerism and activist initiative at the end of the 1920s. With attention falling on the industrial exigencies of the revolution in the build-up to the First Five-Year Plan, the party leadership pushed for the mobilization of a new activist workforce and Komsomol working campaigns. The desire to finally overcome the limitations of existing industry, to cast off the yoke of NEP, and to press ahead with an ambitious production drive, all privileged collectivist forms of worker organization. This was a populist industrial takeover. Amid the waves of new worker-activist recruits, the urban communes and communards increasingly began to equate collectivism and the struggle for *byt* with new labour methods.

It became more common for commune groups to attempt to live and work together as one collective unit. This was a practice that some had already experimented with, drawing on the heritage of the Russian *arteli*. But labour activism took on more importance in the build-up to the First Five-Year Plan. Increasingly, groups vied to demonstrate their socialist credentials through lifestyle and productivity. And as more and more people were mobilized, the urban communes and communards became embroiled in the emergent 'shock-worker' (*udarnik*) movement and the practice of 'storming' (*sturmovshchina*) in industry, which saw teams of new workers, known as brigades (*brigady*), attempt to overturn existing labour practices through intensive collective effects to fulfil or exceed factory quotas. This

---

[23] 'When life and development of man are no longer restricted by oppression, the idea of freedom will also become obsolete.' See A. Bogdanov, *Engineer Menni* (1913), in *Red Star, The First Bolshevik Utopia*, trans. and ed. Loren R. Graham and Richard Stites (Bloomington, IN: Indiana University Press, 1984), 205.

[24] Klaus Mehnert, *Youth in Soviet Russia*, trans. Michael Davidson (London: George Allen & Unwin, 1933), 67–8.

was also the time that local management and leadership, eager to make mobilization a success, started to lend more support to commune groups. The urban commune found a new home within the industrial landscape of the Soviet Union during the onset of the First Five-Year Plan. With heavy industry ramping up, and with new factory barracks emerging across the construction sites of the Soviet Union, working life was becoming more collective in general.

Numbers rose higher and higher, as the urban communes were co-opted into the working strategies of local revolutionary bodies and industrial management. For workers such as Vladimir Molodtsov, entering Soviet industry between 1929 and 1930, the urban commune continued to offer a means of revolutionary self-discovery and participation.[25] But, at the same time, the character of the urban commune also started to change as activists were reminded that shock work, productivity, and the culture of industry should now be among their most pressing concerns. With greater external input, and with more groups forming under the guidance of local Komsomol and party cells, many communes started to look more prescribed. The 'production communes' (*proizvodstvennye kommuny*), as the press had taken to calling the latest incarnations of the commune alliance, emerged as the party leadership pressed all organs to pursue a militarized command economy and a new socialist offensive in industry. These communes subsequently became embroiled in the maelstrom of industrial change surging forward across the factories and construction sites of the Soviet Union. And, largely because the vision of a militarized, socialist economy was based on what David Priestland has termed 'theorized wishful thinking', and not genuine command structures, the urban commune was opened up to the failings of this industrial push. The belief had been that old 'bourgeois science' could be replaced by a new 'proletarian science'; a 'science' that took into account the force of popular willpower and the untapped potential of collective mobilization.[26] But things did not prove to be that simple. Mobilization succeeded in overturning the established order of industry, but it was also unruly, unpredictable, and inconsistent. So, tied up in this socialist offensive at the outset of the First Five-Year Plan, urban communes and communards became susceptible to criticisms of excess and isolation, as industrial policy moved towards privileging one-man management and a return to stability after 1931.

Ultimately, as we have seen, the idea of the urban commune alliance would not survive much beyond this point. Co-opted into the parameters of local mobilization strategies, the urban communes and communards soon found that their alliances had lost their revolutionary relevancy. The idea of the commune had become entwined with a debate about industrial stability and the need for more developed command structures. Indeed, the urban commune seemed to be cast on the wrong side of this debate. While there were reports of some isolated commune groups staying together until 1934, the vast majority of communards increasingly felt

---

[25] V. A. Molodtsov, 'On byl shakhter, prostoi rabochii …', in *Dnevniki i pis'ma Komsomol'tsev*, ed. M. Kataeva (Moscow: Molodaia gvardiia, 1983), 49–68.
[26] David Priestland, *The Red Flag: Communism and the Making of the Modern World* (London: Penguin Books, 2010), 148.

obliged to look elsewhere to continue their revolutionary journeys.[27] There were instances of disappointment and even remonstrance. Some did argue the case for the commune alliance beyond 1931.[28] Some continued on, much as before, but under the guise of a cost-accounting unit (*khozraschet*). Other soon-to-be-former communards, also members or aspiring members of the Komsomol and party, decided to roll with the times. Some expressed opinions that were in accord with the leadership on the matter of prioritizing industrial stability; others, perhaps conscious that the 1930s were turning into a Schmittian world of friend and foe—a place where one did not want to be caught on the wrong side—decided that their ideological ambitions were best served within the increasingly professionalized organs of state.

As the party leadership moved away from voluntaristic schemes in industry, the urban commune alliance faded from existence. Along the way, it had served to provide numerous young activists and wannabe Bolsheviks with a means of engaging in the possibilities of revolution. But, as far as the life cycle of the October Revolution was concerned, this was the end of the urban commune.

HISTORY WILL TAKE SOMETHING GOOD FROM US

What does the story of the urban communes and communards tell us about the early Soviet state? Pogodin's communards wanted to shape the future. Among the activists that inspired his play, Pogodin observed a trait common to many revolutionaries: the self-conscious will to make history. In a sense, the self-worth of many young activists became wrapped up in the idea of the urban commune. This was what provided them with the chance to participate in the modernizing ideology of socialism. Where the early infrastructure of state fell short, urban communes and communards could be found attempting to fulfil revolutionary dreams. This was an example of how would-be radicals, outside or on the cusp of the party apparatus, received and engaged the promises of October.

By uniting in these collective alliances, revolutionary hopefuls sought to elevate everyday life and everyday activities to a science.[29] Experimenting with Soviet Taylorism, groups implemented daily schedules and collective regimens designed to promote a socialist vision of best practice. They also embraced a revolutionary attitude towards 'personal life' (*lichnaia zhizn*) and 'private life' (*chastnaia zhizn*). That is, they promoted what was, at the time, an evolving perception of 'personal life' as something that might be observed—where individuals might be encouraged to follow a path of revolutionary self-improvement—while 'private life' and 'private'

---

[27] For example, see Mehnert, *Youth in Soviet Russia*, 249–51.
[28] See Z. L. Mindlin and S. A. Kheinman (eds), *Trud v SSSR: statisticheskii spravochnik* (Moscow, 1932); S. Samuelii, 'Rabotu proizvodstvennykh kommun i kollektivov—na novye rel'sy', *Partiinoe stroitel'stvo*, no. 15–16 (1931), 12–18; A. Kliushin, 'Proizvodstvennye kommuny kak opyt kollektivnogo truda', *Partiinoe stroitel'stvo*, no. 11 (1931), 23–5.
[29] Cf. Jill Lepore, *The Mansion of Happiness: A History of Life and Death* (New York: Vintage Books, 2013), 97.

(*chastnye*) matters, indicating something that was removed or closed off from the public, were cast as bourgeois or un-revolutionary. For the communards, 'private' matters and spaces ran counter to their desire for 'common' (*obshchii*) experience. Their collective arrangements were panoptic creations established in opposition to any 'private life'. This private–personal dichotomy became a staple of Soviet cultural understanding that long outlasted the urban communes and communards.[30] In their own small way, the urban commune and communards were helping to ground revolutionary ideology.

The urban communes and communards were not restricted to innovations in domestic organization, nor were they merely the offspring of a housing shortage. They tended to combine collective cohabitation with cultural-enlightenment objectives. Urban communards wanted to present themselves as pioneers of revolutionary modernity, enacting and becoming part of the Soviet discourse on collectivism, cultural revolution, the 'new way of life' (*novyi byt*), and working habits. In dialogue with the revolutionary ideas and ideals presented in the Soviet press, they brought socialism to life wherever they were situated. And they did so in a manner that was not always in keeping with the plans and prerogatives of local Komsomol or party representatives. Sometimes taking revolutionary policy in a slightly different direction than was perhaps intended, they displayed their own agency. Sometimes displaying the propensity to change their mind, or go back and forth on particular issues, especially when it came to revolutionary attitudes towards sex and gender equality, they revealed the indeterminacy of revolution in these areas.

The story of the urban communes and communards, then, helps put some of the ambiguity back into Soviet history and shows the role that socialist aspiration played in developing revolutionary ideology across the opening decade of the world's first socialist state. Traditionally, studies of totalitarian regimes have left little room for such considerations. But studying such groups enables us to better recognize what has been referred to as the 'ways people actively appropriate forms and meanings'.[31] Soviet history cannot be distilled to the debilitating and coercive forces enacted on the citizen, no matter how comforting and appealing such narratives might prove when it comes to explaining some of the horrors of that history. At the very least, the story of the urban communes and communards captures a taste of what it was like for young activists to have lived the revolution and experimented with being Soviet.

It should also be noted that the end of the urban commune trend, come 1931–32, signified a change in the politics of the Soviet Union, but not necessarily a complete break with the ideological experimentation and aspiration that sustained it. Former communard Ali Ianbulat, reflecting upon his youthful experimentation, referred to these collective alliances as a 'foundry of education for the [New] Soviet Person'. The activists that united inside the urban communes, Ianbulat insisted

---

[30] Cf. Oleg Kharkhordin, 'Reveal and Dissimulate: A Genealogy of Private Life in Soviet Russia', in Jeff Weintraub and Krishan Kumar (eds), *Public and Private in Thought and Practice: Perspectives on a Grand Dichotomy* (Chicago: University of Chicago Press, 1997), 333–63.
[31] Mark D. Steinberg, *Proletarian Imagination: Self, Modernity, and the Sacred in Russia, 1910–1925* (Ithaca, NY: Cornell University Press, 2002), 13.

some forty years on, were also the people that 'swelled the ranks of [new] specialists' and became 'a considerable force ... in the development of our great motherland'.[32] Likewise, Stepan Balezin seemed to forever equate the 'exemplary practice' (*shefstvo*) and 'social work' (*obshchestvennaia rabota*) he promoted in his communard days with the sense of duty and responsibility he felt as a Soviet citizen.[33] Balezin continued his education in the 1930s, becoming a scientist specializing in corrosion and chemical inhibitors. He served in the war, later sought to aid Khrushchev's scientific revolution in the 1960s, and between 1967 and 1970 was even called upon to lead a team of Soviet scientists as part of a United Nations Educational, Scientific and Cultural Organization (UNESCO) school reform programme in India.[34]

For Ol'ga Komova, too, her commune years proved formative. Alongside Balezin, Komova experimented with collective life and tried to act as a socialist role model. She enrolled in the Faculty of Social Education, attended countless pedagogical meetings, and, having discussed the responsibilities of being a teacher with her fellow communards, decided to go out to the factories and sign up for various Komsomol campaigns in order to offer herself as a mentor and guide to other Soviet youths. This was a way of life that Komova maintained throughout her subsequent thirty-two-year career as a teacher. During this time she received two national awards and four medals for her 'spirit', 'energy', and constant 'commitment to the guidance of youth', as well as the social work that she undertook with the Komsomol.[35]

Vladimir Molodtsov, who left commune life behind in 1932 to chase new revolutionary opportunities, seemed to remember his collective experience fondly. It was the urban commune that allowed him to experiment with socialism, and it was here that he first cut his teeth as an aspiring revolutionary activist and leader. By 1933 he had moved up to the position of assistant director of mine number ten in the Mosbassa coal system. He served as a Komsomol cell secretary, head of agitation and propaganda, and ended up joining the Komsomol district committee. But, like so many of his generation, his life was cut short by the war. Active in an underground resistance movement in occupied Odessa, he was reportedly wounded in a provocation, tortured by Nazi forces, dragged through the streets, and eventually shot in June 1942. He was little over thirty years of age. He was posthumously awarded the title of 'Hero of the Soviet Union'.[36]

For these individuals, the urban commune lived on in some form, staying with them as they moved on to new things and embraced new challenges in the life cycle of the October Revolution and the Soviet Union. In some cases, the ideological causes they helped promote continued on or evolved to become key components of Soviet life. And it might just be that the idea of the urban commune, and the *kommuna* alliance, also lay dormant within Soviet culture. Indeed, it is interesting

---

[32] *Muzei istorii Sankt-Peterburgskogo gosudarstvennogo elektrotekhnicheskogo universiteta, 'LETI'* (hereafter, Muzei istorii SPbETU), KP. osn. 4711, d. 2025, ll. 3–5 (Personal file of Ali Ianbulat).
[33] See MRGPU im. Herzen, d. K-38, l. 20.   [34] MRGPU im. Herzen, d. B-5, ll. 43–40.
[35] MRGPU im. Herzen, d. K-38, l. i; *Sovetskii uchitel'*, 13 December 1983, 3.
[36] Molodtsov, 'On byl shakhter, prostoi rabochii . . .', 49.

that as destalinization was giving birth to a renewed sense of optimism and activism in the late 1950s and early 1960s, a grassroots educational initiative of pedagogues and youth leaders, dissatisfied with the tired old slogans and regimentation of late Stalinism, quickly became known as the 'Communard movement'. This movement and its sources of influence remain greatly in need of research, but, born within the educational institutes of Leningrad, where the urban communes had a key presence in the 1920s, these aspiring revolutionaries sought to revive the creativity and energy that they associated with previous generations of Soviet youth. 'Communard' remained as nebulous a title as it ever had, but it is perhaps telling that as the headquarters of the Leningrad District of Young Pioneers was unofficially renamed the '*Frunzenskaia kommuna*', and as the first communard group of the post-Stalin period started to assemble here, these reformers initiated a tentative discourse revolving around the rebirth of social responsibility, self-initiative, discussion groups, and collective enterprise.[37] Briefly finding their way into the Soviet press, they came to reflect a sense of renewed possibility.[38] It may be that the themes, concerns, and structure intrinsic to the urban communes of the early Soviet state had not escaped the attention of these later would-be radicals.

---

[37] S. Soloveichik (ed.), *Frunzenskaia kommuna* (Leningrad, 1968).

[38] S. Soloveichik, 'Frunzenskaia kommuna', *Komsomol'skaia pravda,* 10 January 1962, 4; cited in Simon Huxtable, 'Revisiting "Governmentality": Journalists and Political Power at *Komsomol'skaia pravda,* 1953–1968' (Unpublished paper, University of Oxford Postgraduate Seminar Series, June 2011); and Simon Huxtable, 'A Compass in the Sea of Life: Soviet Journalism, the Public, and the Limits of Reform after Stalin, 1953–1968' (Unpublished PhD Dissertation, Birkbeck, University of London, 2012), 243–5. For further examples of the communard discourse, see 'On the Multiparty System', in *Samizdat. Voices of the Soviet Opposition,* ed. George Saunder (New York: Pathfinder Press, 1975), 235–9.

Bibliography

ARCHIVES

GARF—State Archive of the Russian Federation (Gosudarstvennyi arkhiv Rossiiskoi Federatsii)
    f. A.2313—People's Commissariat of Education, RSFSR
    f. 5469—Union of Metalworkers
    f. 5515—People's Commissariat of Labour
    f. 7952—History of Factories and Plants (Gorky Archive)
MRGPU im. Herzen—Museum of History, A. I. Herzen State Pedagogical University (Muzei istorii Rossiiskii gosudarstvennyi pedagogicheskii universitet im. A. I. Gertsena)
    B-5—Personal file of Stepan Afanas'evich Balezin
    K-38—Personal file of Ol'ga Sergeevna Komova
    Pedvuzovets—Student newspaper
Muzei istorii SPbETU—Museum of History, St Petersburg State Electro-technical University, 'LETI' (Muzei istorii Sankt-Peterburgskogo gosudarstvennogo elektrotekhnicheskogo universiteta, 'LETI')
    KP. osn. 4711—Personal file of Ali Ianbulat
    KP. osn. 4712—Ali Ianbulat on the LETI communes
    Pamphlet collection
OKhDOPIM—Divisional Repository of the Social-Political History of Moscow (Otdel khraneniia dokumentov obshchestvenno-politicheskoi istorii Moskvy)
    f. 459—Sverdlov Communist University
RGASPI—Russian State Archive of Socio-Political History (Rossiiskii gosudarstvennyi arkhiv sotsial'no-politicheskoi istorii)
    M.1: Division of Youth Organizations
    f. M.1 op. 3—Meetings of the Bureau of the Central Committee of the Communist Youth League, including materials provided
    f. M.1 op. 4—Meetings of the Secretariat of the Central Committee of the Communist Youth League, including materials provided
    f. M.1 op. 23—Documents of the Communist Youth League
TsAG Moskvy—Central State Archive of the City of Moscow (Tsentral'nyi arkhiv goroda Moskvy)
    f. 415—History of the Factories and Plants, Automobile Society of Moscow (AMO)
TsDAHOU—Central State Archive of Public Organizations of Ukraine (Tsentral'nyi derzhavnyi arkhiv hromads'kykh ob'iednan' Ukrainy)
    f. 3198—State Political Directorate
TsGAMO—Central State Archive of the Moscow Oblast (Tsentral'nyi gosudarstvennyi arkhiv Moskovskoi oblasti)
    f. 2614—Department of National Education
    f. 6769—Department of Regional Education

LIBRARIES

British Library (BL)
Russian State Library (Rossiiskaia gosudarstvennaia biblioteka)

Bibliography

State Public Historical Library of Russia (Gosudarstvennaia publichnaia istoricheskaia biblioteka Rossii)
UCL, School of Slavonic and East European Studies Library (UCL SSEES Library)

JOURNALS AND NEWSPAPERS

Bol'shevik
Ekonomicheskaia gazeta
Iunyi kommunist
Iunyi proletarii
Izvestiia
Kommunar
Komsomol'skaia pravda
Krasnaia letopis'
Krasnoe studenchestvo
Krasnyi student
Leningradskii Universitet
Molodaia gvardiia
Partiinoe stroitel'stvo
Pedvuzovets
Pravda
Proletarskaia kul'tura
Rabochnaia gazeta
Ratsionalizatsiia proizvodstva
Revoliutsiia i kul'tura
Smena
Sovetskii uchitel'
Stroitel'stvo Moskvy
Trud
Voprosy truda
Za industrializatsiiu

PUBLISHED PRIMARY SOURCES

VIII Vsesoiuznyi s"ezd VLKSM 5–16 maia 1928 goda. Stenograficheskii otcheta. Moscow: Molodaia gvardiia, 1928.
XVII Konferentsiia VKP(b): stenograficheskii otchet. Moscow: Partiinoe izd-vo, 1932.
50 let VLKSM 1918–1968. Moscow, 1969.
Afanas'ev, K. N., ed. *Iz istorii sovetskoi arkhitektury 1917–1925 gg. Dokumenty i materialy.* Moscow: Akademiia nauka SSSR, 1963.
Andropov, A. *Na novykh putiakh studencheskogo byta.* Moscow, 1930.
Badaev, A. E. *Desiat' let bor'by i stroitel'stva: Prodvol'stv.-kooperativ. rabota v Leningrade, 1917–1927.* Leningrad, 1927.
Balashov, A. *Komsomol v Tsifrakh.* Moscow: Molodaia gvardiia, 1931.
Ber, Iu. *Kommuna segodnia: opyt proizvodstvennykh i bytovikh kommun molodezhi.* Moscow: Molodaia gvardiia, 1930.
Bogdanov, A. *Red Star: The First Bolshevik Utopia.* Trans. and ed. by Loren R. Graham and Richard Stites. Bloomington, IN: Indiana University Press, 1984.

Bonnell, Victoria, ed. *The Russian Worker: Life and Labor under the Tsarist Regime.* Berkeley: University of California Press, 1983.

Bubnov, A. S. et al. *Na ideologicheskom fronte: Bor'by s kontrrevoliutsii.* Moscow: Krasnaia nov', 1923.

Bukharin, N. *Historical Materialism: A System of Sociology.* New York: International Publishers, 1925.

Bukharin, N. *Bor'ba za kadry: Rechi i stat'i.* Moscow-Leningrad: Molodaia gvardiia, 1926.

Bukharin, N. *K novomu pokoleniiu: doklady, vystupleninia i stat'i, posviashchennye problemam molodezhi.* Moscow, 1990.

Bukharin, N. and Preobrazhensky, E. *The ABC of Communism.* Ed. and intro. by Edward H. Carr. Harmondsworth: Penguin Books, 1969.

Chayanov, A. *Osnovnye idei i formy organizatsii sel'skokhozaistvennoi kooperatsii.* Moscow, 1927.

Chernyshevky, N. *What Is to Be Done?: Tales about New People.* Trans. by M. R. Katz. Ithaca, NY: Cornell University Press, 1989.

Chislennost' i sostav rabochikh v Rossii na osnovanii dannykh pervoi vsebshchei perepisi naseleniia Rossiiskoi Imperii 1987 g. St Petersburg: Parpvaia litografiia, 1906.

Chudnovskii, S. L. 'Iz dal'nikh let (Otruvki iz vospominanii)'. *Byloe* no. 9–10 (1907).

Dmitriev, V. and Galin, B. *Na putiakh k novomu bytu.* Moscow, 1927.

Dobroliubov, N. A. 'Chto takoe Oblomovshchina?' In *Sobranie sochinenii.* Vol. 2. Moscow, 1952. 107–41.

Dubner, P. and Kozyrev, M. *Kollektivy i kommuny v bor'be za kommunicheskie formy truda.* Moscow: Gosudarstvennoe izdatel'stvo, 1930.

Engels, Friedrich. *The Origin of the Family, Private Property and the State.* London: International Publishers, 1941.

Eskin, E. *Osnovnye puti razvitiia sotsialisticheskikh form truda.* Leningrad: Sotsekon. izd-vo, 1936.

Feuer, Lewis S., ed. *Karl Marx & Frederick Engels, Basic Writings on Politics and Philosophy.* New York: Anchor Books, 1969.

Filimonov, N. A. *Po novomu ruslu, vospominaniia.* Leningrad: Leninizdat', 1967.

Gosudarstvennoe regulirovanie truda i profsoiuzy. Moscow, 1929.

Gurevich, S. A. *Obzor: Zhilishchno-kommunal'nogo dela v Moskve i deiatel'nosti Moskovskoi zhilishchno-sanitarnoi inspektsii i Sektsii kommunal'noi sanitaria v 1922 g.* Moscow: Izdanie sanitarnoi hasti MOZ, 1923.

Harper, Samuel N. *Civic Training in Soviet Russia.* Chicago, IL: University of Chicago Press, 1929.

Iankovskii, M. *Kommuna sta tridtsati trekh.* Leningrad: Priboi, 1929.

Industrializatsiia SSSR, 1929–1932 gg.: dokumenty i materialy. Moscow: Nauka, 1970.

Kagan, A. G. *Rabochaia molodezh' na otdykhe.* Leningrad: Priboi, 1927.

Kagan, A. G. *45 dnei sredi molodezhi.* Leningrad: Priboi, 1929.

Kaganovich, L. V. *Socialist Reconstruction of Moscow and other Cities in the USSR.* Moscow: Cooperative Pub. Society of foreign workers in USSR, 1931.

Kaganovich, L. V. *O zadachakh profsoiuzov SSSR na dannom etape razvitiia.* Moscow: Profizdat, 1932.

Kaishtat, A., Ryvkin, I. and Sosnovik, I. *Kommuny molodezhi, po materialam obsledovaniia i pod redaktsiei instituta sanitarnoi kul'tury.* Moscow: Molodaia gvardiia, 1931.

Kapustin, A. *Udarniki! Praktika raboty udarnykh brigad v sotsialisticheskom sorevnovanii.* Moscow: Mosovskii rabochii, 1930.

Kavelin, K. *Sobranie sochinenii v 3 tomakh.* Vol. 2. St Petersburg: M. M. Stasiulevicha, 1898.

Kayden, Eugene M. and Antsiferov, Aleksey N. *The Cooperative Movement in Russia During the War.* New Haven, CT: Carnegie Endowment for International Peace, Yale University Press, 1929.

Kokorev, Iu. *Kak rastet novoe: istoriia razvitiia odnoi kommuny.* Leningrad, 1931.

Kollontai, A. *Love of Worker Bees.* Trans. by Cathy Porter. London: Academy Press, 1977.

Kollontai, A. 'The Family and the Communist State.' In *Bolshevik Visions: First Phase of the Cultural Revolution in Soviet Russia.* Ed. by William G. Rosenberg. Ann Arbor, MI: University of Michigan Press, 1990. 67–82.

Komsomol'skii byt. Moscow-Leningrad: Molodaia gvardiia, 1927.

Kosarev, A. *Proizvoditel'no rabotat' kul'turno zhit'. Doklad na 7-I vsesoiuznoi konferentsii VLKSM.* Moscow, 1932.

Kovalevskaia, Sofia. *A Russian Childhood.* Trans. by Beatrice Stillman. New York: Spinger-Verlag, 1978.

Kozyrev, M. *Kollektivy i kommuny.* Moscow, 1930.

KPSS v rezoliutsiiakh i resheniiakh s"ezdov, konferentsii i plenumov TsK. Moscow: Gos. Izd-vo, 1928.

Krupskaya, N. *Zadachi i organizatsiia sovpartshkol.* Moscow: Krasnaia nov', 1923.

Krupskaya, N. *O bytovykh voprosakh.* Moscow: Gosudarstvennoe izdatel'stvo, 1930.

Krupskaya, N. *V pomoshch' kul'tbrigadam: Beseda s brigadami poslannymi NKP RSFSR na posevnuiu kampaniiu.* Moscow-Leningrad: Gos. Izd-vo, 1931.

Larin, Iu. *Stroitel'stvo sotsializma i kollektivizatsiia byt.* Moscow: Gosudarstvennoe izdatel'stvo, 1930.

Larin, Iu. and Belousov, V., eds. *Za novoe zhilishche: Sbornik statei k 5 letiiu zhilishchnoi kooperatsii.* Moscow: Gosudarstvennoe izdatel'stvo, 1930.

Lenin, V. I. *Collected Works.* Vols 29–33. Moscow: Progress Publishing, 1960–70.

Lenin, V. I. 'Articles on Tolstoy'. In *Marxists on Literature. An Anthology.* Harmondsworth: Penguin Books, 1977.

Lenin, V. I. *The State and Revolution.* Intro. by Robert Service. London: Penguin Books, 1992.

Marx, Karl. *Economic and Philosophical Manuscripts of 1844.* Moscow: Progress Publishers, 1959.

K. Marx, F. Engels, V. I. Lenin, On Scientific Communism. Moscow: Progress Publishers, 1976.

Mavrodin, V. V., ed. *Na shturm nauki, vospominaniia byvshikh studentov fakul'teta obshchestvennykh nauk leningradskogo universiteta.* Leningrad: Izd-vo Leningra un-ta, 1971.

Mehnert, Klaus. *Youth in Soviet Russia.* Trans. by Michael Davidson. London: George Allen & Unwin, 1933.

Mehnert, Klaus. *The Anatomy of Soviet Man.* London: Robert Cunningham & Sons, 1961.

Mel'gunov, S. P. *Iz istorii studencheskikh obshchestv v russkikh universitetakh.* Moscow: Izd. Zhurnala 'Pravda', 1904.

Mindlin, Z. L. and Kheinman, S. A., eds. *Trud v SSSR: statisticheskii spravochnik.* Moscow, 1932.

Oganovskii, N. P. *Revoliutsiia naoborot: razrushenie obshchiny.* Petrograd: Tipografiia 'Zadruga', 1917.

Ol'khov, V. *Za zhivoe rukovodstvo sotssorevnovaniem, opyt vsesoiuznoi proverki sotssorevnovaniia brigadami VTsSPS.* Moscow: Izd, VTsSPS Moskva, 1930.

Peterburg, den' mirovogo internatsionala 19 iulia 1920 g. Petrograd, 1920.

Piatiletnii plan narodno-khoziaistvennogo stroitelstva SSSR. Moscow: Planovoe khiziastvo, 1929.

Pogodin, N. 'Derzost'.' In *Sobranie dramaticheskikh proizvedenii.* Vol. 1. Moscow, 1960. 103–98.

Pokrovskii, M. N. *Brief History of Russia.* London: Martin Lawrence, 1933.

Razin, I., ed. *Komsomolskii byt': Sbornik.* Moscow: Molodaia gvardiia, 1927.

Reed, John. *Ten Days That Shook the World.* London: Penguin Books, 1977.

Reznikov, D. *Udarnye brigady sotsializma.* Moscow, 1930.

Rogachevskaia, L. S. *Sotsialisticheskoe sorevnovanie v SSSR: istoriia i ocherki, 1917–1970.* Moscow: Nauka, 1977.

Saunder, George, ed. *Samizdat. Voices of the Soviet Opposition.* New York: Pathfinder Press, 1975.

Sheftel', S. *Deputaty na zavode. O sovetskom aktive zavode 'Kauchuk'.* Moscow, 1932.

Shklovsky, V. *The Knight's Move.* Champaign, IL: Dalkey Archive Press, 2005.

Slutskii, A. G. *Parizhskaia Kommuna 1871 goda.* Moscow: 'Nauka', 1925.

Soloveichik, S., ed. *Frunzenskaia kommuna.* Leningrad: Detskaia literatura, 1968.

Stalin, I. V. *Sochineniia.* Vols 12–13. Moscow: Gos. Izd-vo, 1949–51.

Strong, Anna L. *The Soviets Conquer Wheat. The Drama of Collective Farming.* New York: Henry Holt and Company, 1931.

Sumatokhin, M. *Davaite zhit' kommunoi!* Moscow: Izd-vo Vserossiiskago Tsentral'nago Ispolnitel'nago Komiteta Sovetov RSK i K. Deputatov, 1918.

Tovarishch komsomol. Dokumenty s"ezdov, konferentsii i TsK VLKSM, 1918–1968. Vol. 1. Moscow: Molodaia gvardiia, 1969.

Trotsky, L. 'Voprosy byta'. In *Sochineniia.* Moscow: Gos. Izd-vo, 1927.

Trotsky, L. *The Revolution Betrayed: What Is the Soviet Union and Where Is It Going?* Trans. by Michael Eastman. New York: Pathfinder Books, 1972.

Trotsky, L. *Problems of Everyday Life and Other Writings on Culture & Science.* New York: Monad Press, 1973.

Trotsky, L. 'From the Old Family to the New'. In *Bolshevik Visions: First Phase of the Cultural Revolution in Soviet Russia.* Ed. by William G. Rosenberg. Ann Arbor: University of Michigan Press, 1990. 77–83.

Trud i profdivzhenie v leningradskoi oblasti 1932 g. Leningrad, 1932.

Trud, otdykh, son komsomol'tsa-aktivista. Po materialam vyborochnogo obsledovaniia biudzhetov vremeni aktivnykh rabotnikov RLKSM, vyp. 6. Moscow-Leningrad, 1926.

Trud v pervoi piatiletke. Moscow: Gos. Sotsekon izd-vo, 1934.

Trud v SSSR: Materialy k otchetu Narkomtruda SSSR na IX s'ezda VSPS. Moscow-Leningrad: NKTP, 1932.

Trud v SSSR: Sbornik statei. Moscow: Gostrudizdat, 1930.

Trud v SSSR: Spravochnik 1926–1930 gg. Moscow: Gosplana SSSR, 1930.

Trud v SSSR: Statisticheskii spravochnik. Moscow: Gosplana SSSR, 1932.

Trud v SSSR: Statisticheskii spravochnik. Moscow: Gosplana SSSR, 1936.

Tsikhon, A. *Otchet Narkomtruda IX s'ezdu profsoiuzov.* Moscow: Profizdat, 1932.

Voprosy kul'tury pri diktature proletariat. Sbornik. Moscow: Gosizdat, 1925.

Vorontsov, V. 'Krest'ianskaia obshchina'. In *Itogi ekonomicheskogo issledovaniia Rossia po dannym zemskoi statiskii.* Moscow, 1892.

Webb, Sidney and Webb, Beatrice. *Soviet Communism: A New Civilisation?* London: Longmans, Green & Co., 1935.

Winter, Ella. *Red Virtue. Human Relationships in the New Russia.* London: Victor Gollancz Ltd, 1933.

Winterton, Paul. *A Student in Russia*. Manchester: Co-operative Union Ltd, 1931.
Yarov, S. *Udarnye brigady v Gus'-Khrustal'noi*. Moscow, 1930.
Zarkhii, S. *Kommuna v tsekhe*. Moscow: Molodaia gvardiia, 1930.
Zhiga, I. *Novye rabochie*. Moscow: Moskovskii rabochii, 1929.
Zvedin, Z. K. *Politicheskii i trudovoi pod"em rabochego klassa SSSR, 1928–1929 gg: Sbornik dokumentov*. Moscow: Gospolitzdat, 1956.

BOOKS, ARTICLES, AND CHAPTERS

Acton, Edward, Cherniaev, V. Iu. and Rosenberg, William G., eds. *Critical Companion to the Russian Revolution 1914–1921*. London: Edward Arnold, 1997.
Ahmed, Sara. *The Cultural Politics of Emotions*. Edinburgh: Edinburgh University Press, 2004.
Aldanov, Mark. 'A Russian Commune in Kansas'. *Russian Review* no. 1 (Spring 1944): 30–44.
Althusser, Louis. *Essays on Ideology*. London: Verso, 1984.
Andrle, Vladimir. *Workers in Stalin's Russia, 1928–1941*. London: Pluto Press, 1986.
Andrusz, Gregory D. *Housing and Urban Development in the USSR*. Basingstoke: Macmillan, 1984.
Aralovets, N. A. *Gorodskaia sem'ia v Rossii, 1927–1959 gg*. Tula: Rossiiskaia akademiia nauk, 2009.
Atkinson, Dorothy. 'The Statistics on the Russian Land Commune, 1905–1917'. *Slavic Review* no. 4 (December 1973): 773–87.
Atkinson, Dorothy. *The End of the Russian Land Commune, 1905–1930*. Stanford, CA: Stanford University Press, 1983.
Attwood, Lynne. *Gender and Housing in Soviet Russia. Private Life in a Public Space*. Manchester: Manchester University Press, 2010.
Audoble, Eric. *'Le Communisme, tout de suite!' Le Mouvement des Communes en Ukraine soviétique, 1919–1920*. Paris: Les Nuits Rouges, 2008.
Badcock, Sarah. *Politics and the People in Revolutionary Russia. A Provincial History*. Cambridge: Cambridge University Press, 2007.
Barber, John. 'The Establishment of Intellectual Orthodoxy in the USSSR, 1928–1934'. *Past and Present* no. 2 (May 1979): 141–64.
Baron, Samuel H. 'Plekhanov on Russian Capitalism and the Peasant Commune, 1883–1885'. *Slavic Review* no. 4 (December 1953): 463–74.
Bartlett, Roger, ed. *Land Commune and Peasant Community in Russia. Communal Forms in Imperial and Early Soviet Society*. London: Macmillan, 1990.
Bartlett, Rosamund. *Tolstoy, A Russian Life*. London: Profile Books, 2010.
Bauman, Zygmunt. *Modernity and The Holocaust*. Ithaca, NY: Cornell University Press, 1989.
Bauman, Zygmunt. *Modernity and Ambivalence*. Oxford: Blackwell Publishers, 1991.
Bauman, Zygmunt. *Intimations of Postmodernity*. London: Routledge, 1992.
Beer, Daniel. *Renovating Russia, The Human Sciences and the Fate of Liberal Modernity, 1880–1930*. Ithaca, NY: Cornell University Press, 2008.
Bernstein, F. L. *The Dictatorship of Sex: Lifestyle Advice for the Soviet Masses*. DeKalb: Northern Illinois University Press, 2007.
Best, Steven and Keller, Douglas. *Postmodern Theory: Critical Interrogations*. London: Macmillan, 1991.
Bezzubtsev-Kondakov, A. E. 'Kommuny Leningrada'. *Klio* no. 3 (2004): 158–63.

Bloch, Ernst. *The Principle of Hope.* 3 Vols. Trans. by Neville Plaice, Stephen Plaice, and Paul Knight. Oxford: Blackwell, 1986.

Boym, Svetlana. *Common Places. Mythologies of Everyday Life in Russia.* Cambridge, MA: Harvard University Press, 1994.

Branch, Michael., ed. *Defining Self. Essays on Emergent Identities in Russia Seventeenth to Nineteenth Centuries.* Helsinki: Finnish Literature Society, 2009.

Brandenberger, David. *Propaganda State in Crisis: Soviet Ideology, Indoctrination, and Terror under Stalin, 1927–1941.* New Haven, CT: Yale University Press, 2011.

Brower, Daniel R. *Training the Nihilists: Education and Radicalism in Russia.* Ithaca, NY: Cornell University Press, 1975.

Brown, Edward. J. *Major Soviet Writers. Essays in Criticism.* Oxford: Oxford University Press, 1973.

Brown, Edward. J. *Russian Literature Since the Revolution.* Cambridge, MA: Harvard University Press, 1982.

Brubaker, Rogers and Cooper, Fredrick. 'Beyond "identity"'. *Theory & Society* no. 1 (February 2000): 1–47.

Buchli, Victor. *An Archaeology of Socialism.* New York: Berg, 1999.

Buldakov, V. *Utopiia, Agressiia, Vlast': Psikhosotsial'naiia dinamika postrevoliutsionnogo vremeni Rossia, 1920–1930 gg.* Moscow: ROSSPEN, 2012.

Burke, Paul, ed. *New Perspectives on Historical Writing.* Cambridge: Cambridge University Press, 1991.

Chartier, Roger. *The Cultural Uses of Print in Early Modern France.* Princeton, NJ: Princeton University Press, 1987.

Chartier, Roger. 'Texts, Printing, Readings'. In *The New Cultural History.* Ed. by Lynn Hunt. Berkeley: University of California Press, 1989. 154–75.

Chartier, Roger. *On the Edge of the Cliff: History, Language, and Practices.* Baltimore, MD: Johns Hopkins University Press, 1997.

Chatterjee, Choi and Petrone, Karen. 'Models of Selfhood and Subjectivity: The Soviet Case in Historical Perspective'. *Slavic Review* no. 4 (Winter 2008): 967–86.

Clark, Katerina. *Petersburg, Crucible of Cultural Revolution.* Cambridge, MA: Harvard University Press, 1995.

Clark, Katerina. *The Soviet Novel: History as Ritual.* Bloomington, IN: Indiana University Press, 2000.

Clough, Patricia. T., ed. with Halley, Jean. *The Affective Turn, Theorizing the Social.* Durham, NC: Duke University Press, 2007.

Conquest, Robert. *Industrial Workers in the USSR.* New York: Bodley Head, 1978.

Corney, Frederick. *Telling October: Memory and the Making of the Bolshevik Revolution.* Ithaca, NY: Cornell University Press, 2004.

Crowley, David and Reid, Susan E., eds. *Socialist Spaces. Sites of Everyday Life in the Eastern Bloc.* Oxford: Clarendon Press, 2002.

Dahlke, Sarah. 'Kampagnen für Gottlosigkeit: Zum Zusammenhang zwischen Legitimation, Mobilisierung und Partizipation in der Sowjetunion der zwanziger Jahre'. *Jahrbrücher für Geschichte Osteuropas* no. 50 (2002): 172–85.

David-Fox, Michael. *Revolution of the Mind. Higher Learning among the Bolsheviks, 1918–1929.* Ithaca, NY: Cornell University Press, 1997.

David-Fox, Michael. 'Mentalité or Cultural System: A Reply to Sheila Fitzpatrick'. *Russian Review* no. 2 (April 1999): 210–11.

David-Fox, Michael. 'What is Cultural Revolution?' *Russian Review* no. 2 (April 1999): 181–201.

David-Fox, Michael. (review) 'Obshchestvennye organizatsii Rossii v 1920-e gody'. *Kritika: Explorations in Russian and Eurasian History* no. 1 (Winter 2002): 173–81.

David-Fox, Michael. *Crossing Borders: Modernity, Ideology, and Culture in Russia and the Soviet Union*. Pittsburgh, PA: University of Pittsburgh Press, 2015.

Davies, Robert W., Harrison, Mark and Wheatcroft, Stephen G., eds. *The Economic Transformation of the Soviet Union, 1913–1945*. Cambridge: Cambridge University Press, 1994.

Davis, Natalie. *Women on the Margins: Three Seventeenth-Century Lives*. Cambridge, MA: Harvard University Press, 1995.

Davis, Robert W. and Khelvniuk, Oleg V. 'Gosplan'. In *Decision Making in the Stalinist Command Economy, 1932–1937*. Ed. by E. A. Rees. Basingstoke: Macmillan, 1997.

Davydov, A. Iu. *Kooperatory sovetskogo goroda v gody NEPa. Mezhdu 'Voennym kommunizom' i sotsialisticheskoi rekonstruktsiei*. St Petersburg: Aleteiia, 2011.

De Certeau, Michel. *The Practice of Everyday Life*. Berkeley: University of California Press, 1984.

De George, Richard T. *Soviet Ethics and Morality*. Ann Arbor: University of Michigan Press, 1969.

Dixon, Simon. *The Modernisation of Russia 1676–1825*. Cambridge: Cambridge University Press, 1999.

Dobrenko, Evgeny. *The Making of the State Reader: Social and Aesthetic Contexts of the Reception of Soviet Literature*. Trans. by Jesse M. Savage. Stanford, CA: Stanford University Press, 1997.

Edele, Mark. *Stalinist Society, 1928–1953*. Oxford: Oxford University Press, 2011.

Edgerton, William, ed. and trans. *Memoirs of Peasant Tolstoyans in Soviet Russia*. Bloomington, IN: Indiana University Press, 1993.

Eklof, Ben. 'By A Different Yardstick. Boris Mironov's "A Social History of Imperial Russia, 1700–1917" and its Reception in Russia'. In *What Is Soviet Now? Identities, Legacies, Memories*. Ed. by Thomas Lahusen and Peter H. Solomon, Jr. Berlin: Verlang, 2008. 93–119.

Elias, Norbert. *The Civilizing Process: Sociogenetic and Psychogenetic Investigations*. Trans. by Elias N. Jephcott. Oxford: Blackwell Publishing, 2000.

Engel, Barbara A. *Between the Fields and City: Women, Work, and Family in Russia, 1861–1914*. Cambridge: Cambridge University Press, 1994.

Engel, Barbara A. *Women in Russia, 1700–2000*. Cambridge: Cambridge University Press, 2004.

Fierman, William. 'Kazakh Language and Prospects for its Role in Kazan "Groupness"'. *Ab Imperio* no. 2 (February 2005): 393–423.

Figes, Orlando. *Peasant Russia, Civil War. The Volga Countryside in Revolution, 1917–1921*. Oxford: Clarendon Press, 1991.

Filtzer, Donald. *Soviet Workers & Stalinist Industrialization*. London: Pluto Press, 1986.

Filtzer, Donald. *The Hazards of Urban Life in Late Stalinist Russia: Health, Hygiene, and Living Standards, 1943–1953*. Cambridge: Cambridge University Press, 2010.

Fitzpatrick, Sheila. 'Cultural Revolution in Russia 1928–1932'. *Journal of Contemporary History* no. 1 (1974): 33–52.

Fitzpatrick, Sheila. *The Russian Revolution, 1917–1932*. Oxford: Oxford University Press, 1983.

Fitzpatrick, Sheila. *The Cultural Front: Power and Culture in Revolutionary Russia*. Ithaca, NY: Cornell University Press, 1992.

Fitzpatrick, Sheila. 'Sources on the Social History of the 1930s. Overview and Critique'. In *A Researcher's Guide to Sources on Soviet Social History in the 1930s*. Ed. by Sheila Fitzpatrick and Lynne Viola. New York: M.E. Sharpe, 1992. 3–25.

Fitzpatrick, Sheila. 'Cultural Revolution Revisited'. *Russian Review* no. 2 (April 1999): 202–9.

Fitzpatrick, Sheila. *Tear off the Masks! Identity and Imposture in Twentieth-Century Russia.* Princeton, NJ: Princeton University Press, 2005.

Fitzpatrick, Sheila, ed. *Cultural Revolution in Russia, 1928–1931.* Bloomington, IN: Indiana University Press, 1978.

Fitzpatrick, Sheila, Rabinowitch, Alexander and Stites, Richard, eds. *Russia in the Era of NEP. Explorations in Soviet Society and Culture.* Bloomington, IN: Indiana University Press, 1991.

Fogarty, Robert S. *All Things New: American Communes and Utopian Movements 1860–1914.* Chicago, IL: University of Chicago Press, 1990.

Foucault, Michel. 'On Governmentality'. *Ideology and Consciousness* no. 6 (Autumn 1979): 5–21.

Foucault, Michel. 'The Subject and Power'. In *Michel Foucault: Beyond Structuralism and Hermeneutics* (2nd ed.). Ed. by Henri Drefus and Paul Rabinow. Chicago, IL: University of Chicago Press, 1982.

Foucault, Michel. *Discipline and Punish: The Birth of the Prison.* Trans. by Alan Sheridan. London: Knopf Doubleday Publishing Group, 1991.

Friedman, R. and Healey, D. *Masculinity, Autocracy and the Russian University, 1804–1863.* New York: Palgrave Macmillan, 2005.

Fülöp-Miller, Rene. *The Mind and Face of Bolshevism.* Trans. by F. Flint and D. Tait. New York: Harper & Row, 1927.

Fürst, Juliane. *Stalin's Last Generation: Soviet Post-War Youth and the Emergence of Mature Socialism.* Oxford: Oxford University Press, 2010.

Galkin, I. S. *I Internatsional. Parizhskaia Kommuna.* Moscow: Akademia nauk SSSR, 1963.

Galkova, O. V. 'Militarizatsiia truda, zhizni i byta molodezhi v 20–30x godakh'. In *Voina i mir v istoricheskom protsesse.* Ed. by E. G. Blosfel'd. Volgograd: Permena, 2003.

Gerasimov, Ilya V. *Modernism and Public Reform in Late Imperial Russia: Rural Professionals and Self-Organization, 1905–30.* Basingstoke: Palgrave Macmillan, 2009.

Gerstner, Alexandra, Könszöl, Barbara and Nentwig, Janina, eds. *Der Neue Mensch. Utopien, Leitbilder und Reformkonzepte zwischen den Weltkriegen.* Frankfurt: Peter Lang, 2006.

Getty, J. Arch. *Practicing Stalinism: Bolsheviks, Boyars, and the Persistence of Tradition.* New Haven, CT: Yale University Press, 2013.

Giddens, Anthony. *Capitalism and Modern Social Theory. An Analysis of the Writings of Marx, Durkheim and Max Weber.* Cambridge: Cambridge University Press, 1971.

Giddens, Anthony, ed. *Émile Durkheim, Selected Writings.* Cambridge: Cambridge University Press, 1972.

Gilbreth, Lillian. *The Psychology of Management: The Function of the Mind in Determining, Teaching and Installing Methods of Least Waste.* New York: The Macmillan Company, 1921.

Gildea, Robert. *The Past in French History.* New Haven, CT: Yale University Press, 1996.

Gildea, Robert. *Children of the Revolution. The French 1799–1914.* London: Allen Lane, 2008.

Gill, Graeme. *The Origins of the Stalinist Political System.* New York: Cambridge University Press, 1990.

Ginzburg, Carlo. *The Cheese and the Worms: The Cosmos of a Sixteenth-Century Miller.* Trans. by John Tedeschi and Anne Tedeschi. Baltimore, MD: Johns Hopkins University Press, 1982.

Gleason, Abbott et al., eds. *Bolshevik Culture: Experiments and Order in the Russian Revolution.* Bloomington, IN: Indiana University Press, 1985.

Glickman, Rose L. *Russian Factory Women: Workplace and Society, 1880–1914.* Berkeley: University of California Press, 1986.

Glickman, Rose L. 'Peasant Women and their Work'. In *Russian Peasant Women*. Ed. by Beatrice Farnsworth and Lynne Viola. Oxford: Oxford University Press, 1992. 54–72.

Gnatovskaia, D. Iu. and Zezina, M. P. 'Bytovye kommuny rabochei i studencheskoi molodezhi vo vtoroi polovine 20-kh–nachale 30-z godov'. *Vestnik MGU. Ser. 8. Istoriia* no. 1 (1998): 45–6.

Goldman, Wendy Z. *Women, the State and Revolution: Soviet Family Policy and Social Life, 1917–1936*. Cambridge: Cambridge University Press, 1993.

Goldman, Wendy Z. *Women at the Gates. Gender and Industry in Stalin's Russia*. Cambridge: Cambridge University Press, 2002.

Gooderham, Peter. 'The Komsomol and Worker Youth: The Inculcation of "Communist Values" in Leningrad During NEP'. *Soviet Studies* no. 4 (October 1982): 506–28.

Gordeeva, I. 'Predislovie'. In *Kommunizm svoimi rukami. Obraz agrarnykh kommun v Sovetskoi Rossii*. St Petersburg: The European University of St Petersburg, 2010.

Gordon, Collin, ed. *Power/Knowledge. Selected Interviews and Other Writings 1972–1977*. New York: Vintage Books, 1980.

Gorsuch, Anne E. 'NEP Be Damned! Young Militants in the 1920s and the Culture of Civil War'. *Russian Review* no. 4 (October 1997): 564–80.

Gorsuch, Anne E. *Youth in Revolutionary Russia. Enthusiasts, Bohemians, Delinquents*. Bloomington, IN: Indiana University Press, 2000.

Gorzka, Gabrielle. *Ein Beitrag sur sowjetischen Kulturgeschichte*. Berlin: Verlag, 1990.

Grant, Bruce. *In the Soviet House of Culture. A Century of Perestroikas*. Princeton, NJ: Princeton University Press, 1995.

Grant, Susan. *Physical Culture and Sport in Soviet Society: Propaganda, Acculturation, and Transformation in the 1920s and 1930s*. London: Routledge, 2013.

Guillory, Sean. 'The Shattered Self of Komsomol Civil War Memoirs'. *Slavic Review* no. 3 (2012): 546–65.

Gusiatnikov, P. S. *Revoliutsionnoe studencheskoe dvizhenie v Rossii*. Moscow: 'Mysl', 1971.

Habermas, Jürgen. *The Structural Transformation of the Public Sphere. An Inquiry into a Category of Bourgois Society*. Trans. by Thomas Berger. Cambridge: Polity Press, 1989.

Halfin, Igal. *From Darkness to Light. Class, Consciousness and Salvation in Revolutionary Russia*. Pittsburgh, PA: University of Pittsburgh Press, 2000.

Halfin, Igal. *Terror in My Soul: Communist Autobiographies on Trial*. Cambridge, MA: Harvard University Press, 2003.

Halfin, Igal. *Intimate Enemies: Demonizing the Bolshevik Opposition, 1918–1928*. Pittsburgh, PA: University of Pittsburgh Press, 2007.

Halfin, Igal. *Stalinist Confessions. Messianism and Terror at the Leningrad Communist University*. Pittsburgh, PA: University of Pittsburgh Press, 2009.

Halfin, Igal. *Red Biographies: Initiating the Bolshevik Self*. Seattle: University of Washington Press, 2011.

Halfin, Igal, ed. *Language and Revolution. Making Modern Political Identities*. London: Frank Cass, 2002.

Harris, Steven E. *Communism on Tomorrow Street: Mass Housing and Everyday Life after Stalin*. Baltimore, MD: Johns Hopkins University Press, 2013.

Hazard, John N. *Soviet Housing Law*. New Haven, CT: Yale University Press, 1939.

Hazareesingh, Sudhir. *Political Traditions in Modern France*. Oxford: Oxford University Press, 1994.

Hazareesingh, Sudhir. *From Subject to Citizen. The Second Empire and the Emergence of Modern French Democracy*. Princeton, NJ: Princeton University Press, 1998.

Hazareesingh, Sudhir. *The Legend of Napoleon*. London: Granta Books, 2005.

Healey, Dan. *Homosexual Desire in Revolutionary Russia. The Regulation of Sexual and Gender Dissent.* Chicago, IL: University of Chicago Press, 2001.

Healey, Dan. *Bolshevik Sexual Forensics. Diagnosing Disorder in the Clinic and Courtroom, 1917–1939.* DeKalb: Northern Illinois University Press, 2009.

Heitlinger, Alena. *Women and State Socialism: Sex Inequality in the Soviet Union and Czechoslovakia.* London: Macmillan Press, 1979.

Hellbeck, Jochen. 'Working, Struggling, Becoming: Stalin-Era Autobiographical Texts'. *Russian Review* no. 3 (July 2001): 340–59.

Hellbeck, Jochen. *Revolution on My Mind: Writing a Diary Under Stalin.* Cambridge, MA: Harvard University Press, 2006.

Hobsbawm, Eric. *Bandits.* London: Penguin Books, 1971.

Hoffman, David L. *Stalinist Values. The Cultural Norms of Soviet Modernity, 1917–1941.* Ithaca, NY: Cornell University Press, 2003.

Hoffman, David L. and Kotsonis, Yanni, eds. *Russian Modernity: Politics, Knowledge, Practices.* Basingstoke: Macmillan, 2000.

Holmes, Larry E. *Stalin's School: Moscow's Model School No. 25, 1931–1937.* Pittsburgh, PA: University of Pittsburgh Press, 1999.

Holquist, Peter. '"Information is the Alpha and Omega of Our Work": Bolshevik Surveillance in Its Pan-European Context'. *Journal of Modern History* no. 3 (1997): 415–50.

Holquist, Peter. *Making War, Forging Revolution. Russia's Continuum of Crisis, 1914–1921.* Cambridge, MA: Harvard University Press, 2002.

Hosking, Geoffrey. 'Patronage and the Russian State'. *Slavonic and East European Review* no. 2 (April 2000): 301–20.

Hughes, Richard. *The Chinese Communes.* London: Bodley Head, 1960.

Humphrey, Caroline. 'Ideology in Infrastructure: Architecture and Soviet Imagination'. *Journal of the Royal Anthropological Institute* no. 1 (2005): 39–58.

Il'ina, I. N. *Obshchestvennye organizatsii Rossi v 1920-e gody.* Moscow: Institut rossiiskoi istorii RAN, 2000.

Isaev, V. I. *Kommuna ili kommunalka? Izmeneniia byta rabochikh Sibiri v gody industrializatsii, 1920-kh–1930-e gg.* Novosibirsk: Russian Academy of Sciences, 1996.

Izmozik, V. S. and Lebina, N. B. *Peterburg sovetskii 'novyi chelovek' v starom prostranstve, 1920–1930-e gody.* St Petersburg: Kriga, 2010.

Jakobson, Roman. *Language in Literature.* Ed. by Krystyna Pomorska and Stephen Rudy. Cambridge, MA: Harvard University Press, 1987.

Johnson, Richard. 'Edward Thompson, Eugene Genovese, and Socialist-Humanist History'. *History Workshop Journal* no. 6 (Autumn 1978): 79–100.

Johnston, Timothy. *Being Soviet. Identity, Rumour, and Everyday Life under Stalin 1939–1953.* Oxford: Oxford University Press, 2011.

Kaganovsky, Lilya. *How the Soviet Man was Unmade. Cultural Fantasy and Male Subjectivity under Stalin.* Pittsburgh, PA: University of Pittsburgh Press, 2008.

Kamenskii, A. B. 'Uroki, kotorye mozhno bylo izvlech'. *Odissei: Chelovek v istorii* no. 1 (2004): 408–21.

Kanter, Rosabeth M. *Commitment and Community: Communes and Utopias in Sociological Perspective.* Cambridge, MA: Harvard University Press, 1972.

Kanter, Rosabeth M. *Communes: Creating and Managing the Collective Life.* New York: Harper & Row, 1973.

Kassow, Samuel D. *Students, Professors, and the State in Tsarist Russia.* Berkeley: University of California Press, 1989.

Kelly, Catriona. *Refining Russia: Advice Literature, Polite Culture, and Gender from Catherine to Yeltsin*. Oxford: Oxford University Press, 2001.

Kelly, Catriona. 'The Education of the Will: Advice Literature, *Zakal*, and Manliness in Early Twentieth-Century Russia'. In *Russian Masculinities in History and Culture*. Ed. by Barbara E. Clements, Rebecca Friedman, and Dan Healey. Basingstoke: Palgrave, 2002. 131–51.

Kelly, Catriona. *St. Petersburg: Shadows of the Past*. New Haven, CT: Yale University Press, 2014.

Kelly, Catriona and Volkov, Vadim. 'Obshchestvennost', Sobornost': Collective Identities'. In *Constructing Russian Culture in the Age of Revolution, 1881–1940*. Ed. by Catriona Kelly and David Shepherd. Oxford: Oxford University Press, 1998. 26–7.

Kenez, Peter. *The Birth of the Propaganda State: Soviet Methods of Mass Mobilizations, 1917–1929*. Cambridge: Cambridge University Press, 1985.

Khan-Magomedov, Selmin O. *Pioneers of Soviet Architecture: The Search for New Solutions in the 1920s and 1930s*. London: Thames and Hudson, 1983.

Kharkhordin, Oleg. 'Reveal and Dissimulate: A Genealogy of Private Life in Soviet Russia'. In *Public and Private in Thought and Practice, Perspectives on a Grand Dichotomy*. Ed. by Jeff Weintraub and Krishan Kumar. Chicago, IL: University of Chicago Press, 1997. 333–63.

Kharkhordin, Oleg. *The Collective and the Individual in Russia. A Study of Practices*. Berkeley: University of California Press, 1999.

Kiaer, Christina. 'Delivered from Capitalism. Nostalgia, Alienation, and the Future of Reproduction in Tret'iakov's I want a Child!'. In *Everyday Life in Early Soviet Russia. Taking the Revolution Inside*. Ed by Christina Kiaer and Eric Naiman. Bloomington, IN: Indiana University Press, 2006. 183–216.

Kir'ianov, Iu. I. *Zhiznennyi uroven' rabochikh Rossii*. Moscow: Nauka, 1979.

Kirikov, B. M. and Stieglitz, M. S. *Arkhitektura Leningradskogo avangarda. Putevoditel'*. St Petersburg: Kolo, 2009.

Kirschenbaum, Lisa. *Small Commrades: Revolutionizing Childhood in Soviet Russia, 1917–1932*. New York: Routledge Falmer, 2000.

Koenker, Diane P. *Republic of Labor: Russian Printers and Soviet Socialism, 1918–1930*. Ithaca, NY: Cornell University Press, 2005.

Konecny, Peter. *Builders and Deserters, Students, State, and Community in Leningrad, 1917–1941*. Montreal: McGill-Queen's Press, 1999.

Korol'chuk, E. A. *Rabochee dvizhenie 70-kh godov*. Moscow: Izd-vo politkatorzhan, 1934.

Korol'chuk, E. A., ed. *V nachale puti. Vospominaniia peterburgskikh rabochikh, 1872–1897*. Leningrad: Lenizdat, 1975.

Kotkin, Stephen. *Magnetic Mountain, Stalinism as a Civilization*. Berkeley: University of California Press, 1995.

Kuromiya, Hiroaki. *Stalin's Industrial Revolution. Politics and Workers, 1928–1932*. Cambridge: Cambridge University Press, 1988.

La Vigna, Claire. 'The Marxist Ambivalence toward Women: Between Socialism and Feminism in the Italian Socialist Party'. In *Becoming Visible: Women in European History*. Ed. by Renate Bridenthal and Claudia Koonz. Boston, MA: Houghton Mifflin, 1987. 146–81.

Larrain, Jorge. 'Ideology'. In *A Dictionary of Marxist Thought*. Ed. by Tom Bottomore. Cambridge, MA: Harvard University Press, 1983. 219–23.

Lebedeva, L. V. *Povsednevnaiia zhizn' penzenskoi derevni v 1920-e gody: traditsii i peremeny*. Moscow: ROSSPEN, 2009.

Lebina, N. B. *Povsednevnaia zhizn' sovetskovgo goroda: normy i anomalii, 1920/1930 gody.* St Petersburg: Letnii sad, 1999.

Lefebvre, Henri. *Critique of Everyday Life.* Vols 1–3. London: Verso, 2008.

Lepore, Jill. *The Mansion of Happiness: A History of Life and Death.* New York: Vintage Books, 2013.

Levine, Donald N. *The Flight from Ambiguity: Essays in Social and Cultural Theory.* Chicago, IL: University of Chicago Press, 1985.

Levitas, Ruth. *The Concept of Utopia.* Oxford: Peter Lang, 1990.

Lewin, Moshe. *La paysannerie et le pouvoir soviétique 1928–1930.* Paris: Mounton, 1966.

Lewin, Moshe. *The Making of the Soviet System: Essays in the Social History of Interwar Russia.* New York: Routledge, 1985.

Loewenstein, Karl. 'Obshchestvennost' as Key to Understanding Soviet Writers of the 1950s: *Moskovskii Literator,* October 1956–March 1957'. *Journal of Contemporary History* no. 3 (2009): 473–92.

Lovell, Stephen. *Russia in the Microphone Age: A History of Soviet Radio, 1919–1970.* Oxford: Oxford University Press, 2015.

McAuley, Mary. 'Bread without the Bourgeoisie'. In *Party, State, and Society in the Russian Civil War: Explorations in Social History.* Ed by Diane P. Koenker, William G. Rosenberg, and Ronald G. Suny. Bloomington, IN: Indiana University Press, 1989. 158–79.

McDermid, Jane and Hillyer, Anna, eds. *Women and Work in Russia, 1880–1930: A Study in Continuity Through Change.* London: Routledge, 1998.

Malle, Silvana. *The Economic Organization of War Communism 1918–1921.* Cambridge: Cambridge University Press, 1985.

Malle, Silvana. *Employment Planning in the Soviet Union. Continuity and Change.* New York: St Martin's Press, 1990.

Mally, Lynn. *Culture of the Future: The Proletkult Movement in Revolutionary Russia.* Berkeley: University of California Press, 1990.

Mandel, David. *The Petrograd Workers and the Fall of the Old Regime. From the February Revolution to the July Days, 1917.* London: Macmillan Press, 1983.

Mandelstam, Nadezhda. *Hope Against Hope.* Trans. by Michael Hayward. London: Harvill Press, 1999.

Mazower, Mark. *Dark Continent: Europe's Twentieth Century.* London: Allen Lane, 1998.

Meerovich, M. G. *Nakazanie zhilishchem: Zhilishchaia politika v SSSR kak sredstvo upravleniia liud'mi, 1917–1937 gg.* Moscow: ROSSPEN, 2008.

Meerovich, M. G., Konycheva, E. V., and Khmel'nitskii, D. *Kladbishche sotsgorodov: Gradostroitel'naia politika v SSSR, 1928–1932 gg.* Moscow: ROSSPEN, 2011.

Messana, Paola. *Soviet Communal Living. An Oral History of the Kommunalka.* New York: Palgrave Macmillan, 2001.

Meyers, Alfred G. *The Feminism and Socialism of Lily Braun.* Bloomington, IN: Indiana University Press, 1985.

Miller, Timothy. *The 60s Communes: Hippies and Beyond.* New York: Syracuse University Press, 1999.

Mironov, Boris. 'The Russian Peasant Commune After the Reforms of the 1860s'. *Slavic Review* no. 3 (Autumn 1985): 438–67.

Mironov, Boris with Eklof, B. *The Social History of Imperial Russia, 1700–1917.* 2 vols. Oxford: Westview Press, 2000.

Moon, David. 'Reassessing Russian Serfdom'. *European History Quarterly* no. 4 (1996): 485–526.

Moon, David. *The Russian Peasantry, 1600–1930. The World the Peasants Made*. London: Longman, 1999.

Morrissey, Susan K. *Heralds of Revolution. Russian Students and the Mythologies of Radicalism*. New York: Oxford University Press, 1998.

Morrissey, Susan K. *Suicide and the Body Politic in Imperial Russia*. Cambridge: Cambridge University Press, 2012.

Naiman, Eric. *Sex in Public: The Incarnation of Early Soviet Ideology*. Princeton, NJ: Princeton University Press, 1997.

Nechemias, Carlo. 'The Impact of Soviet Housing Policy on Housing Conditions in Soviet Cities: The Uneven Push from Moscow'. *Urban Studies* no. 1 (1982): 1–8.

Neirick, Miriam. *When Pigs could Fly and Bears could Dance: A History of the Soviet Circus*. Madison: University of Wisconsin Press, 2012.

Neumann, Matthias. *The Communist Youth League and the Transformation of the Soviet Union, 1917–1932*. London: Routledge, 2011.

Nove, Alec. *An Economic History of the USSR*. London: Penguin, 1969.

Nye, Robert. *Masculinity and Male Codes of Honor in Modern France*. Oxford: Oxford University Press, 1993.

Obertreis, J. *Tränen des Sozialismus. Wohnen in Leningrad zwischen Alltag und Utopie 1917–1937*. Cologne: Böhlau Verlag, 2004.

O'Connor, Timothy. *The Politics of Soviet Culture: Anatolii Lunacharskii*. Ann Arbor: UMI Research Press, 1983.

Offord, Derek. 'Lichnost': notions of Individual Identity'. In *Constructing Russian Culture in the Age of Revolution: 1881–1940*. Ed. by Catriona Kelly and David Shepherd. Oxford: Oxford University Press, 1998. 13–25.

Panova, V. F. *O moei zhizni, knigakh i chitateliakh*. Leningrad: Lenizdat, 1980.

Pate, Alice K. 'Workers and Obshchestvennost': St. Petersburg, 1906–14'. *Revolutionary Russia* no. 2 (December 2002): 53–71.

Pearl, Deborah. *Creating a Culture of Revolution: Workers and the Revolutionary Movement in Late Imperial Russia*. Bloomington, IN: Slavica, 2015.

Pershin, N. I. *Kommunisticheskaia partiia—organizator osvoeniia tekhniki proizvodstva v traktornoi promyshlennosti v period stroitel'stva sotsializma*. Volgograd: Nizh.-Volzh kn. izd-vo, 1974.

Pethybridge, Roger. *The Social Prelude to Stalinism*. London: Macmillan Press Limited, 1974.

Petrus, K. *Religious Communes in the USSR*. New York: Research Program on the USSR, 1953.

Pilbeam, Pamela M. *Republicanism in Nineteenth-Century France, 1814–1871*. London: Macmillan, 1995.

Pilkington, Hilary. *Russia's Youth and its Culture. A Nation's Constructors and Constructed*. London: Routledge, 1994.

Pinnow, Kenneth M. *Lost to the Collective. Suicide and the Promise of Soviet Socialism, 1921–1929*. Ithaca, NY: Cornell University Press, 2010.

Pirani, Simon. 'The Moscow Workers' Movement in 1921 and the Role of Non-Partyism'. *Europe–Asia Studies* no. 1 (2004): 143–60.

Pirani, Simon. *The Russian Revolution in Retreat, 1920–24. Soviet Workers and the New Communist Elite*. Oxford: Routledge, 2008.

Plamper, Jan. *The History of Emotions: An Introduction*. Trans. by Keith Tribe. Oxford: Oxford University Press, 2015.

Potekhin, M. N. *Petrogradskaia trudovaia kommuna, 1918–1919*. Leningrad: Leningradskii universitet, 1980.

Pott, Phillip. *Moskauer Kommunalwohnungen 1917 bis 1917: Materielle Kultur, Erfahrung, Erinnerung.* Zürich: Pano Verlag, 2009.

Priestland, David. *Stalinism and the Politics of Mobilization: Ideas, Power, and Terror in Inter-war Russia.* Oxford: Oxford University Press, 2007.

Priestland, David. *The Red Flag: Communism and the Making of the Modern World.* London: Penguin Books, 2010.

Rabinow, Paul, ed. *The Foucault Reader.* New York: Pantheon, 1984.

Raleigh, Donald J. *Experiencing Russia's Civil War: Politics, Society, and Revolutionary Culture in Saratov, 1917–1922.* Princeton, NJ: Princeton University Press, 2002.

Rancière, Jacques. *Nights of Labour: The Workers' Dream in Nineteenth-Century France.* Philadelphia, PA: Temple University Press, 1989.

Ransel, David. 'A Single Research Community? Not Yet'. *Slavic Review* no. 3 (Fall 2001): 550–7.

Read, Christopher. *Culture and Power in Revolutionary Russia: The Intelligentsia and the Transition from Tsarism to Communism.* London: Macmillan, 1990.

Reich, Wilhelm. *The Sexual Revolution: Toward a Self-Governing Character Structure.* Trans. by Theodore P. Wolfe. New York: Farrar, Straus and Giroux, 1969.

Retish, Aaron B. *Russia's Peasants in Revolution and Civil War. Citizenship, Identity, and the Creation of the Soviet State, 1914–1922.* Cambridge: Cambridge University Press, 2008.

Richardson, Curtis. 'Konstantin Kavelin and the Struggle for Emancipation: A Case Study of the Westerners' Role in the Foundation of Civil Society in Imperial Russia'. *The Carl Beck Papers in Russian and East European Studies* no. 2006 (September 2010).

Rolf, Malte. *Soviet Mass Festivals, 1917–1991.* Pittsburgh, PA: University of Pittsburgh Press, 2013.

Rosenberg, William G. and Siegelbaum, Lewis H., eds. *Social Dimensions of Soviet Industrialization.* Bloomington, IN: Indiana University Press, 1993.

Rosenthal, Bernice G., ed. *Nietzsche in Russia.* Princeton, NJ: Princeton University Press, 1986.

Rosenthal, Bernice G., ed. *Nietzsche and Soviet Culture. Ally and Adversary.* Cambridge: Cambridge University Press, 1994.

Ross, Kristin. *Communal Luxury: The Political Imaginary of the Paris Commune.* London: Verso, 2015.

Rowbotham, Sheila. *Dreamers of a New Day: Women Who Invented the Twentieth Century.* London: Verso, 2011.

Sanborn, Joshua A. *Drafting the Nation: Military Conscription, Total War, and Mass Politics.* DeKalb: Northern Illinois University Press, 2003.

Saunders, David. *Russia in the Age of Reaction and Reform, 1801–1881.* London: Longman, 1992.

Savage, Mike. 'The Rise of the Labour Party in Local Perspective'. *Journal of Regional and Local Studies* no. 1 (1990): 1–16.

Sawer, Marian. 'The Soviet Image of the Commune: Lenin and Beyond'. In *Images of the Commune. Images de la Commune.* Ed. by James A. Leith. Montreal: McGill-Queen's University Press, 1978.

Schlögel, Karl. '*Kommunalka*—oder Kommunismus als Lebensform. Zu einer historischen Topographie der Sowjetunion'. *Historische Anthropologie* no. 3 (1998): 329–46.

Schöttler, Peter. 'Historians and Discourse Analysis'. *History Workshop Journal* no. 27 (1989): 37–65.

Schultz, Kurt S. 'Building the "Soviet Detroit": The Construction of the Nizhnii-Novgorod Automobile Factory, 1927–1932'. *Slavic Review* no. 2 (Summer 1990): 200–12.

Schwarz, Solomon. *Labor in the Soviet Union.* New York: Praeger, 1952.

Scott, Joan W. *Gender and the Politics of History.* New York: Columbia University Press, 1999.

Seddon, J. H. *The Petrashevtsty. A Study of the Russian Revolutionaries of 1848.* Manchester: Manchester University Press, 1985.

Service, Robert. 'Russian Populism and Russian Marxism: Two Skeins Entangled'. In *Russian Thought and Society 1800–1917: Essays in Honour of Eugene Lampert.* Ed. by Roger Bartlett. Keele: University of Keele Press, 1984. 92–113.

Shanin, Teodor. *The Awkward Class. Political Sociology of Peasantry in a Developing Society: Russia 1910–1925.* Oxford: Oxford University Press, 1972.

Shearer, David. *Industry, State, and Society in Stalin's Russia, 1926–1934.* Ithaca, NY: Cornell University Press, 1996.

Shweder, Richard A. and LeVine, Robert A. *Culture Theory. Essays on Mind, Self, and Emotion.* Cambridge: Cambridge University Press, 1997.

Siegelbaum, Lewis H. 'Production Collectives and Communes and the "Imperatives" of Soviet Industrialization, 1929–1931'. *Slavic Review* no. 1 (Spring 1986): 65–84.

Siegelbaum, Lewis H. *Stakhanovism and the Politics of Productivity in the USSR, 1935–1941.* Cambridge: Cambridge University Press, 1988.

Siegelbaum, Lewis H. *Soviet State & Society between Revolutions, 1918–1929.* Cambridge: Cambridge University Press, 1992.

Siegelbaum, Lewis H. *Cars for Comrades: The Life of the Soviet Automobile.* Ithaca, NY: Cornell University Press, 2008.

Siegelbaum, Lewis H., ed. *Borders of Socialism: Private Spheres of Soviet Russia.* New York: Palgrave Macmillan, 2006.

Siegelbaum, Lewis H. and Suny, Ronald G., eds. *Making Workers Soviet. Power, Class, and Identity.* Ithaca, NY: Cornell University Press, 1995.

Slezkine, Yuri. 'The USSR as a Communal Apartment, or How a Socialist State Promoted Ethnic Particularism'. *Slavic Review* no. 2 (Summer 1994): 414–52.

Slonim, Marc. *Russian Theatre: From the Empire to the Soviets.* New York: Collier, 1962.

Smith, Mark B. *Property of Communists: The Urban Housing Program from Stalin to Khrushchev.* DeKalb: Northern Illinois University Press, 2010.

Smith, Michael G. *Rockets & Revolution: A Cultural History of Early Spaceflight.* Lincoln: University of Nebraska Press, 2014.

Smith, Stephen A. *Red Petrograd. Revolution in the Factories, 1917–1918.* Cambridge: Cambridge University Press, 1985.

Smith, Stephen A. 'The Social Meanings of Swearing: Workers and Bad Language in Late Imperial and Early Soviet Russia'. *Past and Present* no. 160 (1998): 167–202.

Smith, Stephen A. *Revolution and the People in Russia and China: A Comparative History.* Cambridge: Cambridge University Press, 2008.

Starks, Tricia. *The Body Soviet. Propaganda, Hygiene, and the Revolutionary State.* Madison, WI: University of Wisconsin Press, 2008.

Stedman Jones, Gareth. *Language of Class: Studies in English Working-Class History, 1832–1982.* Cambridge: Cambridge University Press, 1983.

Steinberg, Mark D. *Moral Communities. The Culture of Class Relations in the Russian Printing Industry, 1867–1907.* Berkeley: University of California Press, 1992.

Steinberg, Mark D. *Proletarian Imagination: Self, Modernity, and the Sacred in Russia, 1910–1925.* Ithaca, NY: Cornell University Press, 2002.

Steinberg, Mark D. and Sobol, Valeria, eds. *Interpreting Emotions in Russia and Eastern Europe.* DeKalb: Northern Illinois University Press, 2011.

Stites, Richard. *The Women's Liberation Movement in Russia: Feminism, Nihilism, and Bolshevism, 1860–1930*. Princeton, NJ: Princeton University Press, 1978.

Stites, Richard. *Revolutionary Dreams, Utopian Vision and Experimental Life in the Russian Revolution*. Oxford: Oxford University Press, 1989.

Straus, Kenneth M. *Factory and Community in Stalin's Russia: The Making of an Industrial Working Class*. Pittsburgh, PA: University of Pittsburgh Press, 1997.

Strong, Anna L. *The Rise of the Chinese Communes*. Peking: New World Press, 1959.

Suny, Ronald G. *The Baku Commune 1917–1918. Class and Nationality in the Russian Revolution*. Princeton, NJ: Princeton University Press, 1972.

Suny, Ronald G. *The Soviet Experiment: Russia, the USSR, and the Successor States*. Oxford: Oxford University Press, 1998.

Surh, Gerald D. 'Petersburg's First Mass Labor Organization: The Assembly of Russian Workers and Father Gapon'. *Russian Review* no. 3 (July 1981): 241–62 (pt. 1); and no. 4 (October 1981): 412–41 (pt. 2).

Surh, Gerald D. *1905 in St. Petersburg: Labor, Society, and Revolution*. Stanford, CA: Stanford University Press, 1989.

Thompson, Edward P. 'Time, Work-Discipline, and Industrial Capitalism'. *Past & Present* no. 1 (December 1967): 56–97.

Thompson, Edward P. *The Poverty of Theory and Other Essays*. London: Merlin Press, 1975.

Thompson, John M. *A Vision Unfulfilled: Russia and the Soviet Union in the Twentieth Century*. Toronto: University of Toronto Press, 1996.

Thurston, Robert W. 'The Soviet Family during the Great Terror, 1935–1941'. *Soviet Studies* no. 3 (1991): 553–74.

Timasheff, Nicholas S. *The Great Retreat. The Growth and Decline of Communism in Russia*. New York: E.P. Dutton & Company, 1946.

Tirado, Isabel A. *Young Guard! The Communist Youth League, Petrograd 1917–1929*. New York: Greenwood Press, 1988.

Tolz, Vera. *Russia's Own Orient. The Politics of Identity and Oriental Studies in the Late Imperial and Early Soviet Periods*. Oxford: Oxford University Press, 2011.

Tönnies, Ferdinand. *Community and Civil Society*. Trans. by Jose Harris and Margaret Hollis. Cambridge: Cambridge University Press, 2001.

Toumanoff, Peter. 'The Development of the Peasant Commune in Russia'. *Journal of Economic History* no. 1 (March 1981): 179–84.

Transchel, Kate. *Under the Influence: Working-Class Drinking, Temperance, and Cultural Revolution in Russia, 1895–1932*. Pittsburgh, PA: University of Pittsburgh Press, 2006.

Tucker, Robert. 'Stalinism as Revolution from Above'. In *Stalinism: Essays in Historical Interpretation*. Ed. by Robert Tucker. New York: W.W. Norton & Company, 1977. 77–110.

Turton, Katy. *Forgotten Lives: The Role of Lenin's Sisters in the Russian Revolution, 1864–1937*. Basingstoke: Palgrave Macmillan, 2007.

Velikanova, Olga. *Popular Perceptions of Soviet Politics in the 1920s: Disenchantment of the Dreamers*. Basingstoke: Palgrave Macmillan, 2013.

Vihavainen, Rosa. *Homeowners' Associations in Russia after the 2005 Housing Reform*. Helsinki: Kikimora Publications, 2009.

Viola, Lynne. *The Best Sons of the Fatherland. Workers in the Vanguard of Soviet Collectivization*. New York: Oxford University Press, 1987.

Volkov, Vadim. 'The Concept of *Kul'turnost*: Notes on the Stalinist Civilizing Process'. In *Stalinism: New Directions*. Ed. by Sheila Fitzpatrick. London: Routledge, 2000. 117–41.

Von Bremzen, Anya. *Mastering the Art of Soviet Cooking: A Memoir of Food and Longing*. London: Doubleday, 2013.

Von Geldern, James. *Bolshevik Festivals, 1917–1920.* Berkeley: University of California Press, 1993.

Vorozheikin, I. E. *Ocherki istoriografii rabochego klassa SSSR.* Moscow: Politzdat, 1975.

Vviedenskii, B., ed. *The Great Soviet Encyclopedia.* Vol. 22. Moscow: Foreign Languages Publishing House, 1953.

Waldron, Peter. *Between Two Revolutions: Stolypin and the Politics of Renewal in Russia.* London: University College London Press, 1998.

Ward, Chris. *Russia's Cotton Workers and the New Economic Policy: Shop Floor Culture and State Policy, 1921–1929.* Cambridge: Cambridge University Press, 1990.

Waterlow, Jonathan. 'Intimating Trust: Popular Humour in Stalin's 1930s'. *Cultural and Social History* no. 2 (2013): 211–29.

Wesson, Robert. *Soviet Communes.* New Brunswick, NJ: Rutgers University Press, 1963.

Wildman, Allen K. 'The Russian Intelligentsia of the 1890s'. *American Slavic and East European Review* no. 2 (April 1960): 157–79.

William, Robert C. 'Collective Immortality: The Syndicalist Origins of Proletarian Culture, 1905–1910'. *Slavic Review* no. 3 (1980): 389–402.

Willimott, Andy. 'The Kommuna Impulse: Collective Mechanisms and Commune-ists in the Early Soviet State'. *Revolutionary Russia* no. 1 (June 2011): 59–78.

Willimott, Andy. 'Everyday Revolution: The Making of the Soviet Urban Communes'. In *Russia's Home Front, 1914–1922: The Experience of War and Revolution.* Ed. by Adele Lindenmeyr, Christopher Read, and Peter Waldron. Bloomington, IN: Slavica, 2016. 431–54.

Wolfe, Thomas C. *Governing Soviet Journalism. The Press and the Socialist Person after Stalin.* Bloomington, IN: Indiana University Press, 2005.

Wood, Elizabeth. 'The Trial of Lenin: Legitimizing the Revolution through Political Theatre, 1920–1923'. *Russian Review* no. 2 (April 2002): 235–48.

Wood, Elizabeth. *The Baba and the Comrade. Gender and Politics in Revolutionary Russia.* Bloomington, IN: Indiana University Press, 1997.

Woodcock, George. *Anarchism. A History of Libertarian Ideals and Movements.* Harmondsworth: Penguin Books, 1983.

Worobec, Christine. *Peasant Russia: Family and Community in the Post-Emancipation Period.* DeKalb: Northern Illinois University Press, 1991.

Yurchak, Alexei. *Everything Was Forever, Until It Was No More. The Last Soviet Generation.* Princeton, NJ: Princeton University Press, 2005.

Zaleski, Eugene. *Planning for Economic Growth in the Soviet Union, 1918–1932.* Trans. by Marie-Christine MacAndrew and G. Warren Nutter. Chapel Hill, NC: University of North Carolina Press, 1971.

Zeldin, Theodore. *France 1848–1945.* 3 Vols. Oxford: Clarendon, 1977.

Zhuravlev, S. V. '*Malenkie liudi' i 'bol'shaia istoriia': inostrantsy moskovskogo Elektrozavoda v sovetskom obshchestve v 1920–30 gg.* Moscow: ROSSPEN, 2000.

Zubkova, E. Iu. and Zhkova, T. Iu. *Na 'Kraiu' Sovetskogo obshchestva: Sotzial'nye marginaly kak ob"ekt gosudarstvennoi politiki, 1945–1960-e gg.* Moscow: ROSSPEN, 2010.

Zuikov, V. N. and Vadim, V. V. *Istoriia industrializatsii Urala, 1926–1932 gg.* Sverdlovsk: Sredne-Ural'skoe knizhnoe izd-vo, 1967.

UNPUBLISHED MATERIALS

Guillory, Sean C. 'We Shall Refashion Life on Earth! The Political Culture of the Young Communist League, 1918–1928'. Unpublished PhD Dissertation, University of California, Los Angeles, 2009.

Huxtable, Simon. 'Revisiting "Governmentality": Journalists and Political Power at *Komsomol'skaia pravda*, 1953–1968'. University of Oxford Postgraduate Seminar Series, June 2011.

Huxtable, Simon. 'A Compass in the Sea of Life: Soviet Journalism, the Public, and the Limits of Reform After Stalin, 1953–1968'. Unpublished PhD Dissertation, Birkbeck, University of London, 2012.

Russell, John. 'The Role of Socialist Competition in Establishing Labour Discipline in the Soviet Working Class, 1928–1934'. Unpublished PhD Dissertation, University of Birmingham, 1987.

Index